THE MONEY DOCTOR
FINANCE ANNUAL
2009

John Lowe

Very best wishes & continued success

Gill & Macmillan

Gill & Macmillan Ltd
Hume Avenue, Park West, Dublin 12
with associated companies throughout the world
www.gillmacmillan.ie

Print origination by TypeIT and O'K Graphic Design, Dublin
Printed by ColourBooks Ltd, Dublin
Index compiled by Cover to Cover

The paper used in this book is made from the wood pulp of managed forests. For every tree
felled, at least one tree is planted, thereby renewing natural resources.

A catalogue record is available for this book from the British Library.

1 3 5 4 2

PHOTO CREDITS

The publisher would like to acknowledge the following for the use of their logos: The Independent
Mortgage Advisers' Federation, The Irish Brokers' Association, Professional Insurance Brokers'
Association, Financial Services Ombudsman, AIB, Bank of Ireland, Permanent TSB, National Irish
Bank, Ulster Bank, Bank of Scotland (Ireland), the Credit Union, VHI Healthcare, Hibernian
Health and Quinn Healthcare.

All photographs © Imagefile.

Whilst every effort has been made to ensure accuracy, no legal or other liability
on the part of the author or publishers can be accepted for any information
or advice given.

CONTENTS

Preface   xix
Is this book for you?   xxiii
Getting the most out of this book   xxiv
The Money Doctor website   xxiv
Acknowledgements   xxvi

PART 1 HOW TO BECOME FINANCIALLY FIT IN 2009

1   All it takes is a little planning   5
    How your financial plan will make you better off   5
    Why you need a financial plan   5
    Supposing you *don't* plan?   6
    Instant savings and more   8
    What does a financial plan look like?   9
    How long should a financial plan last for?   10
    If you think you need help   10

2   Writing a financial plan   12
    Everything you need to know to write your own financial plan
        (or to get someone else to do it for you) 12
    How do you decide what your financial objectives should be?   12
    Prioritising your financial objectives   14
    Ten universal needs   15
    Setting realistic aims   16
    How far have you got?   17
    Your monthly income and outgoings   18
    Your assets   19
    Your liabilities   20
    The importance of making assumptions   21
    Where do you need to take action?   23

3   Money is a family affair   25
    How families can work together to achieve long-term
        financial security   25

Problem? What problem?   25

Are you and your partner financially compatible?   26

Opening a dialogue   27

Anything to declare?   28

Building a joint approach to money   29

Sharing out the chores   30

The importance of involving and educating your children   31

4   Getting help   35

How far should you go?   35

Getting help   36

   How to get help from someone you can trust   36

   What can you expect from your independent professional

     Authorised Advisor or mortgage intermediary?   37

   Saving tax   39

   A very short history lesson   39

PART 2 YOUR FINANCIAL RIGHTS

5   Your right to social welfare   42

How the system works and how to make sure you receive

   your entitlements   42

The difference between contributory and non-contributory

   payments   43

The different types of social welfare   44

So, what is means testing?   45

What are you entitled to? Social welfare payments in detail   46

   Social welfare pensions   46

   Pensions for widows and widowers   47

   Other age-related benefits   47

   Supplementary welfare allowance   48

   One-parent family payment   48

   Deserted wife's benefit   49

   Guardian's payment (contributory)   49

   Guardian's payment (non-contributory)   50

   Invalidity pension   50

   Medical cards   50

   Treatment benefits   51

Maternity benefit   51
Adoptive benefit   51
Asylum seekers   51
Habitual Resident's test   52
Child benefit   52
Early childcare supplement   52
Jobseeker's benefit   53
Jobseeker's allowance   53
Back-to-work allowance and back-to-work enterprise
  allowance   53
Carer's benefit   54
Disability and injury benefits   54
Bereavement grant   54
Widowed parent's grant   55
Family income supplement   55
Drugs payments scheme   55
Nursing home subvention   55
Disabled persons   56
Free travel   56

6   **Your employment rights**   60
You may be more protected than you imagine   60
Minimum wage   60
A Sunday bonus   61
Annual leave entitlement   61
Holiday pay   61
Your working week   61
On-call workers   62
Dismissal rights   62
Time off work   63
What to do if you are unhappy with your employer   64
Redundancy   65

7   **Your rights as a 'financial' consumer**   66
Your basic rights   66
How to complain   66
If you're unhappy with your bank, building society,
  credit union or insurance company   67

If you're unhappy with your financial advisers   67
If you're unhappy with your pension company   68
Have you been turned down for a loan or credit card for
    no apparent reason?   68
If you're worried about Big Brother   69
If you're still unhappy and want to take it further   70

PART 3 BANKING, BORROWING AND GETTING OUT OF DEBT

8   Banking   74
How to enjoy the best banking in Ireland   74
Understanding the banking system   74
    Making the banking system work for you   75
What banks do best   76
Basic banking services explained   78
    Standing orders   78
    Direct debits   78
    Laser cards (debit cards)   78
    Overdrafts   79
What price banking?   79
Cutting the cost of your current account   80
Other types of bank account   82
    Other bank services to consider   82
The building society option   83
The An Post option   84
The credit union option   84
Banking on holiday   85

9   Getting out of debt   87
How to pay off all your loans – including your mortgage
    – quickly and easily   87
You may not even realise you have a problem   87
Sizing up the problem   88
Debt comes in many disguises   88
Beware the minimum payment trap   91
Debt threatens your future freedom   92
Seven excellent reasons to become debt free   93
The first step to getting out of debt   95

Taking stock of your situation 96
The art of debt elimination 98
   The consolidation approach 99
   The sniper approach 100

10 Borrowing 103
How to borrow sensibly and inexpensively 103
   Look at the difference! 103
So, what is 'sensible borrowing'? 104
Never borrow for longer than you have to 105
Build up a good financial/credit rating history 105
Why rates differ so widely 105
The first rule of borrowing 106
   Secured loans 106
   Unsecured loans 106
Choosing the best loan for your needs 107
The Money Doctor best loan guide 107

PART 4 COMPLETE GUIDE TO INSURANCE

11 Protecting yourself and your family 114
How to buy the medical, income and life insurance you
   actually need – at the lowest possible price 114
Spend time, not money 115
Income protection cover 117
Critical or serious illness insurance 118
Life cover 118
   Term insurance 119
   Whole of life assurance 120
Private medical insurance 120
Which types of cover should you choose? 121
How much life cover do you need? 123
   Life cover tax tip 123
Keeping the cost down 124

12 Protecting your possessions 125
Insider tips on how to keep the cost of your general insurance
   to a bare minimum 125
The importance of proper cover 125

The different types of 'general' insurance 126
Don't just rely on brokers 126
Home insurance 127
    Buildings cover 127
    Contents cover 128
Motor insurance 128
Insider tips on buying other general insurance 129

PART 5 A-Z OF PROPERTY PURCHASE

13 Mortgages 132
How to secure the best-value mortgage in Ireland 132
Taking advantage of the mortgage revolution 132
Throwing out the traditional 'mortgage rules' 134
Interest: all the difference in the world 135
Two mortgage options: repayment versus interest only 136
    Repayment/annuity mortgage 136
    Interest-only mortages 137
Fixed or variable rate? 139
A word about 'current account' mortgages 140
Why you should try to make mortgage overpayments 141
How the right professional adviser will save you money 142

14 Sub-prime Lending 144
Self-certification 147
The Lenders 147
Interest Rates 147
Charges 148
How to avoid the sub-prime market 149

15 Loans for the Over-60s 152
The lifetime mortgage 153
    The interest rate on a lifetime mortgage 153
Home reversion schemes 155
Home reversion fixed and variable share agreements 155
    How it works 156
Lifetime mortgages and home reversion scheme costs 157
The providers and their rates 158

| | Lifetime mortgages | 158 |
| | Reversion schemes | 159 |

16	Property questions	160
	Answers to your property and mortgage questions	160
	Should I buy or rent?	160
	How much can I borrow?	162
	What is APR?	162
	Is it worth switching my mortgage to get a lower rate?	163
	Help! I'm self-employed	163
	What will it cost for me to buy my home?	163
	What tax relief will I receive on my home loan?	165
	Does it make sense to buy a second property as an investment?	166
	What are the benefits of owning a home in a designated area?	166
	What's the story with local authority loans?	166
	What other state housing grants might be available to me?	167
	Is it worth repaying my mortgage early?	168
	What different types of home insurance will I need?	168
	If I have trouble making my mortgage repayments what should I do?	169

PART 6 GUARANTEED SAVINGS AND INVESTMENT SUCCESS

17	Saving for a rainy day	173
	The quickest, most efficient way to build up an emergency fund	173
	Good, old-fashioned savings	173
	Saving made simple	174
	How much is enough?	174
	Your savings strategy	175
	Emergency fund: three basic requirements	176
	Deposit accounts	176
	An Post accounts	176
	Membership of a credit union	177
	Savings and tax	177

| 18 | Investment strategies you can count on | 179 |
| | How to make your money grow and grow and grow | 179 |

Basic investment planning 180
   How much money is involved? 180
   How long can you tie your money up for? 181
   What type of return are you looking for? 181
   What risks are you willing to accept? 182
   To what extent is tax an issue? 182
   A proven investment strategy 182
   When long term means long term 183
Pooled investments 184
   Tracker bonds 185
   Unit trusts 186
   Unit-linked funds 186
   Managed funds 186
   Specialised funds 186
   Indexed funds 186
   With-profit funds 186
   Stock market 'baskets' 187
Alternative investments 187
   A low-risk, medium-term investment option 189
Investing in stocks and shares 189
   How to read the financial pages 191
   Dividend payments 191
   Shares and tax 192
   Choosing a stockbroker 192
   Bonds 193
   Gilts 194
Property 194
Tax-efficient investment options 196

PART 7 PLANNING FOR A RICHER RETIREMENT

19 Retirement basics 200
How to take advantage of the pension options open to you 200
Why you should make pension planning your number
   one priority 200
It is never too early or late to begin 201
Start by taking stock 202

Where do you go for the answers to all these questions? 202

How much will you need when you retire? 203

The good news 204

What to do if you work in the private sector 205

What to do if you work for yourself 206

20 Pensions made easy 208

Step-by-step instructions on how to make your retirement
dreams come true 208

A quick guide to pension schemes 208

Let's being at the very beginning 209

   Employee 209

   Self-employed 211

   Directors 212

More on PRSAs/personal pensions 212

   Small self-administered pension schemes (SSAP) or
   self-directed trusts 212

Big tax relief – the Revenue Commissioners are on your side 213

What happens to your pension contributions? 214

What is it going to cost? 215

What benefits should you be looking for? 217

What happens when you retire? 217

PART 8 WHY PAY MORE TAX THAN YOU HAVE TO?

21 Tax basics 222

Getting to grips with the tax system 222

Keeping it legal 223

Get to know your tax liabilities and the Revenue
Commissioners in the process 223

   Income tax 223

   Capital gains tax 224

   Capital acquisition tax 224

   Stamp duty 224

   Pay Related Social Insurance (PRSI) 225

   Value Added Tax (VAT) 225

Do you have to fill in a tax return? 225

22 Income tax basics 227
The first steps towards reducing your income tax bill 227
What sort of income do you have? 227
A quick explanation of income tax rates 228
Some good news for anyone on a low income 229
Taking advantage of marginal relief 230
Personal credits and tax allowances 231
PRSI – another form of income tax 231

23 All about income tax credits 233
How tax 'credits' and 'allowances' can help you save money 233
How tax credits work in practice 233
Check your tax credits every year 234
A complete guide to personal tax credits and
allowances for 2009 234
Single person's credit 234
Married person's credit 235
One-parent family credit 235
Widowed parent credit 235
Special age credits 235
The home carer's credit 235
Incapacitated child credit 236
Dependent relative credit 236
Incapacitated person's allowance 236
Blind person's credit 237
PAYE credit 237
Medical insurance 237
Permanent health insurance 237
Medical expenses relief 238
Rent relief 238
Relief for long-term unemployed people 238
Third-level college fees 239
Charitable donations 239
Trade union subscriptions 239
Loan interest relief 239
Relief on deeds of covenant 241
Pension contributions 241
Service charges 241

Investment relief	242
Seafarer's allowance	242

24 PAYE — 243

How to make the Pay As You Earn (PAYE) tax system work in your favour	243
The ins and outs of PAYE	243
Emergency tax	245
Getting your tax back! PAYE refunds	245
Making sure your expenses are tax free	247
Motor and travelling expenses	247
A chance to claim more	248
Other tax-free and tax-efficient perks	248
Daily and overnight allowances	249
Free or inexpensive accommodation	249
Staff entertainment	249
Communal transport to your place of work	250
Presents!	250
Meals	250
Lump sum payments	250
Educational fees	250
Injury or disability payments	250
Work tools	251
Pension scheme payments	251
Life cover	251
€250 bonus!	251
Health insurance	251
Medical cover	251
Season tickets	252
Childcare	252
Relocation expenses	252
Sports and recreational facilities	252
Mobile telephones	252
Car parking	252
Exam payments	253
Membership fees	253
Health screening	253
Long-service presents	253

Has your employer offered you an opportunity
   to buy shares? 253
Revenue online service (ROS) 255

25 Income tax for the self-employed 256
How to reduce your income tax bill if you work for yourself 256
   First things first 256
Self-assessment system 256
Preliminary tax 257
The mystery factor! 257
   A quick aside about accounting dates 258
Make your payments on time... or else 258
   Revenue Online Service 259
Do you need to register for VAT? 261
   Don't forget your PRSI 261
   Self-employment comes in many forms 262
Working out your profits 262
Expenses 263
A word about capital expenditure 264
Other tax-saving possibilities 264

26 Tax and property 265
Property investor? How to ensure you keep your tax bill
   to a minimum 265
The tax advantages of property investment 265
A word of warning 266
Tax incentives 266
'Generous' expenses 267

27 Tax and the company car 268
How working motorists can drive down their tax bill 268
How to slash the cost of your benefit in kind 269
   Another clever way to cut your benefit in kind 270
Should you have a company car at all? 270
100% tax free motoring! 271

28 Capital gains tax 272
Don't pay a penny more capital gains tax than you have to 272
How the tax works 272

Basic capital gains tax planning 273
One more useful way to reduce your bill 274

29 Capital acquisition tax 275
Don't allow your gifts and inheritances to be taxed
    unnecessarily 275
Take full advantage of the tax-free thresholds 275
Five completely tax-free categories 276
Two useful ways to avoid capital acquisition tax 277
Farms 278
Businesses 278

30 Love, marriage and lower taxes 279
Extra tax benefits for those who are married 279
Marriage brings greater flexibility 279
Other tax concessions made to married couples 280
Even better news if you're married and self-employed 280
    Turn your children to a tax advantage 281

31 Tax for the ex-pat 282
Tax planning tips if you're living and working abroad 282
It's all about residency and domicile 282
What happens when you move abroad? 283
A money-back offer: tax rebates 283
What is your tax status? 284
Your personal tax credits and reliefs 285
Get professional help! 285

32 Special tax advice for farmers 286
Income tax 287
Capital acquisitions tax 287
Capital gains tax 288
VAT 289
Stock relief 289
Compulsory disposal of livestock 290
Capital allowances 290
Milk quotas 290
Stamp duty 290
Farm consolidation relief 291
Leasing of farm land 291

PART 9 WHEN THE LAST THING YOU WANT TO THINK

ABOUT IS MONEY

33 Redundancy   294
    Top tips, including advice on your rights should you
        experience redundancy   294
    Background briefing on 'redundancy'   294
    How much are you entitled to?   295
    What happens if the employer doesn't pay up?   295
    What's the tax situation?   295
    Claiming tax relief on a redundancy payment   296

34 Separation   298
    The financial consequences of separation   298
        The implications of living apart   299
    What happens when you 'live apart'?   299
    What happens when you get a 'legal separation'?   300
    What is a judicial separation?   301

35 Divorce   303
    The financial consequences of divorce   303
    The importance of budgeting   304
    How your situation will have changed   305
    Making proper pension provision   305

36 Coping with bereavement   307
    What to do about the money side of things when someone
        close dies   307
    A short list of definitions   307
    When there is a will   309
    When there is no will or no valid will   309
    The right of the spouse to inherit   309
    Status of children under a will   311
    Non-marital children   312
    Non-marital relationships   312
    The role of the personal representative   313
        Obtaining the Grant of Representation   313
        The importance of notifying the tax office   314
        What the personal representative could be liable for   315

How the assets are passed on 315
The benefits of Joint Ownership 316
How is it that assets can pass outside of the will or intestacy? 317

Appendix 1 Learn to speak the language 319
A quick guide to the most important 'personal finance' terminology 319
Percentages made easy 320
    You are not alone 320
    What is a percentage? 320
    How to work out percentages 320
The vital difference between capital and income 323
    All money is not equal 323
    And then there is 'interest' 323
The miracle of compound interest 324
    A financial concept that can make–or break–you 324
    Compound interest in one easy lesson 324
    No wonder lenders love you 325
Gearing 325
    Allowing other people to make you rich 325

Appendix 2 The Money Doctor's jargon buster 328

Appendix 3 100 top tax tips 347

Appendix 4 Decision trees 371
What to do about your pension arrangements if you
    are self-employed 371
What to do about your pension arrangements if you are
    an employee 372
How to generate a regular income from a lump sum 373
How to create a financial plan 374
Do you need life cover? 375
Do you need income protection insurance? 376
Do you need private medical insurance? 377
How to maximise the value of regular saving 378
Inheritance on intestacy (no will in existance) 379

Appendix 5 Tax rates   380

Appendix 6 Tax computation template   382

Appendix 7 The Money Doctor's annual budget account   383

Appendix 8 Money Doctor Advisers   385

Appendix 9 Useful addresses   392

Appendix 10 Important tax dates   396

Appendix 11 Budget 2009   399

Appendix 12 20 cracking ways to beat the credit crunch   407

Index   422

Your Financial Notes   436

PREFACE

Welcome to the 2009 edition of Ireland's most comprehensive finance guide.

Unfortunately, we came down to earth with a bang in 2008, and it's not over yet. We were caught *on the hop* by the effects of the sub-prime crisis, which started in the US early 2007, resulting in a very significant decline in liquidity for Irish financial institutions over the last few months in particular.

So, not only did the cost of money increase as banks found it increasingly difficult to buy funding, but when they did they had to buy at much higher rates e.g. European Central Bank base rate towards the end of the year steadied at c. 4.25%, while lenders were forced to buy funding at 5% + before their margin or *profit* was added. As a result, borrowers became scarce and lenders were happy to close up shop for a month or two. It was also easier to turn down an application than trying to fund it.

As if that was not bad enough, the Irish stock market suffered the worst one-year decline in the history of public markets. However, it was the ferocity and speed of the worldwide, and Irish, economic decline that took us all by surprise. Bear Stearns and Lehman Brothers were just two of the major financial giants that failed. *Doom and gloom* became the buzz words. But, don't panic, there are still some of us who beat a more positive drum.

In this 2009 edition, I have included my own solution to the current economic downturn with a new appendix titled 20 Cracking Ways to Beat the Credit Crunch. This takes a look at the consumer's personal finances rather than the macro-economic picture. What is important is how it is going to affect you personally and what you can do about it. The chapters Sub-Prime Lending and Loans for the Over 60s have especially been revised as a result of the credit crunch impact. Plus, the usual Budget '09 summary (see Appendix 11) and updates from the past year throughout the book, along with a revised 100 Top Tax Tips (see Appendix 3) and the revamped Money Doctor's Jargon Buster (see Appendix 2).

I have also included a new section in this year's annual for those wanting to *press the flesh* when it comes to financial advice – Money Doctor advisers (see Appendix 8). These are professional financially experienced advisers whom I have carefully selected, vetted and appointed as my personal representatives. All these men and women are qualified (QFA) or qualify under the 'grandfather rule' (have at least 15–20 years experience with a financial institution) and are employed by Providence Finance Services Limited trading as The Money Doctor, **or** are self-employed financial advisers (having their own authorisation from the Financial Regulator and their appointment letter from The Money Doctor).

Therefore, if you do need a **personal one-to-one financial review**, or someone to give you solid, independent advice, consider the advantages of a consultation with a **Money Doctor adviser**. You can go directly to the website (www.moneydoctor.ie) or email me (jlowe@moneydoctor.ie), or contact the Administration Manager (01 278 5555) to organise an appointment with myself or your own **Money Doctor adviser**.

I often use the following analogy to explain why financial planning is so important:

If you were driving from, say, Cork to Belfast you wouldn't choose a road at random and hope that it would take you where you want to get. Rather, you would plan your journey *in advance*. If, as you travelled, you encountered diversions, you'd get out the road map and decide on the new route. Throughout the journey you'd check your progress.

This book will act then as both a planner and a map on your journey to sound finances.

For many years I have felt that Ireland lacked an annual finance guide that offered genuinely helpful, accurate and independent money advice in language that anyone could understand. I believe that this book fills the gap. Why?

- It is **comprehensive**. Every possible subject has been covered – from getting the best deal on your mortgage to saving for retirement and from slashing your tax bill to working overseas.

- No less importantly, it is packed with **practical** advice. Whatever your circumstances, whatever questions you need answered, whatever your financial goals – you'll find the answers in the following pages.

- All the information here is presented in **plain, jargon-free** English and accompanied by **action-oriented** tips. You'll find real-life examples, checklists and a comprehensive index, too.

- The book has also been written for 2009 – and so it is 'bang up to date'.

MORE THAN A BOOK

Actually, I am referring to this as a 'book' – but really it is more of a 'service'. Because there is also a website with lots of extra information and an 'Ask The Experts' service. So if you need personalised advice you can always email me additional questions at: info@moneydoctor.ie.

THE BIGGER PICTURE

Another advantage that this book has over anything else available in Ireland is that it provides lots of guidance on financial planning. So you can use this book to resolve specific issues (such as paying off all your loans or cutting the cost of your insurance) or to create your own money plan.

WHY THE MONEY DOCTOR?

The short answer is that I aim to do for your wealth what a medical doctor will do for your health. That is to say, I will show you how to overcome any financial 'illnesses' you may be suffering from and also how to improve your financial fitness dramatically. I don't want to stretch the analogy too far … but you can rely on me – as you would rely on a good doctor – to be honest, trustworthy and professional. I'm qualified and I'm experienced.

That's the short answer. Now let me give you the slightly longer answer.

In 1999, at the age of 47, I resigned from my job as senior manager of an Irish bank and turned my back on 27 years of working for mainstream financial institutions. I gave up job security, a pension, a company car and five weeks a year paid holiday. This wasn't the act of the mad man, but the act of someone who had had enough of 'selling' and wanted to start 'telling'.

There is a lot that's right with our financial services sector. It is stable, well regulated and offers both choice and value. But it has one major flaw: it is sales driven, not *solution* driven. Banks, building societies and insurance companies always promote their own products rather than someone else's – even if their products are less appropriate and/or more expensive. This has led to a great deal of consumer cynicism and – quite frankly – suspicion. The reason why I gave up my job and changed direction was because I wanted to be above such suspicion. I wanted to be independent – free to do what was best for the 'patient'.

With my first book and this, my fourth finance annual – together with the www.moneydoctor.ie website – I aim to fill what I perceive to be a real gap in the market. That is to say:

- reliable, up-to-date and accurate personal finance information
- unbiased, easy-to-understand and relevant financial advice.

In particular, I cover both the principles of better financial management and the practical aspects of taking financial decisions. *The Money Doctor* will answer all your questions about how to make the most of your money. If there is something you feel I have left out please let me know so that I can include it in future editions.

ONE FINAL POINT

Dealing with money shouldn't be a chore, but a pleasure. Whether you read this book from cover to cover or dip in and out, I hope it will inspire you in all your future financial dealings.

John Lowe
Dublin, October 2008

IS THIS BOOK FOR YOU?

To get the most out of this book …

- You will find this book relevant, regardless of your financial position, age or gender.

- One of the most important aspects of the guide is that it concentrates on 'how to' information, as in: how to cut the cost of your mortgage, how to get rid of your debts, how to build up savings, how to save tax, and how to protect your family.

- If there is a particular subject you want to learn about, then check the detailed contents page or the index.

- The book is written in plain English and contains plenty of:
  - case histories
  - real-life examples
  - checklists
  - action-orientated advice.

- The book is divided into nine sections covering every aspect of personal finance. It is an annual handbook so the information it contains will be up to date, and include the latest budgetary and legislative changes.

- Each chapter begins with a summary and ends with a list of action points.

- Decision trees (Appendix 4) are designed to help you make a decision by setting out the logic process graphically and allowing you to easily retrace the steps made in coming to that decision. While they are not a substitute for proper research, they can enhance the user's ability to implement what they know.

Look out for the symbols used throughout the book:

Money Doctor Wealth Warning This symbol is used to warn you about something that may have an adverse affect on your financial wealth!

Money Doctor Wealth Check This symbol is used to highlight something that could really improve your financial fitness.

GETTING THE MOST OUT OF THIS BOOK

The Money Doctor says this book will be of relevance to you if you …

- have money questions and don't know to whom to turn for an honest, accurate, unbiased answer
- want the latest financial information
- want to reduce your tax bill
- worry about money
- have, or plan to get, a mortgage
- have credit cards, store cards, hire purchase agreements, an overdraft, personal loans, a mortgage or any other borrowings because it will show you how it is possible to pay all these debts off in a matter of years simply by following a simple, proven, logical plan
- have money on deposit or save money on a regular basis
- want to build up your capital worth and guarantee yourself a comfortable (and possibly an early) retirement
- have capital and don't know how to invest it
- have dependants and you are worried about their well being
- have (or think you should have) any sort of life or critical illness cover
- worry about the quality of financial advice you are receiving
- are separating, or thinking of it.

THE MONEY DOCTOR WEBSITE

The Money Doctor is not just a book: it is a complete service. Visit the free Money Doctor website at www.moneydoctor.ie The Money Doctor website offers you:

- extra articles and checklists covering a huge range of personal finance topics
- the latest personal finance tips, advice and information
- 100 top tax tips (updated regularly)
- up-to-the minute mortgage and investment rates
- special calculators allowing you to see (at the press of a button) what your mortgage or other loan will cost you – as well as how much

your savings will earn you

- an online monthly budget planner
- timely information such as the current tax rates and allowances
- the chance to arrange a consultation with the Money Doctor or one of the Money Doctor advisers
- podcasts on a variety of financial subjects
- an opportunity to receive the Money Doctor's free monthly newsletter or ezine.

The website is updated daily and all the information it contains is available *free* – without charge and without obligation.

You should only deal with an Authorised Advisor to provide insurance, investment and pension advice and deal with a mortgage intermediary who has formal authorised agencies with *all* the lenders to provide credit services. This will mean that they are legally obliged to provide you with the best possible or most appropriate advice.

You can be certain that any individual or firm who is authorised will not only have had to pass a stringent series of tests to qualify, but that their performance will be strictly monitored on an ongoing basis.

Extra consumer protection

You should be aware that there are a number of professional bodies covering the financial services industry. My own belief is that you should only deal with members of these bodies. These are:

- The Independent Mortgage Advisers' Federation (IMAF).

- The Irish Brokers' Association (IBA).

- Professional Insurance Brokers' Association (PIBA).

- Life Insurance Association (LIA).

Your financial adviser should ideally be a QFA (Qualified Financial Adviser) as well as having substantial financial experience. Individual membership of other professional bodies, such as the Institute of Bankers in Ireland, is also desirable.

Finally, if you are looking for advice on buying company shares then you should deal with intermediaries who are members of (or affiliated members of) the Irish Stock Exchange or an Authorised Adviser.

Don't allow yourself to be talked into accepting advice from someone who isn't both independent and qualified. If in doubt visit my website – www.moneydoctor.ie

ACKNOWLEDGEMENTS

There are many people who deserve a clap on the back for their personal help and support to me and who have guided me throughout my career. Included are family, friends, mentors and colleagues. Special mention and special thanks go to the following for their great assistance in the production of this my fourth book:

- My family who continue to support and love me.
- Jonathan Self (writer, novelist and mentor).
- George Butler (Money Doctor).
- John P. Carlin (friend, accountant and Co. Tyrone supporter).
- Simon Carty (Solicitor).
- Frances Brennan (Ciaran Ryan & Co. Accountants).
- Monica McInerney (best-selling novelist) for her introduction to my publishers Gill & Macmillan.
- Winifred Power (Copy Editor), Aoife O'Kelly (Managing Editor) and all the talented team at G&M – every one a gem.
- Fergal Tobin (Gill & Macmillan) for his fantastic help and for giving me the excuse to tell my friends I was having lunch with my publisher!
- Special thanks to RTÉ, Newstalk 106FM, Today FM, East Coast Radio, Dublin's Country Mix, Q 102, FM 104 and the myriad of radio stations around the country for their great support.

PART 1

HOW TO BECOME FINANCIALLY FIT IN 2009

IT ALL COMES DOWN TO BELIEF PATTERNS

I am far too practical a person to be taken in by 'psycho-babble'. However, I do believe that *if you want to be financially better off than you are at the moment then you simply must come to grips with your own belief patterns as they relate to money.* One method of explaining what I mean is to quote some of the different things people have said to me about money:

- 'I would always shop around for a better deal on most things – but not on financial products.'
- 'I hate talking about money. I find it embarrassing.'
- 'Money seems to slip through my fingers.'
- 'I worry about money all the time but I don't do anything about it, because I am not sure what to do.'
- 'Money is boring. We have enough. Why think about it?'

In my experience almost everyone has deeply held beliefs in relation to money – usually negative beliefs. Most can be attributed to one or more of the following factors:

Formative experiences. Take, for instance, the case of someone whose family suffered financial hardship when they were growing up. Naturally, it would influence their attitude to money.

Parental influence. Some parents talk about money, others don't – but either way children can end up being worried about there not being enough. By the same token, some parents are spendthrift while others are positively tight-fisted – again influencing their children's beliefs.

Lack of education. Though there have been recent moves to change the national curriculum, 'personal finance' is still not really taught properly in our schools.

The mystification of money. Financial institutions seem to conspire to make money as mysterious a subject as possible.

Lack of trust in personal finance professionals. Bank managers are viewed as 'fair weather friends' and the institutions they work for as impersonal and greedy. Insurance and pensions salespeople are hardly revered in society. People are suspicious of the experts they rely on to give them advice.

Society's attitude to money. There are some societies where money is discussed openly. In Ireland, however, it is considered rude to talk about money and crass to spend too much time managing it.

The link between belief and behaviour

There is no doubt in my mind that there is a direct link between (a) what you believe about money, (b) your behaviour in relation to money and (c) how much money you end up having. The fact is if you view money in a negative way, you are reducing your chances of a financially stable life. You aren't giving yourself a proper chance.

What's more, if you think that sorting out your personal finances will take more time and effort than *not* sorting them out, think again. Not paying attention to money is likely to result in you:

- wasting a vast amount of energy worrying
- wasting a vast amount of cash
- putting yourself and your dependants at risk
- reducing your standard of living
- lengthening the number of years you have to work
- suffering a shortfall in your pension fund when you reach retirement age.

If you start to *think* positively about money, I guarantee that you will begin to behave more positively about money. And if you behave more positively about money, I guarantee that you will find yourself able to build up much greater wealth.

What are your financial dreams?

- To own your own home without a mortgage?
- To have enough money to retire early?
- To be wealthy enough to pay for all the things you want – such as an education for your children or a second home – without going into debt?

Whatever your dreams, unless you are very, very lucky the only way to make them come true is to make a proper plan. Such a plan – a financial plan – will help ensure that you get from where you are to where you want to be. Creating one is a lot simpler and quicker than you may imagine, as I explain in this section of the book. Furthermore, I guarantee that the process of writing a plan will – in itself – make you substantially better off. Why? Read on and you'll find out.

MONEY DOCTOR WEALTH CHECK

The section on financial planning explains:

- what a financial plan is
- why you need a financial plan
- the different stages involved in writing a financial plan
- practical tips on writing your own plan
- where to get professional financial planning help you can trust
- sample financial plans.

And more besides. Everything, in fact, you need to make financial planning easy.

1

ALL IT TAKES
IS A LITTLE PLANNING

Many people are under the impression that financial planning is a complex process requiring great expertise. In fact, creating a financial plan is a remarkably straightforward activity involving three easy steps:

1 Decide what your financial or money objectives are, and prioritise them.

2 Assess what resources you have available to you now, and consider what resources you may have in the future.

3 Work out what actions you need to take to make your financial (or your 'money') objectives come true.

This short chapter explains the 'ins and outs' of writing a first-class financial plan. The next chapter explains, in greater detail, how to write your own.

WHY YOU NEED A FINANCIAL PLAN

Your financial plan should have the same qualities as the road map analogy as described in the introduction. That is to say, it should help you reach your destination; make your journey as fast as possible; and prevent you wasting time or energy.

MONEY DOCTOR WEALTH CHECK

A little planning brings big rewards

Having a financial plan will bring both *material* and *emotional* rewards. From a **material** perspective a financial plan will make it possible for you to meet your financial objectives. These might include some or all of the following:

- wiping out all your personal debts
- paying off your mortgage years earlier
- never having to borrow again
- having enough money to afford the things that are important to you, such as an education for your children or a second home
- having enough money to retire early
- knowing that you and your dependants are protected against financial hardships
- being wealthy enough never to have to worry about the future – whatever it may bring.

And the **emotional** benefits? You'll feel a tangible peace of mind once you have your financial affairs in order. In addition, a well-considered financial plan guarantees that you will never need to waste energy worrying about money again.

Some people's circumstances, of course, may be such that they will not manage to achieve any or all of these objectives. For these people, financial planning is crucial to getting the maximum advantage from limited resources.

SUPPOSING YOU *DON'T* PLAN?

Suppose you don't bother with a financial plan at all? Leaving something as important as your financial future to chance is risky. True, we live in a country with a relatively generous state benefit system. But would you really want to rely on it? You probably wouldn't starve, but you wouldn't have an easy time of it.

Incidentally, many people assume that the worst thing anyone can do is ignore financial planning completely. In fact, in my experience the people who are worst off are those who *compartmentalise* their money decisions. Let me give you just three examples:

1 When you want to buy a home, you look for a mortgage.

2 When you begin to think about retirement, you start a pension.

3 When you have a young family, you take out life insurance.

The trouble with a **compartmentalised** approach to money is that it is both wasteful and risky because you may:

- end up spending more than you have to on borrowing money
- by default, pay more tax than you need to
- end up with inferior and expensive financial products
- risk your capital, your income, and the standard of living of you and your dependants
- miss opportunities and
- make yourself unhappy worrying about your financial security.

A symptom of this approach is responding to ad hoc situations in a knee-jerk manner, for example, subscribing for newly issued shares on a whim, or paying for education fees when you hadn't expected to do so.

INSTANT SAVINGS AND MORE

Incidentally, one of the key benefits of creating a financial plan is that it will involve a review of your existing financial products. Such a review is bound to result in all sorts of savings as you identify products that are either over-priced or unnecessary. Let me give you just one real-life example:

> One of the Money Doctor's 'patients', Tony, an ex-banker, told me that he'd spent more time choosing his last car than choosing his mortgage. As a result he was, without realising it, paying 1% above the home loan market rate. He'd also allowed himself to be sold a very expensive life insurance plan. I calculated that, over the 25-year term of Tony's €210,000 mortgage, these two products alone would cost him a staggering additional €38,000 in unnecessary loan and insurance payments.

Frankly, because people pay less attention to their finances than to other areas of their lives, they tend to get 'ripped off'. With a financial plan in place, you'll know that you aren't:

- accepting lower rates of return on your savings
- paying more tax than you have to
- paying more to borrow than you have to
- taking out insurance policies that you don't need, or that don't provide you with the protection that you want, and that may well be over-priced
- making poor investment decisions
- failing to plan properly for your retirement or
- putting your money at risk.

WHAT DOES A FINANCIAL PLAN LOOK LIKE?

Your financial plan may be no more than a single piece of paper on which you've jotted down appropriate notes. You might think of it in the same way that you think of a career plan or any other sort of life plan. It is to guide you, save you time, and ensure that none of your effort is wasted. Or, if you are comfortable using spreadsheet software, you could also do it electronically. Whatever way you choose to complete a financial plan, remember it is essential for giving you a map for your financial road to the future.

HOW LONG SHOULD A FINANCIAL PLAN LAST FOR?

Obviously, there is no set period for a financial plan. My general advice is to write it so that it covers the **current** and **next phase** of your life. For instance, if you've just left university and you're starting your first job, then you might write a financial plan designed to take you through to when you own your home. Bear in mind that financial plans need to be *flexible*. You may change your own ideas about what you want or circumstances may intervene and require a change of direction.

A financial plan that only covers a specific, short-term requirement (for instance, saving for your retirement) isn't going to bring you lasting financial success.

IF YOU THINK YOU NEED HELP

You will find everything you need to write your own financial plan in this book. However, you may decide you'd like some professional help. There are any number of people who would like to help you with your personal finances, from bank managers to life insurance salespeople, from credit brokers to pension specialists.

The golden rule is: the fewer options the 'experts' can offer you, the less you should trust them.

Let me give you one pertinent example. If you go to your bank and express an interest in taking out a pension, whoever you speak to is duty bound to offer you something from the bank's own range of products, if they have their own tied agency, even if he or she knows that you would get a better deal elsewhere. If, on the other hand, you go to an independent financial adviser (an authorised adviser for insurance and investments or a mortgage intermediary who has access to agencies with *all* the lenders) he or she will recommend the best and most competitively priced product for your needs.

For more tips on getting professional help, see p. 36.

THE MONEY DOCTOR SAYS...

- There is nothing in the least bit complicated about writing a financial plan. It is simply a matter of working out what your money ambitions are, how far you have got to date, and what action you need to take to get to where you want to go.

- Unless you are very, very lucky, the only way you are going to make your financial dreams come true is by planning.

- Your plan may be a single piece of paper with a few notes.

- The process of writing a plan is likely to bring big savings as you identify financial products you have already bought that are either (a) over-priced or (b) not really necessary.

- Everything you need to write a financial plan is in this book. But if you want help, use an authorised adviser or mortgage intermediary who has authorised agencies with all the lenders. Their assistance could well be free.

2
WRITING A FINANCIAL PLAN

EVERYTHING YOU NEED TO KNOW TO WRITE
YOUR OWN FINANCIAL PLAN (OR TO GET
SOMEONE ELSE TO DO IT FOR YOU)

If you've put off writing a financial plan because you thought it would
be both time consuming and tedious, then this chapter will reassure you.
Not only is it possible to produce a detailed financial plan in a matter of
hours but as you get involved in the process you may find it
considerably more interesting than you ever imagined.

MONEY DOCTOR WEALTH CHECK

First things first

Many people begin the whole financial planning process
because they want to resolve a particular financial question. But
you shouldn't look at financial needs in isolation. Every
financial decision you make should be part of an overall plan.
Thus, a particular product – such as a mortgage, loan,
insurance policy or investment – should not just be judged on
its own particular merits but also in terms of how it moves you
closer to your financial objectives. For this reason, no financial
plan can be created until you have set and prioritised your
financial objectives.

HOW DO YOU DECIDE WHAT
YOUR FINANCIAL OBJECTIVES SHOULD BE?

My advice is to start by **dreaming**. Consider what you'd like to be doing
in, say, five years time, ten years time, and twenty years time. Consider

what work (if any) you'll be doing, where you'll be living, and how you'll be spending your leisure time. What will your family situation be? Once you have a clear picture of the future life you'd like to have, start expressing it in financial terms.

Your possible financial objectives might include:

- owning your own home, outright, without a mortgage
- making sure you have sufficient income to retire (possibly early) and live in comfort
- ensuring that you and your dependants will not suffer financial hardship regardless of any misfortunes that may befall you
- having sufficient wealth to pay for things that you consider important, whether it's charitable donations, an education for your children, or some other item such as a second home or a caravan
- having sufficient wealth to allow you to spend your time as you wish, for instance, having the money to start your own business.

PRIORITISING YOUR FINANCIAL OBJECTIVES

Having produced a list of financial objectives, your next task should be to put them in **order of priority**.

What you consider important will be determined to a great extent by your personal circumstances. For instance, if you're in third-level education, you'll have a very different view of money to someone five years away from retirement. Someone with a lot of debts will have different concerns to someone with a lump sum to invest.

Nevertheless, regardless of your age, existing wealth, health, number of dependants, or – for that matter – any other factor, I would recommend that you keep the following principles in mind when deciding what your financial priorities should be:

1 For most people, their greatest asset is their **income**. Unless you are fortunate enough to receive a windfall, it is almost certainly your income which you will use to achieve your financial objectives. Under the circumstances you don't want to risk it and you don't want to waste it. There are all sorts of inexpensive insurance policies designed to protect your income. And by making sure that you don't waste a single cent (especially when buying financial services) you can ensure that it's used to optimum purpose.

2 **Personal debt** – by which I mean everything from store cards to mortgages – will be the biggest drain on your income. If you've borrowed money (and, obviously there are many circumstances under which this makes excellent sense) then you should make it a priority to repay your loans as quickly as possible. This is easily achievable as I explain in Part 3.

3 It's vital to have a safety net or **emergency fund** to deal with those little trials, tribulations and extra expenses that life often throws our way. In Part 6, I suggest how much this fund should be, and the best way to build it up.

4 If you've got a good, secure income, it doesn't actually matter what other assets you own. Emotionally, it's nice to have the security of owning your own home. Financially, it certainly makes sense. But,

actually, the best investment that most people could ever make is in a really decent pension plan. With a good pension plan you can leave work early and – if you live to 100 or more – never have to worry about money again. One of the best things about modern pension plans is that they are both flexible and diverse.

5   It is not inconceivable that we will live to a very old age and in some cases suffer a reduction in our mental ability to handle money matters. Before this may arise it is worth considering setting up an enduring power of attorney. This is a document providing for the management of a person's affairs in the event of their becoming mentally incapacitated. The appointed person (the 'attorney') may be allowed to take a wide range of actions on your behalf in relation to property, business and social affairs. He or she may make payments from the specified accounts, make appropriate provision for any specified person's needs and make appropriate gifts to the donor's relations or friends. You can appoint anyone you wish to be your attorney, including a spouse, family member, friend, colleague, etc.

6   Know thyself! There's no point in setting financial objectives that you're going to find impossible to attain. Your financial objectives may involve modest changes in your behaviour, but they shouldn't require a complete change in your personality!

TEN UNIVERSAL NEEDS

Ultimately, financial planning is about tailoring a solution to meet your precise requirements. Having said this, there are a number of 'universal' needs that most of us face. To my mind they are:

1   Having an emergency fund to cover unexpected expenses.

2   Paying off any expensive personal loans and credit card debt.

3   Short-term saving for cars, holidays, and so forth.

4   Income protection, in case you are unable to work for any reason.

5   Life assurance for you (and, if relevant, your partner).

6   Starting a pension plan (in my opinion it is never too early).

7   Buying a home with the help of a mortgage.

8   Saving for major purchases.

9   Planning for education fees (if you have children), whether for private school or university.

10   Building up your personal investments.

To this, I suppose I might add long-term care planning if you're worried that your pension and/or the state may not provide for you sufficiently in retirement.

SETTING REALISTIC AIMS

If you had unlimited funds, then you could achieve all your financial ambitions without difficulty and you wouldn't need a financial plan. As it is, for most of us life is more complicated. Since we can't have everything we want instantly, we need to set realistic targets and work towards them in easy stages. To make sure we have realistic targets we must test them. Let me give you an example:

David is 40 and self-employed. His objective is to be financially independent by the age of 55. At that point he wants to be able to live comfortably without working. His current income is €40,000 a year and he feels that he'll be able to manage on much less, say €25,000 a year, once he retires. To achieve this, he'll need capital resources of between €500,000 and €600,000. At this point in time he has a pension fund worth €100,000 which, if it grows in real terms (i.e. after the effects of inflation) by 5% a year, will be worth some €208,000 in 15 years. He also has €25,000 of stocks and shares, which he expects to grow at a slightly faster rate, say 7% a year, which would mean an extra €74,000 in 15 years.

In other words, David has a shortfall of between €212,000 and €312,000. To fill this shortfall, he would have to save at least €600 a month (assuming a growth rate of at least 7%) until he reaches 55. However, €600 a month, or more, is a lot of cash to find, so he may have to adjust his expectations. Perhaps he could live on less? Or postpone his retirement an extra five years? Or earn additional money?

Note: this example is just to give you a feel for what I'm talking about. Inflation would need to be taken into account when deciding what to do.

Once you settle on your overall objectives, you'll have to decide which is the most important to you. For instance, would you rather pay off your mortgage ten years early, or take an annual holiday overseas? Is being able to retire early more important than putting your children through private school?

You must also weigh up other priorities. I always recommend that those with dependants take out income protection insurance before they take out life cover. Why? Anyone under retirement age is 20 times more likely to be unable to work for a prolonged period due to sickness than they are to die. Another recommendation I often make is that people with high personal debt pay it off or consolidate it before they start saving money. This is because it costs more to borrow than you can hope to earn from most forms of low-risk investment.

Anyway, the two key points I want to make are:

1   Keep your financial expectations realistic.

2   Test them to make sure.

HOW FAR HAVE YOU GOT?

If the first stage of a financial plan involves deciding what you want, then the second stage is all about working out where you've got to so far. You need to produce an honest and realistic assessment of:

- what resources you have
- what demands there are on your resources and
- what action you are already taking to meet your targets.

Once you have this information you'll know what surplus is available to you and whether you have a shortfall that needs to be made up.

If you visit my website – www.moneydoctor.ie – you'll find several aids to helping you make and reach your goals. Otherwise, you can use the questionnaire that follows.

YOUR MONTHLY INCOME AND OUTGOINGS

I usually suggest that people start with their income and – if relevant – their spouse/partner's income. The best way to calculate it is as follows:

Monthly income – gross	You	Spouse/partner
	€	€
Salary or wages	_____	_____
Profits from business	_____	_____
Investment income	_____	_____
State benefits	_____	_____
Pensions	_____	_____
Other earnings	_____	_____
Anything else	_____	_____
Subtotal A	€_____	_____
Less tax (PRSI and income tax)	_____	_____
Subtotal B	€_____	_____

The resulting figure (Subtotal B) is your disposable income. You now need to consider how you spend it.

Monthly outgoings	You	Spouse/partner
	€	€
Rent/mortgage	_____	_____
Utilities (gas, electricity,	_____	_____

telephone, etc.) _____ _____

Food _____ _____

Household items _____ _____

Drink _____ _____

Car(s) _____ _____

Home insurance _____ _____

Life insurance _____ _____

Other insurance _____ _____

Clothes _____ _____

Child-related expenses _____ _____

Credit cards _____ _____

Other loan repayments _____ _____

Spending money _____ _____

Pension contribution _____ _____

Regular saving plans _____ _____

Anything else _____ _____

Subtotal C €_____

By subtracting your monthly outgoings (Subtotal C) from your disposable income (Subtotal B) you will arrive at your available surplus. Don't despair if this is a 'minus' figure. That's why you are reading this book – and, together, we are going to do something about it!

YOUR ASSETS

Working out what assets you have involves the same process as working out what your surplus income is. You need to tot up the value of everything you own and subtract any debts or other liabilities you may have.

Start with a list of the assets themselves:

Assets	You €	Spouse/partner €
Home	_____	_____
Personal belongings	_____	_____
Furniture and contents of home	_____	_____
Car(s)	_____	_____
Other property	_____	_____
Other valuables	_____	_____
Cash	_____	_____
Savings	_____	_____
Shares	_____	_____
Other investments	_____	_____
Subtotal D	€_____	

With regard to any investments you have – savings plans or a pension, for instance – you may want to work out what they will be worth at whatever point in the future you intend to cash them in. This can be a complex business. A pension fund, for instance, may grow by more or less than the predicted amount. Therefore, it could be well worth your while to get professional assistance with your calculations.

YOUR LIABILITIES

Liabilities	You €	Spouse/partner €
Mortgage	_____	_____
Credit card debts	_____	_____
Personal loans	_____	_____

Hire purchase   _____ _____

Overdraft   _____ _____

Other loans   _____ _____

Tax   _____ _____

Other liabilities   _____ _____

Subtotal E   €_____

By subtracting your total liabilities (Subtotal E) from the value of your assets (Subtotal D) you will arrive at what financial experts call your 'net worth'. While it not good if this is a 'minus' figure, once again you shouldn't despair. The whole purpose of a money plan is to strengthen your finances.

THE IMPORTANCE OF MAKING ASSUMPTIONS

All financial planning requires 'assumptions'. Some of these assumptions will be personal to you, such as how much income you expect to earn in the future or how many children you anticipate supporting. Other assumptions will be related to factors only partly within your control, such as the return you can expect to receive for a particular investment. You'll also need to allow for financial factors beyond your control, such as the state of the economy.

When making assumptions, the longer the period you're planning for, the less accurate your assumptions will be. It's very hard to predict exactly what you'll be earning in, say, five or ten years, let alone what you'll be earning in twenty years.

In order to improve the quality of their assumptions, many people use historic figures for guidance. Below, I've detailed some statistics that you may find of help.

Inflation. There was a time when inflation had the single greatest influence on the economy and thus on financial planning. Although inflation has been quite low for the last few years, it still has a marked effect on the cost of borrowing and the value of your investments. Over the last ten years inflation has averaged 3.2% a year in Ireland. Over the last twenty years it's averaged 3.5% a year. At its peak, in the 1970s, inflation was running at 18% a year.

Interest rates. Interest rates vary enormously, especially when you are borrowing. For instance, in 2007, when a typical mortgage cost 4.95% per year, you could pay up to 24% on a typical store card. Over the last ten years the average mortgage rate has actually been 7% a year, though in 1995 it did reach 12% a year. During the same period the average personal loan rate has been 12% a year, and the average rate for deposits in a bank or building society has been 3% a year.

Investments. Not only do the returns on different types of investment vary dramatically, so do the returns within each sort of investment vehicle. So, while investing in the stock market could bring a better average return than investing in property, an individual investor might do substantially better or worse in one or the other. In general, it is best to spread your money between different types of investment, and to assume an average return of between 4% and 7% a year in real terms. For instance, over the last ten years the average return from government bonds has been 4.7% a year, while the average return on the stock market has been 10.1% (not including 2008).

MONEY DOCTOR WEALTH CHECK

How much capital will you need?

One of the hardest calculations anyone has to make is how much capital they need to provide a sufficient income for their needs. There are different factors affecting this: inflation, tax and investment performance.

On the whole, my advice is to assume a 2.5% return after inflation and tax. This means that for every €1,000 of annual income you require, you'll need €40,000 of capital. Put another way, if you want an annual income of €20,000 a year you'll need at least €800,000 worth of capital.

MONEY DOCTOR WEALTH CHECK

An important reminder

Do you have a will? If you do, when did you last update it? Are you taking *full* advantage of all the tax allowances and exemptions to make sure that your beneficiaries don't have to pay unnecessary inheritance tax?

If you are over 18 (or if you are younger, but married) you should draw up a will because if you don't your money will be distributed in accordance with the Succession Act of 1965. This means that your estate could end up not going to your chosen beneficiary or beneficiaries and could even end up filling the government's coffers.

You'll find more information about using your will to save capital acquisition tax on the Money Doctor website (www.moneydoctor.ie). Don't forget, both you and your partner should draw up a will and you should also consider:

- giving a power of attorney to someone you trust should you become physically incapacitated
- a living will explaining anything you would like done should you become so unwell as to be unable to communicate.

WHERE DO YOU NEED TO TAKE ACTION?

Which areas of your personal finances should you be dealing with first? Answer the questions below with a 'yes', 'no', or 'maybe'. Every question you answer with a 'no' or 'maybe' suggests an area where you need to take action.

- Do you spend less than you earn each month?
- Are you satisfied with your standard of living?
- Do your pay your credit card and charge card bills in full, on time, every month?
- Have you taken out sufficient life cover to ensure that your family's

lifestyle won't be adversely affected if you die?

- Are you happy with where you live? Is it costing more than you can afford?
- If you had to manage without an income, would you be able to support yourself for at least three months using money you have saved?
- Do you have a clear sense of financial goals? Have you spent any time thinking about how you're going to achieve them?
- Do you have a pension? Will it be sufficient to support you in reasonable comfort?
- Do you have a will?
- Do you have other investments designed to bring you long-term capital growth?

THE MONEY DOCTOR SAYS...

- If you are not sure where to begin – begin at the beginning. Work out what you want from your money – what your priorities are.
- Although everyone's circumstances are different, we all have the same basic needs – to secure our future regardless of what happens. This is done through a combination of saving, investment and insurance.
- Take a little time to work out where you are financially – it may be the most profitable half hour you ever spend.
- Don't be shy about asking for help. If you know you want to sort out your finances, but find it difficult, call in expert help.

3

MONEY IS A FAMILY AFFAIR

HOW FAMILIES CAN WORK TOGETHER TO ACHIEVE LONG-TERM FINANCIAL SECURITY

Anyone who has been in a settled relationship will know that money and love can be a potent combination – both good and bad. If you and your partner share the same attitude to money, then obviously you'll be able to build a secure future for yourselves faster, more efficiently and more enjoyably than if you are in conflict.

However, it would be ridiculous not to acknowledge that many relationships are blighted by arguments about money and that reaching a compromise isn't always easy. In this chapter we look at how couples – and families – can work together to reach their financial goals. And we also look at the importance of educating children about money.

PROBLEM? WHAT PROBLEM?

All relationship money problems tend to boil down to one or more of the following issues:

- how the money is earned and who is earning it
- how the money is spent and who is spending it
- how the money is being managed and who is managing it
- how the money is being saved (if it is being saved at all) and who is doing the saving

- how the money is being invested (if it is being invested at all) and who is handling the investment decisions
- what debts you have – both individually and jointly – and why they were incurred.

Of all the subjects which couples argue about – from the choice of holiday destination to who should do the washing-up – money arguments are the hardest to resolve. This is because our money beliefs tend to be (a) firmly held, (b) unconscious and (c) non-negotiable.

Couples who are serious about building a financially secure future for themselves need to keep an open mind regarding their partner's viewpoint. One of you may be a saver, the other a spender, but that doesn't mean a compromise isn't possible.

ARE YOU AND YOUR PARTNER FINANCIALLY COMPATIBLE?

When a couple disagree about money, it is almost always because they each hold different money beliefs. Which of the following categories best describes you and your partner?

Worry warts. People who worry so much that they never really enjoy money – even when they have plenty.

Big spenders. People who spend money whether or not they have it. They don't mind going into debt to fund their lifestyle.

Careful savers. People who are committed to saving. Sometimes they can be obsessive about it to the point of miserliness, however.

Optimistic dreamers. People who believe that through some miracle – perhaps an unexpected legacy or a lottery win – all their financial worries will be solved overnight.

Outright fools. People – sorry to be harsh – whose spending and borrowing is reckless.

Clever planners. People who plan for a secure financial future but still manage to enjoy a good lifestyle now.

Where a couple consists of two 'clever planners' you tend to get minimum friction. Otherwise, sooner or later, disagreements are bound to arise.

In an ideal world ...

In an ideal world, one would discuss money with a future partner before making any sort of commitment as this would allow you to check that you are financially compatible. However, we don't live in an ideal world and so most couples will find themselves tackling financial issues *after* they have been together for some time. Looking on the bright side, maybe this is preferable. After all, you now know and understand each other better.

OPENING A DIALOGUE

The first and most important step for anyone in a relationship is to open a dialogue with their partner. If you don't communicate you won't know what they are thinking, and they won't know what you are thinking. My advice is to have a gentle discussion in which you discuss some or all of the following topics:

- Your individual values in relation to money. What do each of you think is important?

- Any assumptions either of you may have. One of you may assume that finances should always be joint, the other may have fixed ideas about keeping them separate.

- *Your* dreams and desires and *your partner's* dreams and desires. How do you both envisage the future?

- *Your* fears and *your partner's* fears. What are you both most worried about?

Both of you will have inherited traits and you need to recognise what they are before any sort of agreement can be reached between you.

ANYTHING TO DECLARE?

There are so many tricky areas when it comes to discussing personal finance with your partner that it is hard to decide which is potentially the most controversial. One subject which never fails to cause problems is that of 'secret debts' and 'secret savings'. By this I mean:

- One or both partners have borrowed money without telling the other one.
- One or both partners have tucked money away without telling the other one.

Other 'secrets' which couples keep from each other include:

- How much one or other really earns.
- Money that one or the other has given away or promised (this often arises where one or other has been married before).

If you are harbouring a money secret from your partner, my advice is come clean. The longer you leave it, the worse it will be if you are discovered. Also, it is much harder (and sometimes impossible) to tackle your joint financial position if one of you is holding out.

MONEY DOCTOR WEALTH CHECK

The gentle art of confession

You have a money secret that you need to tell your partner. How can you do it without risking a break-up? Here are some tips:

- The longer you leave it, the worse it will be and the more chance that it will cause a serious rift.
- Pick your moment. No one likes to receive bad news just when they have to go to work or do something else. Better to raise the topic when you are alone and there is a chance to talk about it.
- If appropriate, don't forget to say 'sorry'.

- A medical doctor once told me that he always prepares family members for news about the death of a loved one a day or two before it is likely to happen with the words 'I am afraid you should expect the worst' – this gives them time to get used to the idea. If you start by saying you have a confession to make and it may shock or anger them, the conversation is unlikely to be as acrimonious.

- Don't fool yourself that – say – borrowing or spending money without telling your partner won't upset them. But, equally, remember that it is only money. The important thing is that there should be honesty in your relationship.

BUILDING A JOINT APPROACH TO MONEY

Disagreements about personal finance can be very divisive – I have seen figures that suggest half of the couples who break up do so because of a disagreement about money. So when I say that you need to agree a joint financial strategy with your partner I don't say it lightly. One approach that I have found works well is to:

- **Look for common ground.** It is likely, for instance, that you both want the same thing – to be free of debt and have plenty of spare cash.

- **Communicate freely and honestly.** Assess where you are and how each of you have contributed to the current state of affairs. Be honest. Discuss each of your strengths and weaknesses – the things you are doing right, and the things you are doing wrong.

- Compromise. Don't allow past behaviour and events to poison your chance of success. Put grievances behind you. Start afresh and in doing so accept that you will both have to agree to do things differently in the future.

SHARING OUT THE CHORES

There are certain basic money chores that have to be done and one of the most useful things any couple can do in relation to their personal finances is agree who is going to take on which responsibilities. My recommendation is that all major decisions are made jointly and that each partner should keep the other informed about what they are doing. The tasks that need to be divided up include:

- paying household bills
- filing and organising financial paperwork
- doing the household shopping
- checking the bank accounts and reconciling the balances
- looking after the spending money and accessing cash
- shopping for larger purchases
- saving money and arranging any loans
- investment decisions
- keeping an eye on investments
- dealing with financial institutions, banks, insurance companies and so forth.

In many relationships, one or other partner will take over management for the financial affairs. Even where this works without a hitch I feel it is not entirely a good idea. Supposing one of you should die unexpectedly – how would the other cope? Also, what happens if you go your separate ways at some point? I can't stress how important it is to share information and decisions.

MONEY DOCTOR WEALTH CHECK

How to make yourself financially compatible

Here are some valuable tips on handling joint finances – whether with your partner or with someone else, such as a flatmate or friend.

- Maintain your independence. A joint account is perfect for joint responsibilities but it is a good idea to keep an account for yourself so that you have money available to spend as you want. Decide which areas are joint expenditure and which you are each going to handle alone.

- If one half of a partnership takes over all the money management it can lead to big trouble. The person 'in charge' may end up resenting the fact that he or she is doing all the work … and he or she may also become controlling. The person not involved is leaving himself or herself vulnerable and is adopting an essentially childlike position. Both of you should take decisions together – even if one of you does the day-to-day accounting.

- Be honest about how you each feel. If one of you wants to save and the other wants to spend … admit it and work out a strategy that allows each of you to do as you please. Compromise!

- Plan for a future that isn't completely dependent on staying together. I realise that this may seem pessimistic but I frequently find myself counselling people who unexpectedly find themselves having to deal with money for the first time.

THE IMPORTANCE OF INVOLVING AND EDUCATING YOUR CHILDREN

How did your parents' approach to money influence you? Now consider how your attitude will influence your own children. Regardless of your level of wealth, everything you say or do in relation to money will have an effect:

- If you don't discuss money in front of them they won't learn anything about it.
- Whatever emotions you display – such as fear, worry or indifference – will colour their own relationship with money.
- If you are mean with money or overly generous, if you never waste a penny, or if you spend like there's no tomorrow ... your children will be watching and learning.

Given that they are unlikely to learn much about money from any other quarter – and given the way debt is spreading through society like some super virus – it is obviously important that you educate your children about personal finance. You need to teach them the key principles, including how to:

- save for a specific purpose
- stick to a budget
- choose competitive products
- shop around
- spend money wisely.

THE MONEY DOCTOR SAYS...

My upbringing was fairly typical for Ireland in the 1960s. There were six of us squeezed into a three-bedroom house. My father was a manager and although we never went without, money was always tight. I am reminded of the comedian Les Dawson's self-deprecating quip, 'We were so poor, the first time I saw a butcher's shop, I thought there'd been an accident!' Of course, we didn't have the luxuries that today's generation are now so used to and come to expect. In Ireland today, our children really do not appreciate some of the hardship their parents went through and, in some respects, this is a pity, because parents' values are so much different to their children's.

Clearly, what you *don't* want to do is worry your children about money. Still, I believe there is a lot to be said for showing them where your income comes from, and what you then do with it.

When your children realise how well you manage money they can't fail to be proud of you. Naturally, they will grow up not just wanting to be debt free and rich enough to retire when young – but actually understanding how this can be achieved. What better legacy could you leave?

THE MONEY DOCTOR SAYS...

- If you are in a relationship, it is vital that you discuss your financial objectives together, sort out your differences and formulate a joint plan.
- Honesty is vital! You have to work together, not against each other.
- Remember, two heads are better than one. If you are working together you'll reach your objectives sooner – and it will be more fun, too.

- Don't forget, it is important to educate your children about finance. Don't let them leave home without good money habits and a genuine understanding of how money works.

4

GETTING HELP

Should you adopt a DIY approach to your financial planning or should you get professional help? And, if you seek help, who can you trust to give you the best advice?

Are you the sort of person who relishes the challenge of managing their own financial welfare? Or are you the sort of person who would feel happier passing the whole task to someone else?

HOW FAR SHOULD YOU GO?

You want to make the most of your money. In practical terms this means:

- keeping the cost of your borrowing (including your mortgage) to a bare minimum and making sure that you have the most suitable mortgage for your needs
- earning the highest possible return from your savings and investments without taking undue risk or paying unnecessary fees or commission
- obtaining the best possible pension plan
- taking out only the most appropriate insurance at the lowest possible price
- not paying a penny more tax than you have to
- not paying a penny more for any other financial services or products that you have to
- not being caught by any unscrupulous operators.

With the help of this book (and by visiting my website www.moneydoctor.ie) you will certainly be able to achieve all of the above by yourself. However, does the DIY approach make sense for you? The following questions may help you to decide:

Have you got the right temperament? Financial planning can be stressful and time consuming. If you hate figure work, don't like making decisions and worry about taking risks then maybe you would be better off seeking professional assistance.

Do you have the time? Are you willing to give up a few hours a month to make sure you are optimising your finances? Do you see this as being quite good fun? If not, then maybe the DIY approach isn't best for you.

Can you access the information you need? Financial planning requires access to information. If you can't gain access to the web, and if you aren't near a good library, then it is possible you should let someone else do the legwork for you.

Getting help

How to get help from someone you can trust

Whenever I do a radio phone-in as the Money Doctor I find that the question I get asked most is: 'Who can I turn to for help with my money problems?'

Consumers, understandably, want independent and expert advice. The trouble is that most people offering advice actually work for financial institutions and have products to promote. Bluntly, if you talk to a life assurance salesperson about your retirement planning you know she or he isn't going to recommend anything except one of the products her or his own company sells.

The only solution is to get your advice from someone who isn't under any pressure to *sell* anything, but is in a position to do what is best for you.

For insurance and investments, about 500 such professionals exist in Ireland. They are called Authorised Advisors and they are legally obliged to do the best for you by giving 'best advice'.

This book is designed to give you all the information you need to organise your finances, save you tax and find the most appropriate products for your needs. (If you have any questions, remember you can also take advantage of my web-based service at www.moneydoctor.ie)

However, if you want to discuss your situation through with someone – face to face – make sure you talk to a professional who is experienced in all financial areas. In other words, contact an Authorised Advisor or for credit issues (mortgages, loans) an adviser who deals with and has access to all the lenders.

What can you expect from your independent professional Authorised Advisor or mortgage intermediary?

One of the key advantages to appointing an Authorised Advisor (someone who is independent, professional, qualified and stringently regulated) for insurances and investments is that they owe their allegiance to you and not to any particular financial institution or investment house. *Your needs* will be paramount. As a result, you can expect them to provide you with the following services:

Strategic planning. They will look at your complete financial position, agree your financial objectives with you, and advise you on how to reach your money targets. When doing this he or she should also assess your existing position and review any financial products you have in place to make sure they meet your requirements.

Competitive analysis. Having decided what products you need, your adviser should search the market for the best product offering the best value for money.

Negotiation services. When an insurance company quotes a rate, it isn't necessarily fixed in stone. In fact, it is possible to negotiate discounts on a huge range of financial products. Your adviser will know what else is available in the market and should negotiate to get you the best possible deal.

Background information. Your adviser should provide you with background information on any products or companies they recommend.

Administration. Your adviser should deal with all the paperwork on your behalf and will assist with the filling-out of any forms.

Regular reviews. Your adviser should monitor your needs without being asked. They should constantly be thinking about your situation and making sure that whatever they have recommended is performing in the desired manner.

Your adviser should also be able to look after all your financial and money needs, including:

- mortgages
- re-finance
- commercial loans
- personal loans
- asset finance and leasing
- life cover
- income protection and other insurance
- health cover
- all savings and investments
- pensions
- property and other general insurance.

Where even more specialised advice is needed (say in the selection of shares to build a portfolio, or specific tax planning), then your adviser should be able to recommend other professional experts.

Saving tax

A first-class financial adviser will be able to advise you on tax-saving products. Keep in mind though that for specialist tax advice you should always go to an accountant or qualified tax consultant. If the size of your tax bill doesn't warrant appointing an accountant, then your financial adviser should still be able to assist you. Tax is a big part of financial planning. After all, what's the point of making a better return on your investments only to lose it through poor tax advice? *Always* check that your adviser is taking your tax position into account and is properly qualified to assist you.

A very short history lesson

Prior to November 2001 there were over 9,000 'insurance brokers' offering financial advice. After that, the Central Bank took over regulation and forced them to register.

- Six thousand dropped out immediately, mainly because the scale of their operations meant they did not have the time or resources to provide the level of product research required.

- Of the two new authorisations available, there are currently around 400 Authorised Advisors, who must give 'best advice' irrespective of agencies held.

- The balance of about 2,500 are called **multi-agency intermediaries** (originally called RAIPIs, then 'restricted intermediaries') and they can only give advice on the insurance and investment appointments held.

Then, in 2003, in order to make sure that consumers receive reliable and independent advice the government set up the **Irish Financial Services Regulatory Authority** (IFSRA now called the 'Financial Regulator'), an independent agency set up to take over the regulatory role previously filled by the Central Bank.

One of the first things to do when considering any professional adviser is to check:

- that they are regulated by the Financial Regulator
- what services they are authorised to provide and at what cost.

Financial advisers must give you a Terms of Business booklet, which outlines their terms of business, appointments with product providers, Financial Regulator authorisation and notification of the Investors' Compensation Act.

MONEY DOCTOR WEALTH WARNING

Some things are best not delegated

There is an enormous amount to be said for getting a really good professional adviser to sort out everything for you. You'll save money. You'll save time. And you will end up with the best possible products for your needs. But no matter how good your adviser, you should always take time to:

- understand what he or she is proposing, and why
- learn about the products you are committing to
- check up on the financial institutions who will be supplying those products.

THE MONEY DOCTOR SAYS...

- It is possible to handle all your financial decisions without reference to anyone else. However, it requires time and commitment.
- If you do decide to use a professional adviser, make sure that they are fully authorised and don't be shy about asking them questions.
- Remember, it is important to have clear financial objectives.

PART 2
YOUR FINANCIAL RIGHTS

Are you entitled to claim any government benefits? How does the law protect you as an employee? What do you do if you buy something and are unhappy with the way you have been treated?

This section of the book will answer all your questions with regard to your financial rights. In Chapter 5 you'll discover how the Social Welfare system works and be able to assess what you may be entitled to. In Chapter 6 you'll learn about your rights as an employee. And in Chapter 7 you'll find out what your consumer rights are. I've also included useful sources of additional information and important contact information.

5

YOUR RIGHT
TO SOCIAL WELFARE

HOW THE SYSTEM WORKS AND HOW TO MAKE
SURE YOU RECEIVE YOUR ENTITLEMENTS

The Irish state provides its citizens with one of the most advanced, generous and comprehensive social welfare systems in the world. It isn't, however, what you would call a simple system, being made up of a bewildering array of:

- assistance payments
- benefits
- supplements
- allowances
- grants, and
- pensions.

Many of the financial benefits available are 'contributory', meaning that you are only entitled to them if you have made **PRSI** (pay related social insurance) contributions in the past. Others are available to everyone, including people who have moved here from abroad.

As one would expect, the state only provides social welfare when certain conditions are met. Sometimes these conditions are very straightforward. For instance, with very few exceptions, a special grant of €4,000 is paid to widows or widowers with dependent children following the death of their spouse. In other instances you have to meet stringent requirements, often related to the size and number of your PRSI contributions. A good example of this is the invalidity pension, which is payable if you have been 'incapable of work for at least twelve months and are likely to be incapable of work for a further twelve months, or you are permanently incapable, or you are over age 60 and suffering from a serious illness or incapacity'. Furthermore, to claim this pension you must have paid PRSI at Class A, E or H for at least 260 weeks, and you must have had at least 48 weeks PRSI paid or credited in the last tax year before you apply!

I am afraid the system is made even more confusing by the fact that the government frequently changes the nature, value, names and conditions attached to the various benefits available.

So, how can you discover exactly what you are entitled to?

In this chapter I outline, in broad terms, all the various forms of social welfare that are available, along with the more important conditions which must be fulfilled in order to claim them. Using this, you should be able to ascertain benefits to which you *might* be entitled.

Your next step should be to contact your local Social Welfare office or Citizens Information Centre for further assistance. You'll find both listed in your local phone book.

Another approach is to write directly to:

> The Information Service, Department of Social & Family Affairs
> Áras Mhic Dhiarmada, Dublin
> Tel. (01) 704 3000.
> or
> Retirement/Old Age Contributory & Non-Contributory Pensions
> College Road, Sligo
> Co. Sligo
> Tel. (071) 916 9800/914 8371/LoCall: 1890 50 00 00.

Or, if you have access to the internet, you can go to www.welfare.ie

THE DIFFERENCE BETWEEN
CONTRIBUTORY AND NON-CONTRIBUTORY PAYMENTS

The terms 'contributory' and 'non-contributory' are bandied about a good deal in relation to social welfare benefits. The terms are slightly misleading because they imply that you have to have contributed personally to be eligible for certain payments. The contribution being referred to is generally assumed to be PRSI payments, the health levy, and the employment and training levies. However, a completely different system operated prior to 1974, a third system was in place until 1953, and both may entitle you to contributory benefits.

The word 'contributory' is confusing in another respect, too. You may well be eligible to receive a contributory benefit if you are married to someone who has made contributions, or if you are the child or dependant of someone who has made contributions.

Another point to bear in mind is that you may have been in regular employment but earning so little that you were not liable to make any PRSI payments. If you are a public servant your entitlements will be linked to when you joined, and if you're self-employed a completely different set of regulations applies.

My advice is, therefore, never to assume that you won't be entitled to a particular form of social welfare until you have fully investigated each and every one of the conditions attached to it. Don't ever assume that because something is 'contributory' or 'non-contributory' it won't apply to you.

THE DIFFERENT TYPES OF SOCIAL WELFARE

I've already listed off all the different names used to describe the variety of social welfare payments. What do these various terms mean?

On the whole, social welfare benefits tend to be available only to those who have made PRSI contributions. Furthermore, though there are a few exceptions, social welfare benefits are not affected by your level of wealth.

Social welfare assistance, on the other hand, is given only to those who satisfy what's called a 'means test'.

A good example of the difference is unemployment benefit, which has PRSI conditions attached to it but for which there is no means test, and the non-contributory old age pension, which is classified as social assistance and *is* subject to means testing.

So, what is means testing?

In order that financial assistance only goes to those who are most needy, the government checks each claimant's financial circumstances first. This check is called a 'means test'.

Your means are considered to be:

- any cash income you have
- the value of your assets (your home will be excluded, but if you own a farm that would be included)
- your savings and investments.

In some cases your residential situation will be relevant. For instance, if you are unemployed but live at home with your parents and you are under the age of 27, this could reduce your entitlement.

When you apply for a means-tested form of social assistance, a 'means test officer' will consider your case. The criteria he or she uses in order to assess your entitlement will vary – of course – according to the form of social assistance you are applying to receive. You should expect, however, to be asked about your entire financial situation. This could include:

- your income
- your spouse's income
- your partner's income (if co-habiting)
- your farm income (if relevant)
- any savings, investments or other assets you may own, such as property
- your general circumstances, such as where you live, whom you live with, who is dependent on you, and so forth
- any debts you may have
- your weekly outgoings, including rent
- any other benefits you may be receiving.

Naturally, any information you provide will be treated in the strictest confidence.

There will, of course, be other conditions as well. For instance, you have to be genuinely unemployed to claim unemployment assistance. But it is your means that will be the deciding point. Note that even if you're not eligible for the maximum amount of assistance, you could still be entitled to a reduced amount.

WHAT ARE YOU ENTITLED TO?
SOCIAL WELFARE PAYMENTS IN DETAIL

Below is a summary of all the main social welfare payments. You'll also find an explanation of what they could be worth to you, together with some of the more notable conditions.

Remember, the Department of Social & Family Affairs is there to help you. You shouldn't hesitate to ask their advice about what you are entitled to.

Social welfare pensions

The state makes available two different types of social welfare pension:

Contributory pension. So-called because your entitlement is linked to the amount and class of PRSI you have paid during your working life.

Non-contributory pension. Means tested and available to those who haven't made any contributions during their working lives.

Contributory pensions in turn also fall into two categories: retirement pensions (paid if you're aged 65 and over and have actually stopped working) and contributory old age pensions (paid from the age of 66 with no requirement that you should have stopped working).

The maximum amount for a contributory pension is €223.30 per week, but the actual sum you receive will be determined by the number and value of contributions you made during your working life – and your age. Additional sums are payable if you have dependent children and live alone.

The maximum amount payable as an old age non-contributory pension is currently €212.00 per week. Again, you may be able to claim more if you have dependent children or live alone.

Regardless of whether you have made contributions or not, additional amounts may also be available if you're blind, or if you live on certain offshore islands.

Pensions for widows and widowers

If you are – or become – a widow or widower then you will also have pension entitlements. These are:

The contributory widow(er)'s pension. This – as its name implies – is available to widows or widowers where sufficient PRSI contributions have been made and is worth up to €223.30 per week.

The non-contributory widow(er)'s pension. This is means tested and could be worth as much as €212.00 a week (€222 for those aged over 80).

In both instances if you have a dependent child, live alone and/or are resident on certain offshore islands you may be entitled to receive an additional sum.

Other age-related benefits

If you are aged 66 or over and you qualify for a contributory or non-contributory pension – or you satisfy a means test – you may be entitled to a number of other household benefits, including:

- free travel
- free electricity
- a natural gas allowance
- a free television licence
- a telephone rental allowance.

These benefits are referred to as the Household Benefits Package Scheme.

MONEY DOCTOR WEALTH CHECK

You don't have to be retired to claim free electricity and other benefits

The Household Benefits Package Scheme is also available to those entitled to other payments such as an invalidity pension or a carer's allowance (see below). Under these circumstances your age will not be relevant to your eligibility.

Supplementary welfare allowance

Supplementary welfare allowance provides a basic weekly allowance as a right to eligible people who have little or no income. If you have a low income, you may also qualify for a weekly supplement under the scheme to meet certain special needs. In addition, payments can be made in respect of urgent or exceptional needs.

There are four types of payments – basic payments, supplements, exceptional needs payments and urgent needs payments. To find out more about the scheme, contact the:

> Supplementary Welfare Allowance Section
> Department of Social & Family Affairs
> Áras Mhic Dhiarmada
> Store Street, Dublin 1
> Tel. (01) 704 3000.

One-parent family payment

If you are bringing up a child (or children) without the support of a partner, you may be eligible to apply for the one-parent family payment, which is available to both men and women. You may earn up to €201.80 per week and still qualify for the full payment, while a

reduced payment will be made to you if you earn between €146.50 per week and €400 per week. If your weekly income exceeds €400 a week, a half-rate payment will be made to you for six months.

Deserted wife's benefit

Deserted wife's benefit is a payment made to a woman deserted by her husband. Entitlement to payment is based on social insurance contributions paid by the wife or her husband. The deserted wife's benefit scheme was closed off to new applications with effect from 2 January 1997, when the one-parent family payment was introduced.

Guardian's payment (contributory)

This allowance is payable where both parents have died, or one parent has died and the other has abandoned the child. Being a contributory allowance, one or other of the parents must have made sufficient PRSI contributions. The payment is made up to the age of 18, or 22 if the child is in full-time education. It can be as much as €170 a week.

Guardian's payment (non-contributory)

If a child does not qualify for the contributory guardian's allowance, he or she may instead be eligible for the **non-contributory guardian's payment**. This pension is means tested. It can be as much as €170 a week.

Invalidity pension

This is a contributory pension, so it is only available to those who meet the PRSI payment qualifications. It is payable instead of a disability benefit if you've been incapable of work for at least 12 months and are likely to be incapable of work for a further 12 months, or if you're permanently incapable of work, or you're over the age of 60 and suffering from a serious illness or incapacity.

As with many other pensions, the amount you receive will increase if you have dependent children, live alone, or live on certain offshore islands. If you are eligible for an invalidity pension you may also be able to claim an additional sum if you support someone else. It can be as much as €223.30 a week.

Medical cards

Medical cards entitle you to a range of free medical care. Eligibility is normally means tested, although there are a number of exceptions including for those aged 70 or over, and anyone drawing a state pension from other EU countries. Different income limits exist for those aged under 66 and those aged between 66 and 69 and vary depending on the number of children or dependants and whether they are aged over 16 and in full-time education. Although your circumstances may not entitle you to a medical card, you could still be eligible for a doctor visit card, which would allow you to receive free care from your GP. If this section is relevant to you, you should seek assistance from the Department of Social & Family Affairs – see contact details on p. 43.

Treatment benefits

The state provides a range of contributory treatment benefits covering dental care, eye testing, glasses, contact lenses, and hearing aids. In some instances, the benefits are entirely free and in others you must pay a part of the cost. There may also be upper limits on the amounts which can be claimed.

Maternity benefit

A contributory maternity benefit is payable to women in current employment or self-employment who have been paying PRSI. It is only payable where the mother has been making contributions – the father's contributions have no bearing on eligibility. It can be as much as €280.00 a week.

Adoptive benefit

If you adopt a child you may still be eligible for a payment equivalent in value to the maternity benefit. This is a contributory benefit. It can be as much as €280.00 a week.

Asylum seekers

If you are applying for refugee status, you can obtain rent-free accommodation at a regional centre. Each adult is entitled to a personal allowance of €19.10 per week and €9.60 for each child. Child benefit may also be applicable. More information can be obtained from:

Reception and Integration Agency
2nd Floor
94 St Stephen's Green
Dublin 2
Tel. (01) 418 3200, LoCall: 1890 777 727.

MONEY DOCTOR WEALTH WARNING

A tightening-up of the rules: Habitual Resident's Test

Since 2004 the government has introduced a new **Habitual Resident's Test**, which means that in order to receive a whole range of payments you must be able to prove that you are 'habitually resident in Ireland'. However, the rules do allow you to be resident in the UK, Channel Islands, and Isle of Man, too. Payments affected by this include unemployment assistance, old age contributory pension, one-parent family payment, and supplementary welfare allowance.

Child benefit

Child benefit is not means tested, nor do you have to make any contribution in order to receive it. It is paid each month, and the amount you receive will depend on the number of qualifying children living with you and their ages. In some instances the payment may be made until the children reach the age of 19. For the first and second child it can be as much as €166.00 each per month and €203.00 for the third and subsequent children (2008 rate). It also pays to have multiple births – up to double the child benefit rate for each child and three one-off payments: at birth, aged four and aged 12, or €635 for each child.

Early childcare supplement

The **Early childcare supplement** is a state payment to families in Ireland with children under 6 years of age. The purpose of the supplement is to financially assist families with the cost of raising children, providing childcare, etc. This payment was announced in the 2006 Budget and has been effective since April 2006. The early childcare supplement is worth €1,100 per child per year.

Jobseeker's benefit

Jobseeker's benefit is only paid to those who satisfy the PRSI conditions. The amount you receive will be linked to your age and the amount of PRSI paid. It can be as much as €185.80 a week.

If you are under 18 you can only receive this benefit for up to 6 months, but if you're aged between 18 and 65 it will be paid to you for up to 15 months.

Note that if you receive a redundancy payment in excess of €19,046 you may have to wait for up to nine weeks before you can receive unemployment benefit.

Jobseeker's allowance

This is a means-tested payment available to those who are unemployed and have not made sufficient PRSI payments to be eligible for unemployment benefit. It can be as much as €197.80 a week but on a descending scale depending on your circumstances.

If you want to find out why you have been turned down for a benefit or considered not eligible, contact the:

> Social Welfare Appeals Office
> D'Olier House
> D'Olier Street, Dublin 2
> Tel. (01) 673 2800.

Back-to-work allowance and back-to-work enterprise allowance

Two different schemes exist for those who have been unemployed for a period of time and then return to work: back-to-work allowance and back-to-work enterprise allowance. The first is available if you move into paid employment after being unemployed; the second is given if you become self-employed. Note that other support is also available to those who start their own businesses, including training grants, loans, and assistance towards the cost of public liability insurance. Apply to:

Employment Support Services
Department of Social & Family Affairs
PO Box 3840
Dublin 2
Tel. (01) 704 3165.

Carer's benefit

If you leave work in order to look after someone in need of full-time care and attention, then you may well be eligible for the **contributory carer's benefit**. Additionally, you may be entitled to an **annual respite care grant**, which would be paid to you in June each year. This grant is, in fact, available to all carers providing full-time care, subject to certain conditions. The respite care grant is currently worth €1,500 per person cared for. The carer's benefit can be as much as €322.10 a week if you are caring for more than one person.

Disability and injury benefits

A range of disability and injury benefits – all contributory – is available to those unable to work due to a disability, injury, or some form of disablement. If you are disabled, suffer an injury or have some form of disability you may also be eligible, without means testing, for a range of other benefits including **medical care**, and a **constant attendant's allowance**. If you are a public servant and have to give up work due to ill health, you will be eligible for an **early retirement pension**. These benefits can be worth anything up to €228.90 a week.

Bereavement grant

A **bereavement grant** of €850 is available subject to certain conditions based on PRSI contributions.

Widowed parent's grant

In addition to the bereavement grant mentioned above, a special grant of €6,000 is available to widows or widowers with dependent children following the death of their spouse. This is not means tested and only minimal conditions are attached to it.

Family income supplement

The purpose of this scheme is to help families on low incomes. However, to be eligible it is necessary for one member of the family to be working at least part time, and for the family income to be below a certain level. Although the family income supplement is based on the family's weekly income, once it has been set it doesn't normally fluctuate. However, if your circumstances change (for instance, if you have another child) you can apply to have it increased. The supplement is based on 60% of the difference between your net family income and the income limit that applies to your family circumstances (see Department of Social & Family Affairs leaflet **SW19**).

Drugs payments scheme

Even though you may not be eligible for a medical card, you could well be eligible to receive support under the **drugs payment scheme**. Once you are registered, no individual or family is expected to pay more than €90 a month for prescription drugs included on the list of 'essential medicines'. In order to register you should contact your GP, local pharmacy, or health board.

Nursing home subvention

Someone aged 65 or over needing nursing home care may be eligible to have some or all of it paid for by the local health board. Financial support is only forthcoming if:

- The claimant clearly needs to be in a nursing home.
- He or she is unable to pay for it himself or herself.

In other words, it is linked to need and is means tested.

With regards to the means testing, if the claimant has recently (within the past five years) sold or given away assets then he or she may cease to be eligible. This is because many elderly people were voluntarily changing their financial circumstances in order to avoid paying nursing home fees.

A family home, if occupied by a dependent spouse, child or other close relative will not count as an asset for means testing.

Disabled persons

A host of grants and allowances exist for disabled and incapacitated persons. These include the blind welfare allowance, blind person's pension, carer's allowance, disability allowance, motorised transport grant, domiciliary care allowance and many more. Various tax credits and allowances are also available to disabled people.

Free travel

Free travel on public transport is available to almost everyone aged 66 or over. It is also available to anyone receiving an invalidity pension, a disability allowance, a blind person's pension or a carer's allowance. Note that if you are entitled to free travel, and you're married or co-habiting with someone, they may travel with you free of charge at the same time.

MONEY DOCTOR WEALTH CHECK

What you're entitled to elsewhere in the EU

As Ireland is part of the European Union, you are entitled to a wide range of benefits in other EU member states. However, since EU member states each have their own social welfare system, claiming entitlements in other countries can be fraught with problems. Keep in mind too that contributions made in one member state do not necessarily qualify you for benefits in another. For instance, if you have been working overseas and return home to Ireland, you will not automatically be eligible for unemployment benefit. However, if you have been registered as unemployed for four weeks in Ireland you are then entitled to move to another EU country to look for work and still receive the benefit for up to three months.

If you are thinking of living or working in another EU member state, then you should ask at your local Social Welfare office for a special leaflet describing the benefits which will be available to you.

Incidentally, not only are you legally entitled to look for work in any EU member state without a work permit, but you can also take advantage of each member state's national placement service. To do this, contact your local FÁS Employment Services office. Details of your application will be sent overseas through the SEDOC system free of charge.

MONEY DOCTOR WEALTH WARNING

Social welfare benefits are not necessarily tax free

Social welfare benefits are not automatically tax free. Whether they are taxable will largely depend on the income level of the recipient. Although tax will not be deducted by the Department of Social & Family Affairs on any payments made to you, the Revenue Commissioners will often take the tax direct from some other source of income which may be payable to the recipient. However, on the plus side, four of the 'taxable benefits' you may be entitled to will also qualify you for the PAYE tax credit. These are:

- contributory old age pension
- retirement pension

- contributory survivor's pension
- guardian's payment.

A number of other benefits may also be liable to income tax. These are:

- invalidity pension
- one-parent family payment
- carer's allowance
- unemployment benefit
- blind person's pension
- non-contributory widow's pension
- non-contributory guardian's pension
- social assistance allowance for deserted or prisoners' wives.

The Revenue Commissioners do, however, make a number of useful concessions:

- If you are receiving a disability benefit the first six days will not be subject to tax.
- If you are receiving social welfare payments, child dependent additions are not taxed (except for invalidity pensions).
- If you are a 'short-term worker' (that it is to say, you work in a trade where short-term employment is the norm) then any unemployment benefit you receive will not be taxed.
- The first €12.70 a week is not liable to tax.

MONEY DOCTOR WEALTH CHECK

Don't forget to apply for a European Health Insurance Card

If you're going to live in another EU member state (excluding the UK), then you should apply for a European Health Insurance Card. This will ensure you are eligible for free health care when overseas. You can do this through your local health board.

THE MONEY DOCTOR SAYS ...

- You may be entitled to all sorts of social welfare payments that you weren't aware of.
- Check through all the allowances, benefits and grants summarised in this chapter to see which might apply to you.
- Contact your local Department of Social & Family Affairs to find out more and to make a claim. Remember, they are there to help you.

6

YOUR EMPLOYMENT RIGHTS

When most people think of 'employee rights' they think of legal rights relating to things like discrimination and redundancy. But if you are an employee you have financial rights, too. For instance, you have the right to be paid a minimum wage and the right to holiday pay. This chapter explains these rights in plain English.

You may be more protected than you imagine.

In the last few years the Irish government has enacted a considerable amount of new legislation to protect employees. One reason for this was that many employers were seeking to get around the existing employment legislation by putting their workers on 'contract'. Seasonal and part-time workers were also at a disadvantage. Since 2003, however, workers on fixed-term contracts must be treated just as well as full-time employees. Furthermore, an employee cannot be expected to work on a fixed-term contract for more than four years.

Minimum wage

Since 1 April 2000 all but a tiny minority of workers over the age of 18 are entitled to be paid a minimum amount of money per hour, known as the national minimum wage. From 1 July 2007 the national minimum wage has been set at €8.65 per hour. However, you should note that:

- If you're in a new job you are only entitled to 80% of the minimum wage for your first year, and 90% in your second year.
- If you're under 18 you also have reduced entitlements (70% until your 18th birthday, 80% between your 18th and 19th birthdays, and 90% for the following year).

- If you are still in training or attending an educational course your employer is also entitled to reduce your wage.

A SUNDAY BONUS

If your employer expects you to work on Sunday, you will be entitled to an increased hourly rate. If you are not automatically receiving this then you should contact the Department of Enterprise, Trade and Employment at the address given on p. 64.

ANNUAL LEAVE ENTITLEMENT

You are entitled to a minimum of four weeks annual leave plus public holidays, of which there are nine per year.

HOLIDAY PAY

If you are in paid employment, then you are legally entitled to paid holidays. The holiday year usually runs from 1 April–31 March. However, your employer is entitled to use an alternative twelve-month period. Broadly speaking, if you're working full time, you should be entitled to a minimum of four working weeks over the year. Of course, if you switch jobs this may have the effect of reducing your entitlement.

YOUR WORKING WEEK

Under something called the 'Organisation of Working Time Act', employees cannot be expected to work more than 48 hours a week. However, there are innumerable exceptions to this. For instance, the Act does not apply to junior hospital doctors, transport employees, fishermen, and family members working on a farm or in a private house, or to the Gardaí.

There are also rules regarding rest periods. You're legally entitled to an 11-hour rest period every 24 hours; one period of 24 hours rest per week preceded by daily rest period – in other words a total of 35 hours in a single block; and rest breaks of 15 minutes where up to four and a half hours have been worked, or 30 minutes where up to six hours have been worked. Slightly different arrangements apply to night workers.

ON-CALL WORKERS

If you are expected to be **on call** for work, then you should be paid for it. The rule is that you are entitled to receive pay for at least a **quarter** of your on-call hours even if you don't end up working. The maximum amount your employer has to pay you is for 15 hours a week.

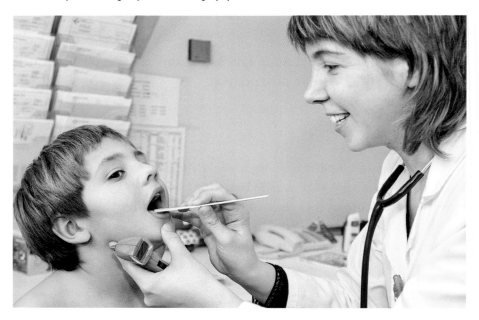

DISMISSAL RIGHTS

Your employer can only dismiss you if he or she can prove that you aren't capable, competent or qualified to do the work you were employed to do. Alternatively, your employer must show that your conduct was in some way unacceptable; or that by continuing to employ you he or she would contravene another statutory requirement. The only other reason an employer may dismiss you if he or she is making you redundant (see below, p. 65). This said, unfair dismissal normally only applies to those who have been employed for at least a year's continuous service with the same employer. Furthermore, there are many exclusions, including those who are aged 65 and over.

If you feel that you've been unfairly dismissed then you must make your complaint within six months.

Note that once you've completed at least 13 weeks with the same employer you are entitled to pre-set periods of notice. This ranges from one week's notice if you've been working for 13 weeks to two years, to eight weeks' notice if you've been working for over 15 years.

Time off work

There are various other reasons why you can legitimately claim time off work. For instance, you can take:

- **Emergency time** off in order to deal with family emergencies resulting from an accident or illness. You are entitled to up to five days over a period of 36 months, and such leave is paid.
- Up to 26 weeks **maternity leave** if you become pregnant, during which time you can claim maternity benefit. Your employer is not obliged to give you any additional income over and above this maternity benefit. When the maternity benefit period ends, you're entitled to take up to a further 16 weeks of unpaid leave.

- Up to 14 weeks parental leave if you are a **new father**, but this is unpaid and without any social welfare entitlement.
- Time off if you are an **expectant mother**, **parent** or **carer** with a special need. For instance, expectant mothers can take time off without loss of pay to go to medical examinations.

WHAT TO DO IF YOU ARE UNHAPPY WITH YOUR EMPLOYER ...

If you feel that your employment rights are being abused, you can obtain further information from:

> The Department of Enterprise, Trade and Employment
> Employment Rights Section
> Davitt House, 65 Adelaide Road, Dublin 2
> Tel. (01) 531 3131/LoCall: 1890 201 615.

The Labour Relations Commission will also assist you. Their address details are:

> Rights Commissioner Service
> Labour Relations Commission
> Tom Johnson House, Haddington Road, Dublin 4
> Tel. (01) 660 9662.

REDUNDANCY

If you have worked for the same employer for at least two years – even if it is part time – and you are made redundant, then you may well be eligible for a redundancy payment. Various conditions apply. For instance, you must be aged between 16 and 66, and you must have normally worked at least eight hours a week. Also, 'redundancy' only covers the situation where you've been dismissed because – essentially – your employer no longer needs your services. This could be for a variety of reasons, including a change in location, or a decision by the employer to carry on the business with fewer employees. The amount you receive will be based on the number of years you've worked. You should receive two weeks' pay for every year of service to a maximum of €600 a week, topped up with one additional week's pay. If you receive a large lump-sum redundancy payment then you may be liable to pay tax on it. For further information about this, turn to Chapter 33.

THE MONEY DOCTOR SAYS...

- Know your financial rights as an employee and don't let your employer bully or cajole you into accepting anything less.
- Remember, there are lots of circumstances where your employer must pay you. And lots of circumstances where your employer must let you have time off.

7

YOUR RIGHTS AS A 'FINANCIAL' CONSUMER

Do you suspect your bank of over-charging you? Have you felt that an insurance salesperson has sold you a product you don't need? Are you worried about personal financial information being used for marketing purposes?

If you have any concerns about the way you've been treated by a financial institution, then this chapter is for you. In it you'll learn how the law protects you and what you can do if there's something you are unhappy about.

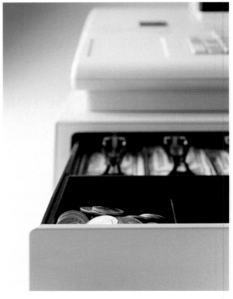

Your basic rights

As the customer of a financial institution you have a wide range of rights. You don't need to suffer poor service, over-charging, mis-selling or fraud. If you're unhappy, there are dedicated, independent organisations which will assist you. Furthermore, if you have lost money you may also be entitled to compensation.

HOW TO COMPLAIN

If you are unhappy and wish to complain then, in the first instance, you should write to the financial institution concerned and offer them an opportunity to redress the situation. If you are not satisfied with the response you receive, follow the appropriate course of action outlined in the relevant section below.

If you're unhappy with your bank, building society, credit union or insurance company

If you're unhappy with your bank, building society or credit union, you can appeal to the Financial Services Ombudsman. This body also covers insurance complaints and is authorised to make awards of up to a limit of €250,000.

All the banks in Ireland now offer a wide range of financial services including insurance and pensions, so this body will cover all that area should you have a complaint to make.

Insurance companies and banks are bound by the Ombudsman's decision but the complainants are not (e.g. a policyholder who does not agree with the Ombudsman's decision).

The Financial Services Ombudsman is a statutory body established in April 2005 and replaced the Ombudsman for Credit Institutions and the Insurance Ombudsman. The details are:

Financial Services Ombudsman's Bureau
Third Floor
Lincoln House
Lincoln Place
Dublin 2
Lo-Call: 1890 88 20 90
Tel. (01) 662 0899
Fax (01) 662 0890
Email: enquiries@financialombudsman.ie

Financial Services
Ombudsman

If you're unhappy with your financial advisers

In order to make sure that consumers receive reliable and independent advice, the government set up the **Financial Regulator**. Before you even consider dealing with any professional adviser, you should check that they are regulated by the Financial Regulator and what services they are authorised to provide. They must give you a Terms of Business letter, which outlines their terms of business, appointments with product providers, Financial Regulator authorisation, and notification of the Investors' Compensation Act. You'll find more information about choosing a professional adviser in Chapter 4.

There are, in fact, four different bodies to which your adviser may belong:

1 The Independent Mortgage Advisers' Federation (IMAF).
2 The Irish Brokers' Association (IBA).
3 Professional Insurance Brokers' Association (PIBA).
4 Life Insurance Association (LIA).

If you're unhappy with your pension company

If you feel that you have been given poor pension advice, then you should contact the Financial Services Ombudsman's Bureau (see address on page 67) and you should also get in touch with the Ombudsman in charge of pensions. The latter can be contacted at:

The Office of the Pensions Ombudsman
PO Box 9324
36 Upper Mount Street, Dublin 2
Tel. (01) 847 1650.

HAVE YOU BEEN TURNED DOWN
FOR A LOAN OR CREDIT CARD FOR NO APPARENT REASON?

If you have been turned down for a loan or credit card, it is probably because of your credit rating. Almost all the lenders in Ireland rely on credit bureaux to provide them with information about their potential customers. If the information that any particular credit bureau holds is incorrect, it can result in you being turned down for credit. The two bureaux which operate in Ireland are legally obliged to advise you of the information they hold about you. Their details are:

The Irish Credit Bureau (ICB)
Newstead House
Newstead, Clonskeagh, Dublin 14.

and

Experian Ireland
Park House
North Circular Road, Dublin 7.

You will pay a small charge for this service. For instance, ICB will charge €6. Do note that they respond only to written requests and the service usually takes no more than three days. You should get in touch with the Ombudsman for Credit Institutions and the Ombudsman for the Financial Services if you're not satisfied with the response you get.

If you're worried about Big Brother

Many of us, with a certain amount of justification, worry that large organisations – such as banks and insurance companies – hold incorrect and unnecessary information about us on their files. Under the Data Protection Act you have the right of access to any personal file relating to yourself held by either a company or other type of organisation. To discover what data a company or organisation holds about you, you simply have to write to them saying that you're making your request under the Data Protection Act. If you encounter any resistance, then you should contact the Data Protection Commissioner at:

The Data Protection Commissioner
Block 6
Irish Life Centre
Lower Abbey Street, Dublin 1
Tel. (01) 674 8544.

If you discover that an organisation has incorrect information about you, you are entitled to have it corrected.

MONEY DOCTOR WEALTH CHECK

The Deposit Guarantee scheme

While it is generally accepted that the banks, building societies and credit unions operating in Ireland are all in healthy shape, you may be reassured to know that the Irish government now guarantees from 30 September 2008, for two years, all deposits for the six Irish-owned deposit takers. These are: AIB, Anglo-Irish Bank, Bank of Ireland, Irish Life and Permanent, Irish Nationwide Building Society, Credit Unions and An Post are guaranteed by the Investor Compensation Scheme up to €100,000. And on 9 October, the Irish government extended the scheme to five other non-Irish-owned banks (Ulster Bank, First Active, Bank of Scotland Halifax, IIB Bank (now KBC Bank) and Postbank – the An Post/Fortis Bank joint venture. *Email me for details on the security of your financial institution* (jlowe@moneydoctor.ie).

IF YOU'RE STILL UNHAPPY AND WANT TO TAKE IT FURTHER

What do you do if you've made a complaint to a financial institution and the relevant Ombudsman and you're still not happy with the result? You have two basic choices:

1 You could institute legal proceedings.
2 You could contact the European Ombudsman.

The European Ombudsman investigates complaints about poor administration by financial institutions and other bodies throughout the EU. You can write to the Ombudsman at:

The European Ombudsman
1 Avenue du President Robert Schuman
BP 403, F-67001
Strasbourg, Cedex.

THE MONEY DOCTOR SAYS...

- If you are unhappy with the service you have received from a financial institution you should, in the first instance, offer them the opportunity to put things right. The best way to do this is to put your complaint in writing.
- If you aren't satisfied with the response you receive – take it further. Complain to the relevant Ombudsman.
- Legal action is always an option – but remember, it will cost you money, whereas there is no charge involved in asking an Ombudsman.

PART 3

This section deals with three extremely important topics. Firstly, it offers a comprehensive guide to modern banking services in Ireland, together with tips on getting the most from your bank at the lowest possible cost. Secondly, it explains how you can pay off all your debts – including your credit cards, loans, overdrafts and even your mortgage – quickly and easily. Thirdly, it looks at the different ways in which you can borrow money and suggests the most inexpensive ways to do so.

8

BANKING

HOW TO ENJOY THE BEST BANKING IN IRELAND

What do you demand from your bank? A first-class service? Free banking? Total security? A range of competitively priced financial products? With a little careful planning, as I will explain in this chapter, you can enjoy the best banking in Ireland.

UNDERSTANDING THE BANKING SYSTEM

The first step to enjoying better banking is to understand how the banks themselves operate.

To begin with, despite the charges they make, banks don't make their profits from providing day-to-day banking services. This is because it is incredibly expensive running a branch network, handling millions of transactions, dealing with vast quantities of cash and providing customers with all the other services we (rightly) demand.

So, how *do* banks make their profits? The answer is by selling their customers a wide range of other financial services – everything from mortgages to credit cards, and from insurance to stockbroking.

Every time you use your bank, whether you are withdrawing cash from a machine, paying a bill, or ordering a statement, you present your bank with another opportunity to sell you something. Much in the same way as supermarkets use 'loss leaders' (popular products sold at below-cost price in order to attract customers), banks offer banking services – especially current accounts – as a way of attracting and keeping customers.

In fact, *operated properly* a current account is one of the greatest financial bargains of all time.

Why have I put the words 'operated properly' in italics? Because in order to recoup some of their expenses banks stipulate that you must follow the terms and conditions relating to your account. If you don't, they hit you with all sorts of extra charges.

MONEY DOCTOR WEALTH CHECK

Loyalty doesn't pay

Don't imagine for a moment that by being loyal to a bank you'll get a better service. The era of 'relationship banking' is long gone. For instance, the decision over whether to lend you money is no longer made at branch level but by a centralised team. Of course, no bank wants to lose its customers, but the threat to take your business elsewhere is no longer as powerful as it once was.

Making the banking system work for you

How, then, can you get the most from your bank? I would offer you four straightforward and easy-to-follow rules:

1   Only buy the services and products you need from your bank. Don't allow them to persuade you into buying something you don't really require.

2   Make sure the services and products you buy are competitively priced. Buying a financial product from your bank may be more convenient – but it could cost you a lot of money.

3   Don't hesitate to shop around or move your business. Banks rely on customer inertia. In other words, they know that many people can't be bothered to ring around for a better price, let alone move their account elsewhere for a better deal.

4   Avoid breaking the terms and conditions attached to any product you purchase from your bank, as the consequences will undoubtedly be expensive.

You may imagine from what I am saying that I am 'anti-bank'. Far from it. Today's modern banks offer customers a fantastic choice and – if you buy wisely – a chance to pay little or nothing for your day-to-day banking.

WHAT BANKS DO BEST

At the heart of all banking lies the current account. This basic bank account should provide you with the following facilities:

- a safe and secure place to deposit cheques or cash
- somewhere convenient to keep your money in the short to medium term, until you need to spend it
- access to your cash via branches and cash machines
- a simple and easy way to pay your bills
- a comprehensive record of all your day-to-day financial transactions.

In order to provide all this, the typical current account will offer you some or all of the following services:

- a cheque book
- an ATM (this stands for automated teller machine) card allowing you to get cash 24 hours a day

- a **direct debit facility** so that you can pay your bills automatically
- a **standing order facility** allowing you to make regular payments
- a **cheque guarantee card**, making your cheques (up to a certain value) as good as cash in the hands of the recipient
- a **debit** (Laser) **card** so that you can arrange direct payments without having to write a cheque both in branch and even overseas
- **regular statements**
- **overdraft facilities.**

Your current account should also give you access to a telephone banking facility and – if you use the internet – online banking. Both should allow you to access your account – and arrange for other transactions – without having to go into a branch.

Although you can obtain some of the services listed above from building societies, credit unions and An Post, only six banks in Ireland offer you full current account banking facilities. These are:

1 Allied Irish Bank (AIB).

Bank of Ireland

2 Bank of Ireland (BOI).

3 Permanent TSB.

✹ Ulster Bank

4 Ulster Bank.

5 National Irish Bank (NIB).

✹ BANK OF SCOTLAND
Ireland

6 Bank of Scotland (Ireland).

BASIC BANKING SERVICES EXPLAINED

There are various banking terms that regularly cause customer confusion. I know, because I used to be a banker. Below, I explain them in plain English.

Standing orders

A **standing order** is exactly that – a regular ('standing') instruction ('order') to your bank to make the same payment to the same person or organisation on an agreed date. For instance, you might order your bank to pay €200 a month to me because you appreciate this book so much. Or, for that matter, you might instruct them to pay me a much larger amount every other month or every quarter, six months or year. You can instruct them to do this until further notice or until a date you specify.

Direct debits

A **direct debit** is basically an authorisation to your bank to pay a regular bill on your behalf. For instance, you might sign a direct debit instructing them to pay your ESB bill when it's presented. With a direct debit you don't specify the amount that is going to be paid and because of this there are some very strict safeguards in place to protect you. One of these is that only reputable organisations are allowed to use the direct debit system.

Laser cards (debit cards)

A **Laser card** works exactly like a cheque book – but using plastic instead of paper. When you pay someone with a Laser card they apply to your bank for the money, which is then transferred to their account. The upper limit for a single payment is €1,500. With cheques, of course, the bank only guarantees payment up to the maximum amount on your cheque guarantee card. You should only make a payment by Laser card if you have sufficient funds in your account or if your overdraft credit is large enough to meet the payment. There is an annual €5 stamp duty charge on Laser cards. Many Laser cards also double as ATM cards. Thanks to Laser cards you no longer need to take cash when shopping or wait for a cheque to clear before collecting goods.

Overdrafts

An **overdraft** is a short-term loan offered by your bank as part of your current account facility. There are two types:

- An **authorised overdraft** is one that has been arranged in advance – though you don't, necessarily, have to use it. The bank normally charges for agreeing this facility.
- An **unauthorised overdraft** is where the bank decides that despite the fact that you have no agreement to borrow from them, they will still make some payment on your behalf. Unauthorised overdrafts attract penalties and high rates of interest.

What many bank customers do not realise is that banks expect your current account to be in credit for 30 days a year and will charge you extra if it isn't.

WHAT PRICE BANKING?

So, what can you expect to **pay** for your current account banking? There isn't an easy answer. All banks have different pricing structures so that what one bank offers for free, another will charge for.

In 2004 the Irish Financial Services Regulatory Authority (now known as the 'Financial Regulator') surveyed bank customers and found that on average they were being charged between €50 and €137 for current account transactions. The level of charges was linked to the customer's choice of bank and level of usage. Today these charges are greater.

A direct comparison of current account charges isn't possible because all six banks offer different products and make different charges. If you want to save money on your own current account fees, the best way is to follow the money-saving tips detailed below.

CUTTING THE COST OF YOUR CURRENT ACCOUNT

There are a number of ways in which you can dramatically reduce the cost of your current account banking. These include:

1 With competition hotting up, all the banks now offer free banking, subject to various conditions. Shop around for the best package to suit your individual circumstances.

2 Don't use a bank overdraft facility. Banks will charge you for setting it up. They'll charge you interest on it and if you exceed the overdraft, a surcharge and an additional cost on top of this interest! Also they'll use it as an excuse to charge you for other facilities.

3 Don't, whatever you do, go overdrawn without formal agreement. An unauthorised overdraft will result in you being charged an extremely high rate of interest plus huge additional fees. Even going overdrawn for a couple of days could result in you paying anything from €20 upwards for the privilege.

4 Don't allow your cheques to 'bounce' referred to as being 'Returned Unpaid'. All six banks make heavy charges if your cheque or direct debit has to be returned unpaid. This happens, of course, if you haven't sufficient money in your account or you don't have a large enough overdraft limit. '**Refer to Drawer**' or '**Payment Stopped**' are stamped on the cheque. With the former, your credibility is shot, and there is a question mark on your ability to honour a debt. With the latter, you might wish to stop payments to a supplier of faulty goods if it is outside the cheque card guarantee (capped at €130).

5 Don't bank a cheque that might not clear. A cheque which is lodged to your account, but not honoured, could cost you as much as €17.14 including unpaid charges and referral fees per transaction.

6 Consider using a building society, An Post or credit union account for limited banking facilities – a far more economical way to do one's banking – see pp 83–4.

7 Consider using a credit card to pay all your bills. If you settle your credit card statement in full every month, this won't cost you anything. See the section on credit cards below for more information about this.

8 Internet and telephone banking eliminate cheque costs and other bank charges by enabling you to make payments and transfers between accounts over the telephone with a secure password.

MONEY DOCTOR WEALTH CHECK

The advantage of a joint account

If I am advising someone who is married, co-habiting or has other dependants I often recommend that they open a joint account and keep a bit of emergency cash in it. Why? When someone dies, it often takes months before his or her affairs can be wound up. During this time all bank accounts and other assets will be frozen. This frequently leaves the bereaved worrying about money. If you have a joint account, however, no such problem arises. Joint accounts are useful in other circumstances too, as everyone named on the account has the right to operate it, subject to the signing authority given.

Note: Joint accounts do not automatically escape inheritance tax.

OTHER TYPES OF BANK ACCOUNT

In addition to offering current accounts, all six banks offer a range of deposit and saving accounts. The usual rule with these is that the longer you leave your money, and the more money you deposit, the better the rate of interest you will receive.

In the current climate of low interest rates, many bank deposit accounts offer an extremely poor return.

To put this in perspective, if you deposited €1,000 with your average high street bank for one year you would earn €10 before tax. Unless you are not liable to income tax, you would have to pay Deposit Interest Retention Tax (DIRT tax) on this at 20%, meaning you would be left with a rather modest €8 for your trouble.

I examine the whole question of what to do with your savings in Part 6. In the meantime, my only comment would be that you should not leave your short-term savings in a current account, where it's unlikely to be earning any interest at all, but instead you should shop around and put any spare money where it gets the best rate.

Other bank services to consider

As already mentioned, all six banks offer a wide range of other services, from credit cards to personal loans, and from pensions to mortgages.

There is a great temptation if you have your current account with a particular bank to use them for one or more of these other services. I would advise you to resist this temptation. Let me give you two examples of why it's such a bad idea.

At the time of writing I checked the market for the best and worst mortgage rates.

- The best 92% mortgage for a first time buyer is at 5.55% (interest-only facility for the first two years).
- The worst 92% mortgage for a first time buyer on a standard variable rate (no interest-only facility) is at 6.45%.

At the same time I also checked credit card interest rates:

- Best credit card interest (after the 'loss leader' rates) is 8.5%.
- Worst credit card is a store card in excess of 23%.

As you can see, it definitely pays to shop around.

MONEY DOCTOR WEALTH CHECK

Switching is easy!

All six banks have adopted a code of practice to make it easier to move from one bank to another. Under this code, it should take you less than ten days to get a new account up and running, and all your standing orders and direct debits should be transferred from your old account within one week after that. If you have any trouble changing your bank you should contact the Financial Services Ombudsman's Bureau. You'll find their address on p. 67.

THE BUILDING SOCIETY OPTION

Building societies are owned by their members or – in plain English – their customers. Over the last decade all but two of Ireland's building societies have been sold to other financial institutions or have gone public. The remaining two, however, the EBS and Irish Nationwide, do offer an alternative to the traditional banks. Because of their slightly unusual status in the Irish financial services market place, they no longer offer current accounts to new customers. Nevertheless, thanks to their ATM network, competitive interest rates and other services, using them for your day-to-day banking can be feasible and may save you quite a bit of money.

THE AN POST OPTION

An Post is another option if you would rather not deal with one of the six major banks. Although they don't have any ATM cash machines, there are 1,400 branches of An Post and, of course, they're open six days a week. An account with An Post pays a higher level of interest than the equivalent bank account, and you can pay a range of household bills and buy money drafts at minimal cost. An Post also offers a bureau de change and electronic money transfer service, in a joint venture with Fortis Bank, called Postbank.

THE CREDIT UNION OPTION

Credit unions, like building societies, are owned by their members. There are 430 credit unions in Ireland – each one serving a local community. Their original role was to help people to save and also to provide inexpensive loans. In the last few years, though, many have  expanded the range of financial services they offer dramatically. For instance, many credit unions now offer budget accounts, which are perfectly suitable for paying regular bills. The main drawback to using a credit union for your day-to-day banking is that you can't take advantage of a national branch network or ATM machines. However, for some people they do offer an acceptable option.

BANKING ON HOLIDAY

You're going abroad, what should you do about money? Here are a few useful tips:

1 Since Ireland is one of the 15 countries that comprise the Euro zone, you can pay with Euro when visiting Austria, Belgium, Cyprus, Finland, France, Germany, Greece, Italy, Luxembourg, Malta, The Netherlands, Portugal, Slovenia and Spain. Like the American dollar, the Euro is widely accepted in many other countries, while not legal tender. Unfortunately, Euro cheques from Ireland cannot, yet, be used for payments when visiting another Euro-zone country.

2 Wherever you're travelling in the world – whether it's in the Euro zone or not – a credit card is probably the least expensive, most secure and most convenient way of paying. Visa and MasterCard are the most widely accepted credit cards overseas. The exchange rate you receive will, broadly speaking, be competitive. However, I would not recommend credit cards as a means of obtaining cash when overseas as all the credit card companies charge a fee for cash advances plus a high rate of interest from the day of withdrawal.

3 If you have an ATM card from one of the six Irish banks you'll find that you can use it extensively all over the world. The advantage of this is that you need not carry a great deal of cash with you, providing you have sufficient funds in your current account. Note, however, that you may not get the best rate of exchange and there could be special charges. Check with your bank before you head off.

4 Traveller's cheques are, in fact, quite expensive. Although they are obviously much more secure than cash, between the commission and exchange charges you could lose as much as 6% of your money – which is a high price to pay in my opinion. In fact, the demand for traveller's cheques has fallen so much that Ireland's biggest bank no longer stocks them.

5   It is possible to purchase something called a **pre-paid cash card**. This is offered by VisaTravel Money and is, effectively, a credit card version of a traveller's cheque. You pre-pay the amount you wish to have in credit and then you withdraw that money in local currency from ATMs wherever you travel. The cost works out about the same as traveller's cheques. Permanent TSB also offers a similar facility with its 3V credit card.

THE MONEY DOCTOR SAYS...

- It is possible to enjoy free or very low-cost banking if you take advantage of the system.

- Unauthorised overdrafts are very expensive and should be avoided if at all possible.

- Bank loyalty doesn't pay. Always shop around for the best deal.

- If you settle up each month in full, a credit card can be a very inexpensive way to manage much of your banking.

- There are alternatives to the banks – building societies, An Post and credit unions.

9

GETTING OUT OF DEBT

HOW TO PAY OFF ALL YOUR LOANS – INCLUDING YOUR MORTGAGE – QUICKLY AND EASILY

The greatest threat to your financial well-being is borrowing. I am not talking about reckless borrowing, either, but ordinary borrowing in the form of personal loans, overdrafts and credit cards. This is because the cost of borrowing money is a huge drain on your most valuable asset – your income.

What's more, the cost of borrowing can't just be measured in terms of the interest you are paying. You must also factor in the opportunity cost – the money you would otherwise be making if you were investing your income instead of spending it on servicing your debts. Let me give you one simple example:

> €10,000 repaid over seven years at an interest rate of 10% will require monthly repayments of €166. Total interest cost €3,945.

> Invest €166 a month into – say – the stock market for the same period and assuming the same sort of growth as we have seen over the last ten years – you'll have a lump sum of almost €20,000 in seven years.

Which is why, in this chapter, I explain the benefits of being debt free, together with two proven methods to make paying off all your loans fast and painless.

YOU MAY NOT EVEN REALISE YOU HAVE A PROBLEM

Most people borrow money but fail to think of themselves as being in debt. The fact is:

- You don't have to be in any sort of financial difficulty to be in debt.

- When you add up the cost of servicing your debt – including your mortgage – it may come to more than you imagine.

- Debt is the single greatest threat to your financial freedom and security. It is sucking away your most valuable asset: your income.

- The first benefit of being debt free is that your money becomes your own to spend or invest as you prefer.

- Not having any debt will make you less vulnerable. You won't need so much insurance, for instance.

Sizing up the problem

Over the last twenty to thirty years consumer debt has increased at a frightening pace. Why should this be? Some borrowing is unavoidable – for instance, loans taken out when ill or unemployed. Some can be attributed to other factors such as changing social values, lack of education at school, our consumer society and 'impulse' spending. However, I believe the main reason for the borrowing boom is that 'debt' has become a hugely profitable business. Bluntly, lenders use clever marketing tricks to 'push' debt onto innocent consumers. They are doing this because the returns are irresistible. Look at how much money they can make:

> If you leave money on deposit at a bank you'll typically earn less than 2% (€2 for every €100) a year by way of interest.

> That bank, however, can lend your money to someone else at anything up to 19% (€19 for every €100) a year.

Under the circumstances, is it any wonder that financial institutions are falling over themselves to lend money? Or that they devote themselves to coming up with new ways to sell loans to their customers?

Debt comes in many disguises

The trouble with the word 'debt' is that it has all sorts of negative connotations. Many people believe that providing they are never behind on their repayments they are not in debt. This isn't true. A debt is when you owe someone money. It could be:

- an unpaid balance on a credit card
- an overdraft
- a personal loan
- a car loan or loan for some other specific purchase
- a mortgage on your home
- a secured loan
- a hire purchase agreement
- an unpaid balance on a store charge card
- a business loan.
- a loan made by a friend or family member.

It is important to remember that just because you are never in arrears and have an excellent credit rating, it doesn't mean you are debt free.

MONEY DOCTOR WEALTH WARNING

It is compound interest that makes debt so expensive

When you are earning it, it has the power to make you very rich. When you are paying it, it has the power to make you very poor. Albert Einstein described it as 'the greatest mathematical discovery of all time'. It is the reason why banks, building societies, credit card companies and other financial institutions make so much profit from lending money. And it is the reason why ordinary investors can make themselves rich simply by doing nothing. It is a fiendishly simple concept called compound interest.

Perhaps the easiest way to understand compound interest is to look at two hypothetical examples:

Imagine that you borrow €1,000 at a rate of 10% a year. At the end of one year – assuming you have made no repayments – you will owe €100 in interest (10% of €1,000) or a total of €1,100. If you wait another year then you will owe an additional €110 in interest (10% of €1,100) or a total of €1,210. In other words you are paying interest on the interest.

Now imagine that you have €1,000 to invest and you deposit it in a savings account, which pays interest at a rate of 10% per year. At the end of one year you will be entitled to €100 interest. If you withdraw this interest but leave your capital, at the end of the second year you will be entitled to another €100 interest. Supposing, however, that you don't withdraw the interest but leave it to 'compound'. At the end of your first year your €1,000 is worth €1,100. At the end of your second year you will have earned €110 interest, meaning that your original €1,000 is worth €1,210. Put another way, your interest is earning you more interest.

When you borrow money, compound interest is working

against you. Supposing, for instance, you borrow €5,000 on a credit card at an interest rate of 15% – which isn't high by today's standards. The credit card company allows you to make a minimum payment of 1.5% each month. After two years you will still owe approximately €4,700, having made repayments of €1,750, of which €1,450 has been swallowed up in interest.

Compound interest is your greatest enemy and your greatest ally. When you are in debt, it works against you. But when you have money to invest you can make compound interest really work for you.

Beware the minimum payment trap

You make your lender happy when you:

- borrow as much as possible
- pay it back over as long a period as possible
- borrow at the highest possible interest rate
- make the minimum monthly payment.

You should be particularly wary of the **minimum payment trap** – where the lender allows you to pay back very little of the debt each month. This is particularly prevalent in the credit card and store card sector. When you opt for the minimum monthly repayment your repayment will be made up almost completely of interest so that the debt itself hardly ever gets reduced. Another thing to watch for is 'revolving credit' – where the lender keeps upping your credit limit or offering you new loans. It can take up to 11 years to repay some credit card debt if you only make the minimum payment each month!

DEBT THREATENS YOUR FUTURE FREEDOM

I certainly wouldn't go so far as to say all debt is bad. There are plenty of instances where borrowing money makes financial sense – in order to buy your own home, for example, or to pay for education. *It is when you are borrowing money to finance your lifestyle that you are getting into dangerous territory.* Living beyond your means threatens your future financial freedom. Let me give you an example:

> Cathal is the manager of a supermarket and earns a good income. However, it isn't enough to cover all the things he and his family like to enjoy, so he borrows frequently. In a typical year he might borrow to pay for Christmas presents, a holiday or just to cover other shortfalls in his monthly expenditure such as clothes or eating out. He views this as 'short-term' debt but the reality is that every year between the ages of 35 and 55 he borrows an average of €4,000 more than he earns. Because this is short-term, unsecured debt he pays an average of 12% a year in interest. His monthly debt repayments (excluding his mortgage) are €360.

> Cathal's twin brother, Ray, is also a supermarket manager and earns exactly the same income. However, he lives within his means. He doesn't eat out as often, go on holiday as frequently or drive such a nice car. He saves the €360 his brother spends each month on servicing his debts and instead he invests the money. He manages a return of 6% a year between the ages of 35 and 55 and so he builds up a tax-free lump sum of €160,000.

The fact is, your most valuable asset is your income and there is only so much that each of us will ever earn during our lifetimes. By spending a large portion of it on servicing debt you are – basically – giving it away to your lenders. Surely your need is greater than theirs?

SEVEN EXCELLENT REASONS TO BECOME DEBT FREE

Here are seven reasons why you should pay off all your debts – including, perhaps, your mortgage.

1 It will make you less vulnerable. If you are in debt and for some reason your income is reduced or stops altogether (suppose, for instance you fall seriously ill and don't have permanent health insurance), then not being able to repay your loans could have serious consequences.

2 It will make your family less vulnerable. I don't want to depress you but when you die your debts won't die with you – your estate will have to pay them all.

3 You won't have to worry about inflation. If you owe money and interest rates rise (as recently as 1981 interest rates were as high as 20%) then you could easily find yourself struggling to make your monthly payments.

4 You won't have the stress which comes with debt. The fact is owing money is stressful.

5 You'll enjoy a genuine sense of satisfaction. There is a real peace of mind which comes with not owing money and with owning your home outright.

6 It will open up new choices. Suddenly all the money you are spending on servicing your debts will be available for you to spend or save as you prefer.

7 It will ensure you have a comfortable retirement. Furthermore, it may allow you to retire early. Why should you have to wait until you are 60 or 65 to give up work?

MONEY DOCTOR WEALTH WARNING

How lenders will try to trick you

With so much profit at stake lenders put a lot of effort into persuading consumers to borrow. There is a catch to every offer! Let me give you just one example:

> Josephine goes to buy a new bed in the local store sale. It is marked down from €1,300 to €1,100 and as she goes to pay the shop assistant persuades her to take out a store card as it will give her an extra 10% saving. So instead of €1,100 she pays just €990. However, Josephine doesn't pay off her store card at the end of the month but instead takes 36 months to do so. The result? Because she is being charged 15% interest, the bed ends up costing her €1,548. Not so much of a saving, after all!

A couple of other things to watch out for. Firstly, loan consolidation. When used properly – as I will explain in a moment – loan consolidation is an excellent way to speed yourself out of debt. However, unscrupulous lenders often lure borrowers into taking out expensive consolidation loans – even encouraging them to borrow extra for a holiday or other luxury item. Secondly, if transferring credit card debt to save money, only too often a low interest or zero interest period is followed by a much higher rate. Check the conditions carefully and don't be taken in by lenders.

THE FIRST STEP TO GETTING OUT OF DEBT

There is one thing you must do before you set out to eradicate all your debt: stop borrowing. After all, you can't get yourself out of a hole if you keep digging. Take a once and for all decision to:

- not just to pay off your debts, but to stay out of debt

- not to borrow any more money unless it is absolutely unavoidable (or there is a very reasonable chance that you can invest the money you borrow to make more than the loan is going to cost you to repay)

- not to live beyond your means

- avoid 'bargains'. In my book a genuine bargain is something you need to buy but which you manage to get at a lower price than you expected to pay for it. Something that you don't need but you buy because it seems to be cheap is definitely not a bargain.

There are various actions you can take to make this easier on yourself. You can:

- Cut up all your credit cards and store cards.

- Cancel your overdraft limit. But remember, most banks will allow a 'shadow' overdraft on your account. This means that informally they may allow your account to overdraw by say €500 before you are contacted. This is costly and may eventually have to be formalised, so you are back in the overdraft trap again. Keep track of all transactions on your account.

- Use a charge card where the balance has to be paid in full at the end of each month.

- Avoid buying any unnecessary items.

- Do not take out any new loans including hire purchase agreements and overdrafts.

- Do not increase the size of any existing loans.

- Pay with cash whenever possible (nothing reduces one's tendency to spend money as paying with cash).

American money expert Alvin Hall (you may have seen him on television) suggests that anyone with trouble curbing his or her expenditure should keep what he calls a **money diary**. The basic idea is that you carry a small notebook with you wherever you go and write down details of every single penny you spend. You should include everything – from your daily newspaper to your mortgage repayments. After a couple of weeks you'll have a precise picture of where your money is going and this, in turn, will help you avoid spending money on things you don't really want or need. If you are prone to impulse spending or if you always spend more than your income I can see the good sense in this approach.

TAKING STOCK OF YOUR SITUATION

Once you have stopped making the situation any worse you need to take stock of your situation. In particular, you want to gather together full details of your debts. The information you require about each of your debts is:

- to whom you owe the money
- how big the debt is

- how long you have to pay it back (the term), if relevant
- what the rate of interest is and whether it is fixed or variable
- whether you will be penalised for paying back the debt early (and if so what the penalties are)
- what the minimum monthly payment is (if this is relevant)
- whether the interest is calculated daily, monthly or annually.

Obviously, it is important not to overlook any possible debts so here is a quick checklist to remind you. Don't forget to include any money that your spouse or partner may owe, too!

- mortgages
- secured loans
- credit cards
- store cards
- overdrafts
- personal loans
- car loans
- hire or lease purchase
- catalogue company loans
- family or friends who may have lent you money
- student loans.

Most of the information you need should be supplied to you each month by your lenders. However, if it isn't then you should telephone or write to them asking for full details.

MONEY DOCTOR WEALTH CHECK

The 'savings' conundrum

The Money Doctor often encounters 'patients' who have debts but who are saving money at the same time. If you cannot make a greater return on your capital than the deposit interest rate on your savings, it may well be to your advantage to reduce debt where the interest rate chargeable is far higher than that of the deposit interest rate.

In most cases, it makes sense to stop saving money and to use any existing savings to pay off some or all of your debts. Why? Because usually what you are earning from your savings will be substantially less than what you are paying out to borrow.

€100 in a savings account may be earning you as little as €2 after tax.

€100 owed on – say – a credit card may be costing you as much as €19 or even more a year.

So if you had savings of €1,000 and used it to pay off €1,000 of credit card debt you could be saving yourself as much as €190 a year. More – as much as €240 a year – if you have borrowed on a store card.

Note, however, it does not make sense to cash in your savings if, for example, you have an endowment policy where you may need to leave it mature. You would be well advised to take professional advice since some are worth more than others.

Overall, however, it does not make financial sense to be investing a small amount of money each month if – at the same time – you are spending a small fortune on servicing a debt.

THE ART OF DEBT ELIMINATION

You've taken the decision not to incur any extra debt. You've got a real grip on the size and nature of your problem. What next? You have two options:

- the **consolidation** approach
- the **sniper** approach.

Option 1 The consolidation approach

The idea behind 'consolidation' is to reduce the cost of your debt dramatically. Instead of having lots of different loans – all at different rates – you have a single loan at one, much lower rate. It works particularly well if you own your own home. What you do is:

- Add up all the money you currently spend making your debt repayments.
- Consolidate all your debts into a single, much cheaper loan.
- Keep on making the same monthly payments.

This is best explained with an example. Below I have listed off all the debts that Brian and Sheila have along with the interest rate they are paying on each one:

Type of debt	Monthly cost	Interest rate (%)
Mortgage	€900	5.5
Home improvement loan	€16	10
Credit card 1	€45	16
Credit card 2	€30	16
Store card	€71	17
Car loan	€225	10

The total amount Brian and Sheila are spending on their debts is €1,287 a month. Since they own their own home they can consolidate all their debts in with their mortgage. At the moment their mortgage is for €128,000 and has 19 years to run. Although consolidating their loans increases their mortgage to €152,000, by continuing to pay €1,300 a month they can shorten the length of their mortgage to just 14 years. At the same time they will save themselves €27,000 in interest! Incidentally, to optimise the benefit of consolidation it may be preferable to take out something called a **current account mortgage**. The full benefits of these mortgages are explained on p. 140.

Please remember, debt consolidation is a once-in-a-lifetime course of action. It only works to your advantage if you carry on making the same monthly payments … otherwise all you are doing is spreading the cost of your short-term debt over the longer term. I believe one should never borrow money for a longer period than the life of the asset you are buying.

Option 2 The sniper approach

If you don't own your own home – or if you don't have sufficient capital tied up in your property to consolidate your debts in with your mortgage – you'll need to take what I call the 'sniper' approach. This involves 'picking off' your debts one at a time starting with the most expensive. What you do is:

- Find some extra money. Just because you don't have a mortgage doesn't mean that you can't consolidate your debt. Move your borrowing to where it is costing you the least.
- Use the money you are saving each month to pay off your most expensive debt – in other words, the one with the highest rate of interest.

Do you sometimes pay more than the minimum amount required each month? If you do then make sure you pay it to whichever of your debts is costing you the most. Incidentally, you may find that one or more of your existing lenders will be open to negotiation.

To use a typical example, imagine that Neil has the following debts:

Type of debt	Monthly/minimum cost	Interest rate (%)
Credit card €4,000	€60	16
Store card €5,000	€75	17
Car loan €8,000	€258	10

Every month he usually pays about €100 more off one or other of the debts – on a purely random basis. Also, he is able to find €100 from other sources (see below) to help speed himself out of debt. In other words, Neil has €200 extra to apply to getting himself out of debt.

Therefore, what he needs to do is pay off his most expensive debt first – his store card. By paying an extra €200 a month he can do this within 20 months. This frees up the store card minimum payment of €75 to help pay of his next most expensive debt – which is his credit card.

MONEY DOCTOR WEALTH CHECK

Put your money to the best possible use...

The secret to getting rid of your debts is in putting your money to the best possible use. Your objective is to get your loans onto the lowest possible rate of interest and then to use the saving to speed up the process of paying off your debt.

Of course, if you could find some extra money each month, then you could get out of debt even faster. One way to find extra money is to look at the way you spend your income and see if you couldn't make some basic savings without necessarily cutting back. For example:

- Many people pay more than they have to for their banking. Review your arrangements. Could you be earning extra interest? Saving interest? Avoiding unnecessary costs?

- Don't pay for anything you neither need nor use. For instance, membership fees, internet charges, and magazines.

- Double check you aren't overpaying your tax. Are your tax credits correct?

- Review all your insurance costs. This is a fiercely competitive market and you may be able to save a substantial amount.

In general, it isn't what you earn but how you spend it that will make the difference to your finances. You could be on an enormous salary but if you are up to your neck in debt (as many high-income earners are) it is useless to you.

THE MONEY DOCTOR SAYS...

- If you only take action on one aspect of your finances make it your priority to get yourself out of debt.
- The first step is to stop borrowing and to get a realistic position of what you owe and how much it is costing you.
- Consider consolidating your debt in with your mortgage.
- Remember, if you save money or have any spare cash you should put it towards paying off your debts.
- Pay your most expensive debts off first.

10

BORROWING

IF YOU DO HAVE TO BORROW I WILL SHOW YOU HOW TO BORROW SENSIBLY

HOW TO BORROW SENSIBLY AND INEXPENSIVELY

There are times when it makes sense to borrow. And times when borrowing is unavoidable. Either way, you want to make sure that you don't pay a cent more than you have to. If there is one area of personal finance where consumers get 'ripped off' regularly, then it is when they borrow.

Look at the difference!

Nothing better illustrates the way in which consumers can overpay for a loan than a quick comparison of rates:

Secured loan from one of the specialist lenders	6%
Personal loan (unsecured) from any high street bank	10%
Credit card from any of the main providers	17%
Store card from any of the major retail outlets	19%

As a consumer it is not impossible that you might simultaneously be paying anything from 6% to 20% to borrow money – which is ridiculous.

MONEY DOCTOR WEALTH CHECK

How to compare loan rates

In order that consumers can compare interest rates, the government insists that the cost of loans is expressed in terms of an **annual percentage rate** (APR).

Confusingly, there is more than one way to calculate the APR – but broadly speaking it is an accurate way of assessing how much a loan is going to cost you including all the hidden costs such as up-front fees.

Clearly, the lower the APR the cheaper the loan the better it is for you.

Remember, financial institutions make enormous profits from lending money. You should never, ever be shy about shopping around or asking for a lower rate.

So, what is 'sensible borrowing'?

There are times when it makes excellent sense to borrow. For instance, if you want to:

- buy, build or improve your home
- finance a property investment
- pay for education
- pay for a car or other necessary item
- start a business.

There are also times when it is impossible not to borrow money – if you are temporarily unable to earn an income, for instance, for some reason beyond your control.

There is no intrinsic harm, either, in genuine short-term borrowing for some luxury item. What is really dangerous, however, is short-term borrowing that becomes long-term borrowing without you meaning it to do so. This is not only extremely expensive but makes you more vulnerable to financial problems. I can't emphasise enough how bad it is for your financial well-being to borrow money to pay for living expenses. In particular, you should definitely avoid long-term credit card and store card debt.

If you have succumbed to the temptation of credit card or store card debt – and you want to pay it off – read Chapter 9 on getting out of debt.

Never borrow for longer than you have to

Making sure that you pay the lowest rate of interest is one way to keep the cost of borrowing down. Paying your debts back quickly is another. Compound interest (see Appendix 1) really works against you when borrowing money. The difference between paying back €1,000 at 15% APR over one year and – say – three years is a staggering €300 in interest!

Build up a good financial/credit rating history

It is vital at all times to be aware that defaulting on loans or credit cards is registered with the Irish Credit Bureau (ICB) and will greatly affect your ability to borrow or borrow at attractive interest rates. Never let unauthorised arrears build up on any loan. If your circumstances change during the term of a loan, inform the lender and come to an agreed and realistic repayment schedule. (See Chapter 16, 'If I have trouble making my mortgage repayments what should I do?' for details of whom to contact to avoid money lenders if you are in dire circumstances.)

Why rates differ so widely

Financial institutions set their charges according to the level of risk involved and prevailing market conditions.

As far as they are concerned loans fall into two categories:

Secured loans. Where, if the borrower fails to make the repayments, there is a physical asset – such as a house or even an insurance policy – that can be 'seized' and sold to meet the outstanding debt. Because of this secured loans should cost considerably less.

Unsecured loans. Where, if the borrower fails to make the repayments, the lender has no security and thus risks never getting paid (though this is rare). Such loans cost considerably more.

THE FIRST RULE OF BORROWING

The first rule of borrowing for less is, therefore, to take out a secured rather than an unsecured loan. This isn't always practicable – but where it is, you'll save a substantial amount of money.

Secured loans

Secured loans include:

- mortgage on your property
- secured loan (which is like a second or extra mortgage) on your property
- asset-backed finance (used, for instance, for major purchases such as cars).

Unsecured loans

Unsecured loans include:

- bank overdrafts
- credit union loans
- personal or term loans – including car loans
- credit cards
- store cards
- hire purchase
- money lenders.

MONEY DOCTOR WEALTH WARNING

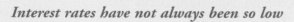

Interest rates have not always been so low

We have enjoyed relatively low interest rate stability up to recently. Things were very different less than a decade ago. Indeed, in the early 1990s mortgage rates went up to 15% at one point, and some people were paying over 30% a year on their credit card debt.

As we have seen in 2008, interest rates rose by nearly 2%. Therefore, don't borrow so much that a change in interest rates (or a change in your personal circumstances) would leave you in crisis.

CHOOSING THE BEST LOAN FOR YOUR NEEDS

With the possible exception of borrowing to fund a holiday or a special event such as a wedding, you should try to make sure that the useful life of whatever you're using your loan for will be longer than the time it takes you to repay it. Remember, the rate of interest you're charged is only part of the equation. The other part is the length of time it will take you to repay the loan. For instance, you might think it was sensible to take out some extra money on your mortgage to buy a car since mortgages are, undoubtedly, the least expensive way to borrow. If, however, your mortgage still has 15 years to run then you'll be paying for your car over all that time. Under the circumstances, you should opt for an alternative method or else ensure that you overpay your mortgage in order to clear that part of the debt sooner.

THE MONEY DOCTOR BEST LOAN GUIDE

Here are the ten most usual ways of borrowing money ranked in order – starting with the least expensive first and ending with the most expensive last.

1   **Loans from family, friends and employers.** Often family members, friends and employers will make interest-free or low-interest loans. My advice is always to regularise such loans with a written agreement so that there is no room for misunderstanding or bad feeling at a later date.

2   **Mortgages and secured loans.** In the current, low-interest climate mortgages and secured loans can be amazingly inexpensive. It may be worth your while to add major purchases into your mortgage in order to reduce their real cost. However, bear in mind that if you

say, buy a car and add it to your mortgage what you should do is increase your monthly repayments so that that bit of your debt is paid off in less time. Otherwise, you could be paying for your car over the whole term of your mortgage. If you do this, however, ensure that your extra payments 'reduce the capital' (loan) rather than credit your repayment account.

3   **Asset finance and leasing.** I am a big believer in asset finance and leasing. Although not as cheap as a mortgage, this can be an economical way to fund major purchases and it has the benefit of being very tax efficient if you are self-employed or running a business. You should ask an authorised financial adviser with access to all providers to find you the best possible rate. Leasing is also very quick and you can receive your cheque within 48 hours of your application.

4   **Overdrafts.** If you have a bank current account you can ask your manager for an overdraft facility. Once approved, you will be able to spend money up to this amount. There won't be a set re-payment period but there may well be an annual arrangement charge. Authorised overdrafts are usually fairly competitive (though you shouldn't be afraid to negotiate). Exceeding your overdraft limit, however, can lead to heavy charges and the embarrassment of bounced cheques – for this reason unauthorised overdrafts should be avoided. Bear in mind, too, that most banks expect your current account to be in credit for 30 days a year and will charge you extra if it isn't.

5   **Credit union loans.** We are fortunate in Ireland to have a network of local credit unions willing to lend money to its membership base at a competitive rate of interest. To qualify for a loan you must first join the credit union and then – normally – save a regular amount with them for a set period of time. Because credit unions are non-profit making they tend to offer much better value for money. Not all credit union rates are the same and while it is worth shopping around, you can only open a credit union account in the nearest office to where you live or where you work.

6   **Personal or term loans.** The cost of personal or term loans can vary enormously. Essentially, when you borrow the money you agree to a set repayment period or 'term'. The rate of interest charged is normally variable and you should always pay close attention to your statements to check that it hasn't risen out of line with market rates. Where a rate is fixed in advance – giving you the security of knowing what your repayments will be – it is likely to be higher.

Where a loan is provided by a dealer or retailer, check the conditions closely. Sometimes you may be offered a low or zero rate for an agreed period that will rise dramatically in cost after the set term. Also, the cost of providing this credit will be built into the price of whatever you are buying.

7   **Credit cards.** Used properly, a credit card will give you as much as 45 days interest-free credit. On a certain day every month your bill will be calculated for the previous 30 days and sent to you for payment by the end of the following month. If your cut-off date is – say – the 17th of the month, all charges between 17 December and 17 January would have to be paid for by the end of February. If you can't pay the full amount then you are given the option of paying a reduced amount. This could be less than 5% of the total outstanding. The catch is that you will be charged an extremely high rate of interest – possibly approaching 20% a year. Credit cards are an extremely expensive way to borrow and credit card companies are very aggressive in their marketing methods. If you are going to use a credit card then don't fall into the trap of making the minimum payment each month. A relatively small balance could take you years to clear.

Note: if your income is high enough your bank may offer you a 'gold' credit card with a built-in overdraft facility at a preferential rate. Your credit card balance will be settled each month using the overdraft. This can be a cost-effective way to borrow and is worth investigating.

8   **Store cards.** I am afraid I am not at all enthusiastic about store cards. They work in the same way as credit cards except – of

course – you can only use them in the store (or chain of stores) that issues the card. Their single advantage is that having such a card may entitle you to an extra discount on first purchase and again during any sales. Their huge disadvantage is that the rate of interest charged on outstanding balances almost always makes normal credit cards look cheap by comparison. My strong advice – unless you are very disciplined with money – is not to use store cards.

9 **Hire purchase.** Hire purchase allows you to buy specific goods over an agreed period of time. In other words, it is a bit like a personal or term loan. The difference is that the rates charged for hire purchase are normally somewhat higher and you might be better looking at alternatives such as a personal loan or a lease. Remember, too, that with hire purchase you don't own whatever you are buying until you have made your last payment. This is not the case with, for example, a personal loan.

10 **Money lenders.** Whether licensed or unlicensed, money lenders are always about the most expensive way to borrow and the rates they charge are outrageous. When they are trading illegally there is the added risk of violence or intimidation if you don't pay what they say you owe them. You should avoid them like the plague! Incidentally, the definition of a money lender – and licensed at that – is an entity or someone who charges you a minimum of 23% interest a year! A list of licensed money lenders is available from The Central Bank.

(See Chapter 16 'If I have trouble making my mortgage repayments what should I do?' for details of whom to contact to avoid money lenders if you are in dire circumstances.)

THE MONEY DOCTOR SAYS...

- Think carefully before you borrow money. Is it sensible to take out a loan for whatever you are planning to buy? Don't borrow money to pay for 'lifestyle' items. No loan should ever last for longer than the thing you are spending the money on!

- Shop around for the most competitive rate. There is a huge difference and you can save yourself – literally – thousands of Euros by making sure you have the cheapest possible loan.

- Read any credit agreement very carefully and seek clarification of any sections you don't fully understand.

- Don't allow your short-term borrowing to become long term by mistake.

- Don't be blindly loyal to any particular lender. Go where the best rate is.

- If in doubt, seek expert help.

PART 4
COMPLETE GUIDE TO INSURANCE

Life insurance…home insurance…pet insurance…medical insurance…product warranty insurance…travel insurance…income protection insurance…there is no shortage of different insurance policies to choose from.

In principle, so much choice is a wonderful thing. It allows you to protect yourself, your family and your possessions from a whole range of risks – at one end catastrophic, at the other mildly irritating.

In practice, of course, so much choice can be confusing and can easily lead to you:

- *not taking out cover you should really have*
- *taking out cover that you don't actually need*
- *taking out the wrong amount of cover (too much or, more worryingly, too little)*
- *paying more than you have to.*

I am afraid the problem is often compounded by the fact that many people end up receiving poor or heavily biased advice.

Anyway, this section of the book has a single purpose: making sure that you have the appropriate cover for your needs and that you aren't paying more for it than is necessary. It is divided into two chapters. In the first, we will consider cover for people, and in the second cover for things.

11
PROTECTING YOURSELF AND YOUR FAMILY

HOW TO BUY THE MEDICAL, INCOME AND LIFE INSURANCE YOU ACTUALLY NEED – AT THE LOWEST POSSIBLE PRICE

First-class medical protection, critical illness cover and life insurance are available at a remarkably low price providing you know how to buy it.

In this chapter you'll discover how to:

- make sure you aren't sold cover you don't need
- decide what cover it is sensible for you to take out
- find out who you can trust to advise you
- make sure you get your cover at the lowest possible price.

American filmmaker Woody Allen quipped that his 'idea of hell is to be stuck in a lift with a life insurance salesman'. Mr Allen is by no means alone in his distrust of both life insurance and the people who sell it. Why should this be? I'm sure it is partly because no one likes to think about anything bad happening to them, and partly because – in order to draw attention to a very real need – life insurance salespeople are forced to bring up uncomfortable subjects with their prospective clients.

However, although it is not something you may rush to tackle, making certain that you have adequate life – and health – insurance will bring you *genuine* peace of mind.

YOU KNOW YOU SHOULD...

It isn't pleasant to dwell on being ill, having an accident or – worst of all – dying. Nevertheless, you owe it to yourself – and those you care for – to spend a little time making sure you are **protected** should the worst happen. This means being:

- *protected* by PHI (permanent health insurance) if you are too unwell to earn an income
- *protected* by private medical insurance if you need medical attention
- *protected* by life cover if you, or your partner, should die.

For a relatively small amount of money you can take out a range of insurance policies designed to:

- provide for you, or your dependants, if you, or your partner, should die
- give you a lump sum or a regular income if you find you have a serious illness, are incapacitated or cannot work
- meet all your private medical bills in the event of an accident or illness.

There are, of course, plenty of facts and figures available proving just how likely it is for someone of any age to fall ill or die. Sadly, such statistics are borne out by everyone's personal experience. The truth is we all know of instances where families have had to face poor medical care and/or financial hardship as the result of a tragedy. We all know, too, that spending the small sum required to purchase appropriate cover makes sound sense.

SPEND TIME, NOT MONEY

The odd thing about the different types of insurance dealt with in this chapter is that none of them is expensive when you consider the protection they offer. The secret is to identify exactly what cover you *really* need and not to get sold an inappropriate or overpriced policy. It is also important to review your needs on a regular basis. What you require today, and what you'll require in even two or three years time could alter dramatically.

The best way to start is by considering what risks you face and deciding what action you should take. Here are three questions that *everyone* should ask themselves, regardless of their age, gender, health or financial circumstances.

Question 1: What would your financial position be if you were unable to work – due to an accident or illness – for more than a short period of time?

Obviously, your employer and the state will both be obliged to help you out. However, if you have a mortgage, other debts and/or a family to support your legal entitlements are unlikely to meet anything like your normal monthly outgoings. If you do have a family then your spouse will have to balance work, caring for you and – possibly – caring for children. Is this feasible or – more to the point – desirable? How long will your savings last you under these circumstances? Do you have other assets you could sell?

Unless you have substantial savings and/or low outgoings then income protection cover (sometimes known as permanent health insurance) and/or critical illness insurance could both make sound sense.

Question 2: Do you have anyone dependent on you for either financial support or care? Are you dependent on someone else financially? Do you have children – or other family members – who would have to be cared for if you were to die?

If you are single and don't have any dependants then the reason to take out life insurance is in order to settle your debts and/or leave a bequest. If, on the other hand, there is someone depending on you – either for money or for care – then life cover has to be a priority.

If you are supporting anyone (or if your financial contribution is necessary to the running of your household) then you need to take out cover so that you don't leave those you love facing a financial crisis.

If you are caring for anyone – children, perhaps, or an ageing relative – then you should take out cover so that there is plenty of money for someone else to take over this role.

Question 3: Does it matter to you how quickly you receive non-urgent medical treatment? If you need medical care would you rather choose who looks after you, where you are treated and in what circumstances? How important is a private room in hospital to you?

We are fortunate enough to enjoy free basic health care in Ireland. However, if you are self-employed or if you have responsibilities which mean that it is important for you to be able to choose the time and place of any medical treatment, then you should consider private medical insurance.

INCOME PROTECTION COVER

If you are of working age then the chances of you being off work for a prolonged period of time due to illness or an accident are substantially greater than the chances of you dying.

It is for this reason that income protection cover is so valuable. As its name suggests, it is designed to replace your income if a disability or serious illness prevents you from working. If you are in a company pension scheme – or if you have arranged your own pension – you should check to see what cover you have already since it is sometimes included.

Incidentally, most policies only pay out after the policyholder has been off work for a minimum of 13 weeks *unless* hospitalised. Also, if you want to reduce the cost you can opt for a policy that doesn't pay out until you have been off work for 26 weeks.

THE MONEY DOCTOR SAYS...

As with anything *you should shop around* for all your insurance cover. Costs vary dramatically. Remember, too, that an Authorised Advisor, regulated by the Financial Regulator, can explain all the policies to you and can steer you to the best for your needs.

MONEY DOCTOR WEALTH WARNING

Don't be sold something you don't need

I don't believe it is advisable to buy insurance from anyone who isn't qualified to inform you about every single option available to you. Salespeople who are tied to one company – or even a small selection of companies – are clearly not going to offer you the same quality of advice as someone who has a detailed knowledge of the entire market. For further advice on this crucial area see Chapter 4.

CRITICAL OR SERIOUS ILLNESS INSURANCE

Horrible as it is to think about, imagine being diagnosed with a serious illness. I am talking about something like cancer, heart disease or multiple sclerosis. Naturally, under the circumstances, you might need special care and/or want to make life changes. This is where **critical** or **serious illness insurance** comes in. (The name of this insurance cover is changing to **specified illness cover**.) Providing you survive for two weeks after your diagnosis you will receive a lump sum of tax-free money to spend however you wish. Clearly, such a sum would allow you to pay off your debts, seek specialist treatment or in some other way ensure that you didn't have any financial problems.

It is important to remember that this cover provides you with a lump sum – not an income.

LIFE COVER

There are several different types of **life cover** – but they are all designed to do one thing. For a relatively low monthly payment they provide a lump sum if the insured person dies. The lump sum is tax free and may go into the insured's estate or may be directly payable to a nominated person (such as his or her spouse). Some of the uses to which this lump sum might be put include:

• paying off a mortgage

- paying off other debts
- being invested to provide a replacement income
- being invested to provide money for childcare or the care of someone else such as an ageing relative.

In the case of more expensive life cover the policy can have a cash-in value after a period of time has elapsed. The cost of life cover will be determined by your age, gender, and lifestyle. If you are a non-smoker and don't drink heavily you will save quite a bit of money.

Below are details of the different types of cover available so that you can decide which is most appropriate to your requirements.

Term insurance

As its name implies, **term insurance** is available for a pre-agreed period of time – usually a minimum of ten years. It is mandatory when you take out most interest-only home loans.

It is particularly useful for people with a temporary need. For instance, if you have young children you and your spouse might take out a 20-year plan giving you protection until your family have grown up and left home. By the same token, you might take out a policy that would pay off the exact amount of your mortgage.

Term insurance is the least expensive form of life cover and you can opt for:

Level term. The amount of cover remains the same (level) for the agreed period. For instance, you might take out €50,000 of cover for ten years. The cost will remain fixed for the same period, too.

Decreasing term. The amount of cover drops (decreases) every year. For instance, you might take out €50,000 of cover that drops to €48,000 in the second year, €45,000 in the third year and so forth. Such policies are almost always taken out in conjunction with mortgages in order to pay off the outstanding debt should the insured die. Note this sort of cover can't be extended or increased in value once you have taken it out.

Convertible term. Although the cover is for a set period of time, a convertible policy will allow you to extend your insurance for a further period regardless of your health. This is a very useful feature because it means that if you suffer some health problem you won't be denied life cover because of it. In fact, if you extend the policy, the insurance company will charge you the same premium as if you were perfectly healthy. Convertible term cover is normally not much more expensive than level term cover and – therefore – is usually the better option.

Whole of life assurance

There are two benefits to taking out a whole of life assurance plan. Firstly, providing you carry on making your monthly payments the plan is guaranteed to pay out. In other words, you are covered for the whole of your life. Secondly, there can be an investment element to the cover. So if you decide to cancel the plan you'll receive back a lump sum.

There are various features you can opt for with whole of life cover. You can vary the balance between actual life cover and the investment element, for instance. Also you can decide to end the cover at a particular point – when you retire, for instance. Some whole of life policies are designed to meet inheritance tax liabilities.

Whole of life cover is more expensive than term cover.

PRIVATE MEDICAL INSURANCE

This type of insurance is designed to meet some or all of your medical bills if you opt to go for private treatment.

Only three companies provide this cover in Ireland. VHI (Voluntary Health Insurance), Quinn Healthcare and Hibernian Health. Between them they offer a wide range of plans with an array of options, conditions and limits.

The basic decisions you have to make are:

- Do you want a choice of consultant?

- Do you want a choice of hospital?

- Do you want private or just semi-private hospital accommodation?

- Do you want outpatient cover?

Discounts can be available if you join through a 'group' – your employer, for instance, or a credit union.

As with all insurance, it is well worth getting expert help in deciding which option is best for your needs.

WHICH TYPES OF COVER SHOULD YOU CHOOSE?

Is it better to take out income protection or critical illness insurance? Should you opt for term life or whole of life cover? If term cover – which sort? If whole of life – what investment element should you include? Do you need private medical insurance, or is it a luxury you can do without?

Although these are personal decisions that only you can make *a professional authorised adviser will be able to guide you.* You can trust these advisers to give you the best possible advice because they are bound – by law – to do so and can be prosecuted for 'mis-selling'.

Keep the following points in mind when making your decision:

- If you have a limited budget I would opt – first and foremost – for either income protection or specified illness cover. Depending on your circumstances you might take out both.

- If you are on a tight budget then take out decreasing term insurance to cover your mortgage.

- If you have joint financial responsibilities – for instance, if you are married – and you have limited resources, it is more important to cover the main income earner.

- Covering a husband and wife together on the same policy often doesn't cost that much more than covering just one person.

- If you are self-employed, private medical cover is not really a luxury but more of a necessity and the premiums are tax deductible for everyone.

MONEY DOCTOR WEALTH WARNING

Six things every life assurance company must tell you...

The sale of life assurance is strictly regulated and your life assurance company must provide you with six important items of information before you sign on the dotted line. These are:

1 The **cost**. Not just the monthly premium but also whether the cost will ever be subject to review. If the cost is fixed, this is referred to as level premiums. There are reasons why the cost could be increased. For instance, it could be because the benefit will be going up at some point in the future.

2 A description of the **main purpose of the product**. For instance, whether it's a savings or protection policy.

3 Full details of all the **charges** and any **commission** that is going to be made to a broker or salesperson.

4 If there is an investment element to the policy, you should be given examples of the **expected return**, together with details of any future **tax liability**. Any guarantees should also be explained.

5 You should be told what will happen **if you cancel** (or 'surrender') the policy early. What will this do to the projected value?

6 **Background information** about the insurer and anyone else involved such as the broker or intermediary.

Note: by law they must also give you a 'cooling-off' period. This is time in which you can change your mind about the policy you have purchased and cancel it, without cost or penalty.

MONEY DOCTOR WEALTH WARNING

You must be truthful

When you complete an application for life cover – in fact, for any sort of insurance – the onus is upon you to advise the insurer of any facts which may affect the risk they are undertaking. Indeed, you'll be asked to sign a declaration to the effect that you haven't withheld any relevant information. If you lie – or even if you fail to reveal something that may be important – your policy may end up being invalid. Clearly, it would be a complete waste of your money if – when you came to claim – the insurer were not legally bound to pay up. In the case of life cover you must provide information about your medical history and also about any risks (such as dangerous sports) that might have some bearing on your life expectancy.

HOW MUCH LIFE COVER DO YOU NEED?

One of the most difficult problems regarding life cover is deciding quite how much you need. If you wanted to replace your income then you will require close to between 10 and 15 times your annual after-tax earnings.

So, if you take home €1,000 a month you should aim to have a minimum of €120,000 cover, which is €1,000 (your salary) x 12 (number of months in the year) x 10 (minimum advisable level of cover).

Remember, it is possible to keep the cost of life cover down by going for a 'term' policy. Bear in mind too that it's better to have some cover than no cover at all.

Life cover tax tip

If you're worried that you may have to pay inheritance tax (see Chapter 29 for further information about this), then one solution is to set up your life assurance policy so that it is not counted as part of your estate when you die. This is done by 'writing the policy under trust' – which is as simple as completing a form your insurer or agent will provide. Incidentally, if you do this not only will the proceeds from your life cover escape inheritance tax, but also the money will be paid to your chosen beneficiaries relatively quickly – usually in a matter of weeks. It doesn't cost anything to put your life assurance under trust, and you can change the beneficiary (or beneficiaries) at any time.

KEEPING THE COST DOWN

There are two ways to keep the cost of your insurance down to an absolute minimum:

1 Always get independent professional assistance from someone who is authorised to look at *every option* for you. This is one purchase where shopping around and expert knowledge can save you serious money.

2 *Refine your needs.* By taking out the *right sort of cover* and the *right level of cover* you won't be wasting money.

THE MONEY DOCTOR SAYS...

- Don't stick your head in the sand, believing that 'it won't happen to me'. Protecting yourself and your family should be one of your key financial priorities.

- Choose an independent, professional Authorised Advisor who you feel comfortable with to advise you.

- Don't get sold cover you don't need.

- Review your needs regularly … every two or three years … to make sure you have adequate protection.

- This is a fiercely competitive market. Having an expert shop around for you could mean big savings.

12

PROTECTING YOUR POSSESSIONS

With the cost of general insurance only going one way it is important to make sure that you are getting value for money. In this chapter you'll discover:

- details of all the different types of cover you should consider
- how to ensure that you aren't paying more than you have to
- other buying tips.

THE IMPORTANCE OF PROPER COVER

The temptation, when insurance premiums rise, is to reduce the amount of cover you have or – where cover isn't obligatory – to cancel the policy completely.

There are two reasons why it is important to make sure that you have adequate 'general' insurance.

Firstly, if you have borrowed money in order to pay for something you should always ensure that there is sufficient insurance to re-pay the debt in case disaster strikes. To quote just one real case history:

> Frank borrowed €15,000 to buy a car and only took out the cheapest motor insurance – third party, fire and theft – he could buy. The car was involved in an accident and completely destroyed. Because Frank didn't have comprehensive insurance he is now saddled with paying off the original car loan plus paying for a replacement car.

Secondly, if you *under*-insure then you always risk receiving less of a pay-out when you come to claim. This is particularly true when it comes to home insurance. Again, let me quote a real case history:

> John and Moira didn't have a mortgage on their house and although they had buildings and contents protection they hadn't bothered to check the amount of cover for many years. Unfortunately, an electrical fault resulted in the house being burned down (thankfully, no one was hurt). When they came to claim because they were under-insured the insurance company would only pay three-quarters of the price of re-building.

Shopping around for insurance is no one's idea of fun. On the other hand, the cost of not taking out adequate insurance can be huge. And if you invest even a small amount of time reading this chapter and acting on it, you will keep the cost to a bare minimum.

THE DIFFERENT TYPES OF 'GENERAL' INSURANCE

So what is 'general' insurance anyway? It is a catch-all expression encompassing some of the following areas:

- home and other forms of property insurance
- motor insurance
- public liability
- insurance for your other possessions such as boats, caravans and mobile telephones
- pet insurance
- travel insurance
- credit insurance
- professional indemnity insurance
- other risk insurance (e.g. Golfsure – for that round of drinks after a hole in one!)

DON'T JUST RELY ON BROKERS

General insurance is the one area where I would suggest that you shouldn't rely solely on brokers to get you the best deal. In many areas there are now 'direct' operations that can undercut brokers substantially. To find details of these direct operations look in your *Golden Pages* and keep an eye out for companies advertising in the national press. Remember, too, that some insurance companies tend to rely on customer inertia when it comes to renewal. So, having won your custom, they may push the cost of cover up in the second year hoping that you won't be bothered to check elsewhere. Telephoning around and filling in extra paperwork is a nuisance, but think of it this way: if it takes you – say – three hours work to save €200 then you are effectively paying yourself nearly €70 an hour after tax.

HOME INSURANCE

Home insurance is divided into 'buildings' cover and 'contents' cover.

Buildings cover

Buildings cover is obligatory if you have a mortgage and you may find that your lender automatically provides this protection (or at the very least a quotation) for you. The insurance will protect the structure of your home (the building itself, outbuildings, fixtures and fittings and so forth) against fire, storm damage, flood, subsidence, and other similar accidents. Most policies also include **public liability** cover so that if something happens to someone on your property (for instance, if they have an accident) you are protected. The main thing to watch for with buildings cover is that you have sufficient protection. The cost is worked out on the value of your home and is linked entirely to the re-building cost. So where your home is located, how old it is, its size and the materials from which it is constructed will all influence the premium. If you would like help deciding how much cover to take out then the **Society of Chartered Surveyors (5 Wilton Place, Dublin 2)** produces an annual guide. Not all buildings policies will cover you for the same things so you should check the small print. One way of keeping the cost down is to make sure you have smoke alarms fitted; another is to join your local neighbourhood watch scheme.

Contents cover

Contents cover is even less standard than buildings cover. The sort of protection you'll receive can vary enormously and when comparing prices you need to bear this in mind. For instance, are you being offered new for old cover, which means that if you claim you'll receive the exact cost of replacement with no reduction on account of the age of your possessions? Also, how much of the loss will you be expected to pay for yourself (known as an excess)? And to what extent are valuables – such as jewellery or cash – actually covered? You'll find that there are all sorts of 'extras' that may or may not be included – from employer's liability to theft of bicycles and from liability to third parties to personal liability. Tedious as it is, the only way to know what you are actually getting is to read the small print. Happily, there are a number of ways in which you can keep the cost of your contents cover down:

- Fit an approved alarm system.
- Fit approved locks to doors and windows.
- Join your neighbourhood watch scheme.

Do note that discounts are sometimes offered to people at home most of the day – for instance, if you are retired.

MOTOR INSURANCE

With such high insurance premiums you may be tempted to try and reduce the cost by any means possible. For instance, city-based car owners usually pay higher premiums than their rural counterparts and some are tempted to pretend that their car actually 'lives' in the country. Remember, if you ever come to claim, many insurance companies now send out an investigator to make independent inquiries and a false statement could result in being taken to court for fraud.

Motor insurance is more expensive if you:

- don't have a full licence
- have a history of motor offences
- are under 25 years old
- have made claims in the past
- have a criminal record.

Obviously, you can't make yourself any older than you actually are but if you don't have a full licence it is well worth putting in the effort to pass the test. By the same token, don't rush to put in a minor claim as it may result in higher premiums. Also, remember that fines may not be the only cost of speeding.

INSIDER TIPS ON BUYING OTHER GENERAL INSURANCE

In my opinion many types of general insurance do not offer value for money. I am particularly suspicious of:

Extended warranties. These cover you against faults developing in your electrical and mechanical goods. Often the retailer makes more money from these insurance policies (by way of commission) than on the sale of the actual product. As legislation offers you 12 months' protection anyway (and as, in general, such goods are much better made nowadays) I am suspicious of such policies.

Mobile telephone insurance. This protects you against loss of or damage to your phone. This is often expensive in relation to the actual cost of replacing your telephone. Furthermore, many people end up buying this cover without meaning to because they don't pay proper attention when completing the contract.

Credit card insurance. There are two types of cover offered by credit card companies. The first protects you against fraud and the second against you being unable to make your repayments due to an accident, illness or redundancy. Both types of cover are expensive and in most cases I would advise against them.

Pet insurance. This protects you against having to pay vet bills if your pet is ill or involved in an accident. Again, I would strongly suggest examining the value for money offered by such policies.

One more point is in relation to buying **travel insurance**. This is often sold by travel agents at highly inflated prices since they earn good rates of commission on every policy sold. Travel insurance is important – but there are many different sources of cover. If you are a regular traveller you may like to consider an annual policy. Also, if you have a credit card a certain amount of cover may be included in with your annual fee.

THE MONEY DOCTOR SAYS...

- Check the small print! All insurance policies are not equal.
- It may not be much fun shopping around but it helps if you think of the saving in terms of effort and reward. Three hours spent saving €200 is worth virtually €70 an hour after tax to you.
- Don't get sucked into buying cover you don't really need.
- Don't be tempted to under-insure ... it could leave you exposed.

PART 5
A-Z OF PROPERTY PURCHASE

I don't think it would be an overstatement to say that property – and, in particular, owning it – has become something of a national obsession. It is easy to understand why: home ownership offers security and the potential to make a capital gain. Indeed, in the ten years up to 2006 residential property prices had grown at an average rate of 12% per annum. Sadly the downturn has taken hold, but there are still opportunities in the property market.

Only the fortunate few can afford to buy a home outright. For the rest of us, saving up until we had the full cost of the apartment or house we wanted to buy would be impractical. Leave aside the fact that it would probably take decades, we would need to live somewhere else in the meantime. The solution is to take out a mortgage or home loan. Such loans are 'secured' against the value of the property being purchased and – because this means the lender faces much less risk – they are normally the least expensive type of borrowing you can undertake.

From a financial perspective, mortgages are the most important consideration when buying a property, which is why the longest chapter in this section is devoted to them. They are not, however, the only thing you need to think about if you own – or are thinking of owning – a property. Just as important are issues such as whether it is better to rent or buy, investing in property, property-related costs, tax and a host of other related topics, all subjects that are covered extensively in what follows.

13

MORTGAGES
HOW TO SECURE THE BEST-VALUE MORTGAGE IN IRELAND

The mortgage maze has become increasingly difficult to negotiate as a growing number of lenders offer an ever-growing range of home loan options. This chapter explains:

- how to take advantage of the demand for your business
- how to make sure you've got the mortgage that suits you best
- how to make sure you are paying the lowest possible price
- who to trust for mortgage advice.

In addition, we look at how mortgages work, re-mortgaging, tax relief and just about every other property-related question you can think of.

TAKING ADVANTAGE OF THE MORTGAGE REVOLUTION

Please put any pre-conceptions you have about buying a home or arranging a mortgage to one side. The truth is:

- Your home is *not* necessarily your most important investment.
- Your home is definitely *not* your most expensive purchase.
- You *don't* have to take 25 years to pay back your mortgage.

- You *aren't* tied to one lender for any longer than you want to be.
- You *don't* have to move to a different lender to get a better mortgage rate.

Also, and this is crucial to keeping the cost of buying your home or investment property to a bare minimum:

- The interest rate your mortgage lender charges you makes a huge difference to the cost of buying your home.
- The type of mortgage you have also makes a huge difference to the cost of buying your home.

Over the last few years there has been a mortgage revolution in Ireland. New products and greater competition mean that there are more opportunities than ever to slash the cost of buying your home. Opportunities which no homeowner – or would-be homeowner – should ignore.

Not necessarily your most important investment. Definitely not your most expensive purchase.

Received wisdom has it that the most important investment most of us will probably ever make is in our home. There is no doubt that owning your home is a significant part of being financially secure:

- The cost is not dissimilar to renting a home – making it a good financial decision.
- You aren't at the mercy of unscrupulous, unpleasant, greedy or inefficient landlords.
- With luck you'll see the value of your property rise – giving you a tax-free gain.

Nevertheless, although it makes sense to buy your own home you shouldn't be fooled into thinking that it is the 'be all and end all' of investments. It is arguable, in fact, that building up your other investments – especially a pension plan – is substantially more important. Furthermore, the stock market has – traditionally – always produced a better return than property. I'm not trying to put you off buying your own home – far from it – but don't forget it is only one part of establishing your personal wealth.

It is also worth remembering that your home won't automatically be your most expensive purchase. Depending on interest rates, that honour could easily go to your mortgage. If you buy a house for €200,000 and take out a traditional, repayment mortgage for €160,000 (80% of the purchase price) and pay it back over 25 years at an average rate of 6%, the total cost of buying your home (including interest) will be €309,265.09. That's €109,265.09 more than the actual cost of your home. Which is why it is crucial you choose the least expensive mortgage option available to you.

THROWING OUT THE TRADITIONAL 'MORTGAGE RULES'

There was a time – not so long ago – when all mortgages were pretty much the same. Loans lasted for 25 or even 30 years; it was unheard of to pay your mortgage off early; borrowers were discouraged from switching between different lenders; and the lenders themselves would not have dreamt of re-negotiating an existing loan.

All this has changed.

There are now 14 different financial institutions offering mortgages in Ireland and thanks to the Euro and greater freedom of financial services within Europe we can look forward to more lenders coming into the market. This means increased competition for your custom with the result that:

- better and better deals are available all the time
- there is much more emphasis on coming up with new, more beneficial home loan products
- lenders are more open to negotiation.

Lenders know that it is now easy to move your mortgage elsewhere – whether or not you are moving your home – and they don't want to lose your business. If you can find a better mortgage deal than the one you are on you may even find that your existing lender will match it rather than see you re-mortgage elsewhere. A mortgage revolution has taken place and – as a consumer – you'd be crazy not to take advantage of it.

INTEREST: ALL THE DIFFERENCE IN THE WORLD

The rate of interest you are charged on your mortgage makes a huge difference to the total cost of your home as the table below indicates:

Cost of €100,000 25-year repayment mortgage: interest payable

Annual interest rate (%)	Cost per month (€)	Total interest over term (€)
3.75	514.13	54,239
4	527.84	58,350
4.25	541.74	65,251
4.5	555.83	66,750
4.75	570.12	71,034
5	584.59	75,377
5.25	599.25	79,773
5.5	614.09	84,225
5.75	629.11	88,730
6	644.30	93,290
6.25	659.67	97,900
6.5	675.21	102,561
6.75	690.91	107,224
7	706.78	112,033

The difference between paying – say – 5.5% and 6.5% (which doesn't sound like much) actually equates to €18,336 of interest over the 25-year term and increases repayments by €161.12 per month. Put another way, think how much extra you would have to earn after tax to end up with €18,336 in your pocket. Paying more mortgage interest than you have to can seriously damage your wealth. Shopping around makes excellent sense.

TWO MORTGAGE OPTIONS: REPAYMENT VERSUS INTEREST ONLY

Although there is a whole range of mortgages to choose from they all fall into one of two categories:

- repayment (annuity) mortgages
- interest-only mortgages.

Repayment/annuity mortgage

The first option is a **repayment** (or **annuity**) mortgage. With this type of mortgage your monthly repayments are divided into two parts. The first is the interest you owe on the total amount borrowed. The second is repayment of part of the capital you have borrowed. The big advantage of this mortgage is that you are guaranteed to have paid off your whole loan at the end of the term. However, in the early years almost all your monthly repayments will be in interest. Let me give you an example:

> Sheila takes out a €200,000 mortgage over 25 years at an interest rate of 5.6%. Her monthly capital and interest payments are €1,240.15. At the end of the first year she will have paid a total of €14,881.80 but will still owe over €196,000 to her lender. In year

ten she will have paid €148,817 and will still owe €150,795. Put another way, in the first ten years roughly two-thirds (66%) of what she pays to her lender will be interest, and only one-third (33%) will be capital.

MONEY DOCTOR WEALTH CHECK

Save extra interest

When choosing a repayment mortgage, make sure the interest is calculated **daily** or at least **monthly** ('monthly rest'). Why? Because over the term of your mortgage this will save you a tidy sum of money. The real thing to avoid is something called the 'annual rest system', which will cost you the most. Some lenders still have customers on their books who are on this system and it can add about 0.35% to your interest rate. If you are in this position, go back to your lender and threaten to move your business if they don't agree to change you to a daily or monthly calculated interest.

Interest-only mortgages

The other sort of mortgage on offer is an **interest-only mortgage**. With this type of mortgage you pay only the interest for the agreed period. With **investment mortgages** you pay interest only on the amount borrowed *and* at the same time you would set up a savings plan, which – it would be hoped – will pay off the capital at the end of the term. Your monthly repayments will, therefore, consist of interest on the loan and a contribution to a savings plan. This is ideal for certain types of loans e.g. commercial loans where the interest remains constant and the tax relief can be maximised (because the capital is not being repaid, you are receiving the most tax relief on the interest in the first year right through to the end of the term).

In the case of both a home or an investment property there are certain circumstances where you might not bother with the savings element, as I'll explain in a moment.

Around 20 years ago interest-only home loans got a bad name because many borrowers were advised to take out **endowment policies** (see below for an explanation) to re-pay the capital at the end of the term. Unfortunately, some of these policies failed to produce a sufficient return to do so. In other words, borrowers found that after 25 years they still owed money to their lenders.

Despite past problems with endowment mortgages, interest-only home loans can make sound financial sense. For instance, if you are self-employed, the tax benefits of a **pension-linked interest-only** mortgage can be very substantial, in particular when taken out for commercial property.

Here is a quick summary of the three main types of interest-only mortgage options available:

Endowment mortgages. There are various types of endowment policy available: these are investments offered by life insurance companies. The money you pay to the life insurance company is partly used to provide you with **life cover** (so that if you die the mortgage itself can be repaid) and partly invested in the **stock market**. If the money is invested well, then obviously your original loan will be repaid and you might even be left with a tax-free sum. However, if the performance of the endowment policy is not good then you could be left with insufficient cash to repay your original loan. There is no tax relief on endowment policy premiums.

Pension-linked mortgages. The difference between this and an endowment mortgage is that the life insurance company (after taking out money to pay for life cover) invests your cash into a **pension fund**. This has very definite tax benefits for anyone who is self-employed or on an extremely high income. Ordinarily, the pension fund is designed to mature on your retirement age at double the original amount being borrowed. Twenty-five per cent of this pension fund is available at maturity for encashment, tax free, and even though you will have to pay tax on the rest of the fund you should have sufficient money to pay off the rest of the mortgage.

New rules on self-direct trusts or **SSAPs** (small self-administered pension schemes) now allow pension funds to borrow on properties. Indeed, there are all sorts of other tax benefits available to those who buy property as part of their pension fund. Some of this is covered elsewhere in the chapters on retirement planning and tax. However, as it is such a complicated area you will need to take specialist advice if you wish to take advantage of the new rules.

Interest-only mortgages. It was possible to borrow money to purchase property at very competitive rates of interest without any obligation to re-pay the capital before the end of the term. For instance, if you took out a 20-year interest-only mortgage all you have to pay each month is the agreed rate of interest. The capital sum isn't due until 20 years have passed. This could suit you for all sorts of reasons. Perhaps you are expecting to receive a lump sum – such as an inheritance – before the 20 years are up. Maybe you intend to re-sell the property during this period. Possibly you have other investments that could be cashed in to repay the loan. Possibly you will win the Lotto! Do note that you will have to take out level term life cover that covers the entire amount borrowed for the full term in association with an interest-only mortgage, so that the loan can be repaid in the event of your death. While the credit crunch rages all around us at the moment, most lenders now only allow up to the first three years interest-only facilities.

Fixed or variable rate?

As if you didn't have enough choice already, another decision you must make when mortgage shopping can be whether to opt for a fixed or variable rate. A **fixed rate** means that the amount of interest you pay is pre-set for an agreed period of time. This offers you the benefit of certainty. Even if interest rates rise your repayments will stay the same. On the other hand if interest rates fall you won't benefit. You incur a penalty should you wish to pay off or part pay off your mortgage while on a fixed rate of interest. Generally, this sum is set at between three and six months interest on the amount being repaid.

A **variable rate**, on the other hand, will move with the market. This is fine while interest rates are low but if they begin to rise you could be adversely affected. There is generally no penalty if you wish to pay off all or part of the loan before the end of the mortgage term.

One other interest rate mortgage option is worth considering. It is called a **mortgage tracker** and the interest rate offered 'tracks' the European Central Bank (ECB) interest rate with the lending's margin (profit) remaining the same for the full term – making it a highly competitive way to borrow money. Only if the ECB rate moves does your tracker rate move. There are discounted tracker rates to consider too.

Currently, the cheapest variable tracker rate for a 50% loan to value is 4.75% – that is 0.5% over the ECB rate, which is currently 4.25%.

THE MONEY DOCTOR SAYS...

Unless you are self-employed, on a high-income or have some other source of funds coming to you in the future, the Money Doctor normally recommends that you take out a repayment or annuity mortgage when buying your main home. This said, there are some interesting variations now available allowing you to combine an interest-only mortgage with a repayment mortgage. The idea is to give you lower monthly payments at the beginning of your mortgage, rising as (hopefully) your income increases and/or your other expenses fall.

A WORD ABOUT 'CURRENT ACCOUNT' MORTGAGES

Currently, one lender offering this facility maintains that 25% of all its home loans are packaged through a **current account mortgage**. Simply, you have two accounts, one where the mortgage or loan is debited and the other where monies borrowed are lodged in this account for withdrawal at later times when required. Other lodgements made into this account (e.g. your monthly salary) are offset against the balance of the mortgage account. This way, you save the interest on that amount which is offset. Over the course of the mortgage term, the savings can be substantial if you are disciplined.

Only two lenders in Ireland offer this product and it is well worth enquiring from those lenders or your financial adviser.

WHY YOU SHOULD TRY TO MAKE MORTGAGE OVERPAYMENTS

Something I have become very keen on in recent years is the idea of overpaying your mortgage each month. This can't be done with all mortgages (for instance, you can't do it where you are on a fixed rate) but where it is possible and your income allows, it brings real benefits. With interest rates low at the moment and potentially likely to stay low for the next few years, it may be also important to remember that if your return/yield is far greater than the cost of the money (the mortgage rate) then investing your surplus monies elsewhere may be more beneficial. Consider these two examples though where overpayment can also be beneficial:

> Mary takes out a repayment mortgage for €250,000 with a term of 25 years at 5.5%. Her minimum monthly repayment is €1535.22. However, she decides that she can afford to pay an extra €235 a month. As a result, her mortgage will be paid off six years earlier and she will save €57,070 in interest.

> John also takes out a repayment mortgage for €320,000 with a term of 30 years at 5.75%. His minimum monthly repayment is €1867.43. He 'overpays' by €320 a month and as a result his mortgage will be paid off nine years earlier and he will save €120,429.31 in interest!

In both instances, by taking out a current account mortgage they could save even more interest. This is because any money on deposit in their current account is offset against their mortgage debt.

THE MONEY DOCTOR SAYS…

With so many mortgage choices available many borrowers worry that they are making the right decision for their needs. This is where a really good independent financial adviser offering a full choice of lenders can help. He or she will be able to guide you to the least expensive, most appropriate mortgage for your needs. See below for further advice on choosing an adviser.

HOW THE RIGHT PROFESSIONAL ADVISER WILL SAVE YOU MONEY

It goes without saying that you should shop around for the best possible mortgage deal as so much of your hard-earned cash is at stake. Two things to watch out for:

1   You may not always be comparing like with like. There is a great deal of difference between a ten-year fixed rate mortgage and a current account repayment mortgage. Each will cost a different amount and each is designed to meet different needs.

2   You may not be offered a full range of options. A bank or building society – for instance – might only have three or four types of mortgage to offer you. Many mortgage advisers deal with less than five lenders.

There are 14 mortgage lenders in Ireland at this point in time. To get the best possible deal you should always deal with an adviser who is **authorised** by the Financial Regulator to act on behalf of every single lender. This professional and independent advice will cost you nothing.

Please remember, too, that even if you are a customer with a particular financial institution, your authorised financial adviser may still be able to negotiate a better deal on your behalf. This is because a professional will know what the best deal available actually is, while the lender will know that the adviser has other options should the lender fall short of the client's requirement.

MONEY DOCTOR WEALTH CHECK

The latest information…

If you want the latest financial information – everything from interest rates to tax-saving tips – then log on to the Money Doctor website at www.moneydoctor.ie

THE MONEY DOCTOR SAYS…

- Don't be complacent. Even a small difference in the rate you pay can make a huge difference to the cost of your mortgage. No lender deserves your loyalty. Go to where the best deal is.

- Don't trust any adviser who isn't authorised to act for all the financial institutions offering home loans in Ireland, or at the very least use an adviser who can tell you where the best deals can be obtained, irrespective of the agencies held. There are 14 lenders and anyone who can't tell you about all of them isn't going to get you the best deal.

- Remember, authorised financial advisers are independent and, in most cases, you only have to pay a nominal fee for their services plus they will definitely find you the best package for your needs.

14

SUB–PRIME LENDING

Firstly, let me define **prime lending**. This is where a lender is able to gain full financial information about the prospective borrower and is able to apply the usual full prudent criteria. This minimises the risk of the loan going bad, and even if it does there will be adequate collateral between asset and income to repay the loan. This type of loan justifies for the lender to keep the interest rate as low as possible.

Mention the words '**sub-prime mortgage**' and most people will run for the hills. Everyone has heard the stories about sky-high interest rates and bailiffs knocking at the door. Of course, the financial disaster that hit the US sector in the summer of 2007 hasn't helped the product's reputation. Every newspaper and TV station across the world told the story of the fall of this sector and the subsequent devastation of the international stock markets. They were scathingly referred to as NINJA mortgages – *No Income, No Job or Assets* – because of the way they were marketed in the US. They were mis-sold in their millions, packaged up and sold on or securitised to other institutions, thus releasing further capital to feed this frenzied lending. Once the housing market there started to falter and values started to drop the bubble burst, leaving many of the large lending institutions holding billions of dollars worth of mortgages on properties that they couldn't even give away.

This one financial product managed to rock the global financial markets and cause countless blue chip companies to close down. However, despite all the media coverage, there remains a lot of confusion about what has happened and how exactly a sub-prime loan **should** work and, to a large extent, has worked in the Irish context.

Sub-prime mortgages, now euphemistically called **specialist**

mortgages, are home loans that are given to people with poor credit histories, at higher interest rates than standard mortgages. They can also apply to self-employed people with insufficient trading history to qualify for a prime mortgage and who can only self-certify their annual income. The interest rate varies depending on the amount of risk associated with your financial status. Applicants who are considered high risk are charged well above the standard mortgage rate.

The problem lies in the fact that people with an unstable financial background end up with even more debt that is charged at higher than average interest rates – a dangerous combination. It is not just first time buyers that apply to these lenders; many existing homeowners go down this route when they want to remortgage their property to pay off other unmanageable debts such as credit cards.

Let me give you an example: David and Jenny have a mortgage with a regular bank. They have four different credit cards that are all maxed to the limit. They also have a personal loan each, a car loan and a holiday loan. They have already remortgaged their home on two occasions. They are sinking quickly under the weight of these loans and decide that they need to consolidate all of their debt and pay off the entire sum by remortgaging their home for the third time. When they apply to their mortgage lender, their request is turned down.

They see an advertisement from a sub-prime lender who promises to listen to their money worries and accept all applications no matter what their financial status may be. David and Jenny switch mortgage providers and pay off their credit card debt and personal loans. They feel a great sense of relief with this debt eliminated and before long they apply for new credit cards and rack up some more high-interest debt. Meanwhile, their sub-prime mortgage lender has slapped them with a whopping interest rate that is double their original rate. With a larger loan and new higher rate, their monthly repayment amount is almost two and a half times what it was previously. And, they have all of that new credit card debt.

More importantly, all of their debt is secured on their home. Once again, they find themselves up to their oxters in loan repayments that they can't meet. The sub-prime lender operates in a high-risk environment and does not have a sympathetic ear. The lender owns the deeds to their house and repossesses their home.

Although the sub-prime mortgage market is just five years old in Ireland, it has been operating in America for far longer. The sector took off there in the mid-1990s and since 1998 over 25% of all mortgage applicants in America have received sub-prime home loans. Many believed this was a pressure cooker on the brink of explosion and they were proved correct. Following a series of hikes that saw interest rates jump from 1% to 5.25% between 2005 and 2007, the number of householders defaulting on their mortgage repayments soared. Weekly repossession figures have now hit staggering proportions. Users of eBay will see well-maintained family homes in good suburban locations for sale due to foreclosure by the banks, for as little as $60,000, but in the end selling for a fraction of this.

Few were surprised when the housing market in America showed signs of collapsing at the end of 2006 and in the first six months of 2007, several major sub-prime mortgage corporations were forced to declare bankruptcy and some even shut down. That decline has continued right through 2008. Not surprisingly, stock prices for many leading institutions in the industry collapsed as investors and lenders ran scared. Freddie Mac and Fanny Mae became household names for all the wrong reasons.

Thankfully, with every grey cloud comes a silver lining. The financial disaster has managed to highlight the dangers associated with borrowing from sub-prime lenders. Industry experts have called for tighter regulations to be enforced on a market which has become renowned for its spurious lending practices. The brokers in this industry have been accused of steering borrowers towards unaffordable loans. However, borrowers have also been criticised for over-stating their incomes on loan applications and entering into loan agreements they could not meet or could never in the first place.

Despite the high risk attached to the industry, it is only in 2008 that this area came under the supervision of the Financial Regulator, following the introduction of enabling legislation in late 2007. Prior to that, the sector would claim that it voluntarily observed the standards laid down for other lenders and, in fairness, it must be said that in comparison with their US counterparts they operated in a responsible manner in the main.

SELF-CERTIFICATION

One of the primary concerns in this type of lending is the issue of self-certification, which enables self-employed people to prove their income without having to meet the normal qualifying criteria. The customer does not have to provide documents such as accounts and pay slips. The lender issues the loans based on the person's own stated income and recent bank statements as proof of that income.

The lenders currently operating in the sector will allow self-certification up to fixed income levels but will lend a substantially smaller percentage of the value of the home than the prime lenders will, and over the last year their lending criteria have become much more stringent. Court Orders for home repossessions by sub-prime lenders, which have received a lot of publicity in the papers of late, are the result of loans granted five to six years ago when interest rates were substantially lower and the economic outlook was universally brighter than it is today.

THE LENDERS

GE Money became the first company in Ireland to introduce the sub-prime mortgage in 2002. During its heyday in mid-2007 there were six lenders operating in the sector, with others in the wings waiting to launch their products. Rationalisation, the high-risk factor of some of these loans and the inability of some of the lenders to keep raising capital to fund their operations has meant that this number has now halved.

INTEREST RATES

The interest rates on sub-prime mortgages vary considerably depending on the current European Central Bank rate and the risk profile of the borrower. Applicants with no outstanding loans, a clean credit history and borrowing less than 60% of the value of the property, will usually receive a competitive interest rate that is just one or two percentage points higher than the main stream lenders' rates.

However, customers with a poor credit rating, unpaid loans or those who have had court judgments registered against them for failing to repay debts, will incur a far higher rate. There are other factors which will incur higher interest rates. For example, interest rates climb in line with the **loan to value ratios**. So, those who want to borrow over 70% of the property value will receive a more expensive rate. Also, people who are self-certifying their income or who apply for an interest-only loan are considered higher risk so they are also given higher rates.

CHARGES

While people with an unstable financial background are often drawn to a fixed rate mortgage, it is not always the best option. Hefty **redemption fees** are often charged when homeowners repay their fixed rate loans earlier than the agreed date. The amount payable is normally calculated based on the mortgage's interest rate. The rate of a sub-prime mortgage is frequently about double that of a standard mortgage, so therefore redemption fees on these loans are particularly expensive. For example, you could be charged a redemption fee of up to six months' interest.

Some sub-prime mortgage lenders often ask their customers to take out an **indemnity bond**. This is a type of insurance policy that works in favour of the lender. It aims to cover any shortfall that might arise between the amount owing and the value of your home if you default. An indemnity bond is usually required when you are borrowing more than a certain percentage of the purchase price – e.g. 75%. Standard mortgage holders are rarely, if ever, asked to buy this cover but sub-prime lenders will sometimes request that it be purchased.

The days of **arrangement fees** are long gone in the mainstream mortgage industry but this is still a common practice amongst sub-prime lenders. **Start Mortgages** (the Irish subsidiary of British Kensington Mortgages) has an arrangement fee of 1% of the value of the mortgage. This means that a person with a loan of €200,000 would have to pay a fee of €2,000. The company's *Flexi Start* product has capped its arrangement cost at €1,800.

GE Money is the only lender that does not have a cap on its arrangement fee. 'The fee is not capped but, in reality, the typical amount drawn down is generally less than €200,000,' said a spokesman. Also be wary of arrears fees or surcharges. Springboard (a joint venture between Permanent TSB and Merrill Lynch) mortgage holders, for example, are charged a fee of €15 for each month that they are behind on repayments.

HOW TO AVOID THE SUB-PRIME MARKET

It's all too easy to stick your head in the sand like an ostrich, but avoiding money problems will land you with a bad credit rating. Once you get a bad name, mainstream lenders will avoid you like the plague. People with good credit ratings get the best rates and that means they pay less than those with a poor rating. All it takes is a few late or missed repayments and your reputation will suffer.

In case you think that it is possible to hide the fact that you have missed a few repayments, think again. Lenders check the credit ratings of applicants by contacting the Irish Credit Bureau (ICB) which holds the personal finance history of all borrowers.

Almost all of the lenders in Ireland send information about borrowers and their repayments to the ICB. According to the bureau, it holds information about borrowers and their loans for five years after the loan is closed. Lenders send details about people who have taken out mortgages, car loans, personal loans, leasing/hire-purchase agreements and credit cards. This information is held in an individual credit report that is kept by the ICB. The bureau reflects a full picture of your credit history, good and bad.

Your report contains the following details: the names of lenders and account numbers of loans you currently hold and previously held within the last five years; details of repayments made and missed for each month on all of the loans; information pertaining to any failure to clear a loan or loans that were settled for less than you owed; legal actions taken against you by a lender.

When you apply for a loan, the **ICB** report is checked and if your credit history is poor it is likely that the application will be unsuccessful even if you have the income to repay it.

If you want to check your rating, contact the **ICB** to receive a full report within a few days of the request. This will cost you €6 and you can get details of the application process over the phone from the Irish Credit Bureau at ICB House, Newstead, Clonskeagh Road, Dublin 14, Ireland, Tel. (01) 260 0388, Fax (01) 260 0390 or online from www.icb.ie.

THE MONEY DOCTOR SAYS...

- The Financial Regulator is at pains to stress the importance of shopping around for the best rate and product. There is a wide variety of choice and rates in the market for borrowers. Just because a loan is being offered to you does not mean it is the only loan available or the best product to suit your needs. Consumers with financial problems should check out all the options and think hard about whether or not borrowing more money is the best solution, particularly if the interest rate is very high.

- As the Regulator says, waiting until you can afford what you want is painless compared with finding yourself trapped with a loan you cannot afford to repay. It can be tempting to take out a loan with lower monthly repayments. But, because it has a longer life term, you end up paying far more in interest. So weigh up what suits you best and how much you can really afford to borrow.

MONEY DOCTOR WEALTH WARNING

- Sub-prime lending should be the last resort. If you do find yourself in this unfortunate position, remember that in the current climate even if you maintain an impeccable payment record with a sub-prime lender and any adverse Credit Bureau rating has expired you may find it difficult to get back into mainline borrowing in the short to medium term. Meanwhile with only three *Specialist Lenders* left in the Irish market, your options have diminished.

15

LOANS FOR THE OVER-60s

Everybody dreams of growing old gracefully in the comfort of their own home or, at worst, in a private, luxury nursing home. The notion of sitting in a dreary state nursing home is not one that many people relish. Unfortunately, by the time we reach retirement age we tend to be somewhat lacking in money. When you consider that the state pension in 2008 is € 223.30 per week and that private nursing home fees can cost up to €1,000 per week, while the price of home help care is potentially even more expensive, it is no wonder that a small number of financial institutions and private equity companies are now targeting the elderly with, what they believe, is the perfect solution to this problem.

Add to this the Irish demographics – by the year 2011, it is estimated that persons aged 65 and over will represent 14.1% of the Republic's population. The percentage in 2002 was 11.13% out of a population of 3,917,203. Over 33% of those aged over 70 years of age live alone. The National Council on Ageing and Older People says that all demographic projections anticipate significant growth in the number of older people in Ireland over the next ten years.

As Irish property prices have soared over the last two decades, many retirees have been left with a substantial nest egg. Releasing equity in a home when you are asset-rich but cash-poor can seem like the ideal way of boosting your quality of life. In recent years, two types of equity-release products have come on the market and both are aimed at older people. As with all financial products, these schemes will not suit everybody and people should seek family and also independent advice before signing on the dotted line.

The lifetime mortgage

The first product, known as a lifetime mortgage, allows you to borrow money against the value of your home. Sound familiar? Well, it works just like a regular equity-release product but there are some fundamental differences. Firstly, before receiving a lifetime mortgage, you have to pay off any existing mortgage on your home in full. The homeowner makes no repayments, and continues to own and live in the house. The loan is usually paid off from the proceeds when the home is eventually sold following the owner's death or when he or she moves out of the home for longer than six months – for example into long-term care. If there are joint borrowers and one owner dies, the mortgage must be paid off when the remaining borrower sells the home.

The financial institutions normally lend between 10% and 45% of your home's value. The older you are, the higher the percentage you can borrow. Depending on certain criteria such as your age, financial situation and the lender itself, customers can draw down the loan in two ways – as a lump sum or in installments. Sometimes, people do both by dividing the loan, taking a lump sum and installments.

Borrowers can end a lifetime mortgage by choosing to pay off their mortgage at any time. This can be done by selling the home and using the proceeds of the sale to pay off the loan or by using any other money they may have to repay the debt. Borrowers should be aware, however, that some lenders charge an early repayment fee if the loan is a fixed rate mortgage.

The interest rate on a lifetime mortgage

Here comes the bad news! Interest rates on lifetime mortgages are usually two or three percentage points higher than those charged on standard mortgage rates because customers are not making regular repayments.

As if that wasn't bad enough – interest is charged at a compound rate. This means that each month interest is charged on the amount the person has borrowed plus the interest added from previous months. So the amount of interest charged increases over time as the amount you owe grows. Your mortgage debt can grow very quickly.

> Let me give you an example: Johnny and Rosie are both 65 years old. They own a house that is valued at €500,000. They decide to take out a lifetime mortgage of 100,000 with a compound interest rate fixed at 6%. After five years, the amount owed has grown to €134,907; after 10 years they owe €192,029; and by the time they are 80 years old they owe the grand total of €245,570.

Just like regular loans, lifetime mortgage are available with both fixed and variable interest rates, the latter changing in line with the European Central Bank (ECB) rate. The ECB dictates the rate of interest for all countries in the eurozone.

There is a big risk associated with this type of loan. By the time the homeowner dies, the interest and repayment due may be so high that the proceeds from the property's sale will barely cover the amount owed and little will be left for the beneficiaries of the will. The home may appreciate in value over the term of the loan which will offset some of the debt but this is never guaranteed.

MONEY DOCTOR WEALTH WARNING

- There are some significant downsides to taking out a lifetime mortgage. The lender can request that you sell your home and pay off the mortgage if you do any of the following:
- Move out of your home for six months or more (unless your mortgage is in joint names and the other owner is still living there).
- You don't insure your home.
- Your home is not maintained to the standard that is set by your lender to keep its value.
- Also, when you receive a lump sum or income through an equity-release scheme, it can affect your right to state benefits such as the means-tested state pension.

HOME REVERSION SCHEMES

Lifetime mortgages are not your only option if you want to take advantage of the growing value of your home. The second type of equity-release product is known as **home reversion**. It allows you to sell part of your home to a property investment company. The big advantage of this product is that you are allowed to remain living in the home until you die. You live in your own home for the rest of your life and use the cash received from the sale to enjoy your retirement in style.

Unlike a lifetime mortgage, you are not borrowing against the value of your home but are actually selling part of it. Applicants must have already paid off their existing mortgage in full to qualify for the scheme. With home reversion schemes you must take the money as a lump sum, and cannot take it in installments.

HOME REVERSION FIXED AND VARIABLE SHARE AGREEMENTS

There are two options available if you enter a contract with a home reversion company. Under a **fixed-share contract**, the company pays you a lump sum in return for a fixed share of your home. The percentage they own and the percentage you keep is fixed from the start and cannot change, no matter how long you live or what your property may be worth in the future.

With a **variable-share contract** you get a bigger lump sum when you first sell your share. However, nothing in life comes for free. In return for the bigger lump sum, the percentage of your home that the company owns automatically increases each year without you receiving any further payments. So, the percentage you own will reduce as time passes. The longer you live, the less of your property you own.

Let me give you a second example: Gerry is 65 years old and sells 25% of his home. By the time he is 80, the company owns 50%.

How it works

Home reversion companies normally buy between 10% and 90% of the property, depending on the person's age and the value of the home.

Now, everyone knows that there is no such thing as a free lunch. This sounds like a dream product but it comes with a hefty price tag! The price paid by the investment company for a chunk of your home is significantly less than the market value of the share of the home that is sold. This is because the person remains living in the house and the home reversion company may have to wait several years before they can cash in their share. The difference between the market value and the lump sum you receive for the share you sell is the real cost of this product. You'd want to live well into your golden years to get good value from the scheme.

> Here's a third example: Dorothy is 65 and owns a house worth €500,000. The estimated market share of 50% of her home is €250,000. According to the Financial Regulator, she can expect to receive €112,450 from a home reversion company.

> If Dorothy was 10 years older, however, she would receive €146,580. The older you are when you start the scheme, the bigger the lump sum you receive for selling the same share. This is because the company expects they will be able to cash in their share sooner for the obvious reason.

Well, at least that's one thing you can look forward to as you creak into your golden years. Financial institutions will be falling over themselves in a bid to give you big, fat cheques. You deserve it – you have worked hard enough for it.

Due to different average life expectancies, a single man of the same age would receive more than a single woman. A couple will receive less, as people in relationships live longer than those who live alone. So, start looking after your spouse if you want to reap the rewards later.

As soon as the homeowner dies or moves into a nursing home, the house is sold and the proceeds are divided between the property investment company and the homeowner or their estate, depending on the percentage owned by each.

If the home reversion company bought a 40% share of your home, they would later on receive 40% of the proceeds from selling your home – either when you move out or after your death. The other 60% would go to you or your estate after your death.

There is no back-tracking once you enter a home reversion contract. If you sell a portion of your home and decide a year or two later that you want to end the agreement, the only option is to negotiate with the company to buy back the share you sold. You can also gain consent from the company to sell your home on the open market. This would allow you to cash in the value of the percentage of your home you still own.

When you die, your family or other beneficiaries may be given the option to buy back the percentage that the home reversion company owns. If the value of your home has increased due to inflation, it may be difficult for them to raise enough money to do this.

MONEY DOCTOR WEALTH WARNING

- The Financial Regulator warns consumers that the firms which provide home reversion schemes are not regulated. This means that consumer credit laws and the Consumer Protection Code do not apply to the activities of the company. So, you cannot refer any complaints to the Financial Services Ombudsman. The only recourse you have is to take legal action if there is a serious problem.

LIFETIME MORTGAGES AND HOME REVERSION SCHEME COSTS

Like most financial products, these schemes come with significant hidden costs. Depending on the type of scheme you choose, you may have to pay some added costs such as a valuation fee, legal fees and costs for transferring ownership or arranging your mortgage. Some companies have a fixed 'set-up' fee to cover legal and valuation fees. A budget of €1,500 to €3,000 should cover these costs.

Be careful it you are offered an option to pay the fees through your lifetime mortgage as compound interest will be charged on the bill over the life of the mortgage, which means it will cost far more in the long run.

For all equity release schemes you must keep your home in a good state of repair and take out insurance noting the percentage owned by the lender or home reversion company.

Maintenance costs can be high and usually increase over time. The lender or home reversion company can inspect your home from time to time, and has the right to carry out any necessary repairs that it believes is necessary. The company usually adds any repair costs to the amount you owe, so compound interest would be charged on those extra costs.

You should also bear in mind that some schemes may restrict you from making certain renovations, for example installing a stair lift, as they may reduce the market value of the property.

THE PROVIDERS AND THEIR RATES

Lifetime mortgages

Bank of Ireland sells a lifetime mortgage known as **LifeLoan**. Applicants must be at least 65 years old and have paid off their mortgage in full. The product enables them to borrow between 20% and 30% of the value of their home.

LifeLoan customers can borrow up to €400,000 at a fixed annual interest rate of 6.9% APR for 15 years. The minimum amount that a homeowner can borrow is €20,000. The LifeLoan interest rate is expensive compared with current standard mortgage rates. If the homeowner lives a long time and the property only increases slowly in value, the rolled-up interest plus the capital could eventually exceed the value of the home.

This product has a number of provisions which have been criticised by the Law Society. Bank of Ireland demands that you to make a will and give the bank the names of your executor, beneficiaries and next of kin.

The property must be worth at least €400,000 in the Dublin region, €250,000 if it is in Cork, Limerick of Galway cities and €200,000 if it is located elsewhere. At the end of the term, customers are offered a choice of either a new fixed rate or a variable rate. Penalties may apply if the loan is repaid early but, unlike most fixed rate mortgages there are no penalties if the borrower dies, sells or moves out early.

Sixty Plus Finance (formerly known as Residential Reversions Limited), is launching a new-interest only mortgage for all homeowners over the age of 60. Single applicants must have a minimum annual income of €20,000 and couples should have a joint income of €30,000. The company believes the product will attract homeowners in the 60 to 70 age bracket. As they get older they can switch to other products, such as a home reversion scheme, if the need arises.

Reversion schemes

Sixty Plus Finance also offers a home reversion scheme. The company buys a percentage of the value of the house; the amount it will offer to buy depends on the value of the property and the age of the homeowner. Essentially, when the homeowner dies, the property is sold and the percentage bought by Sixty Plus Finance is repaid. However, the minimum amount it will pay a 65 year old is €50,000 and the maximum amount is €500,000.

If a house is worth between €500,000 and €1m, the maximum amount it will buy is 60% of the value of the property. Residential Reversion will buy a maximum of 40% of a property worth between €1m and €1.5m. If the scheme ends within four years, or if house price inflation is exceptional, the company will provide additional cash benefits.

Residential Reversions recently introduced a house price inflation guarantee, which slightly restricts its share of the profits from a house sale if the house increases significantly in value.

A number of other companies operating lifetime loans and reversion schemes have had difficulties, either in coping with the volume of business or in securing long-term financing and have temporarily stopped accepting new business.
So, whatever you decide, ensure you have the best of family, legal and tax advice before you embark on that little bit of comfort in your twilight years. And remember, you deserve it!

16
PROPERTY QUESTIONS
ANSWERS TO YOUR PROPERTY
AND MORTGAGE QUESTIONS

This chapter contains detailed answers to all your property and mortgage questions, including:

- Should I buy or rent my home?
- How much can I borrow on my income?
- What is 'APR'?
- Is it worth switching my mortgage to get a lower rate?
- Help! I'm self-employed. How do I get a mortgage?
- What will it cost for me to buy my home?
- What tax relief will I receive on my home loan?
- Does it make sense to buy a second property as an investment?
- What are the benefits of owning a home in a designated area?
- What's the story with local authority loans?
- What other state housing grants might be available to me?
- Is it worth repaying my mortgage early?
- What different types of home insurance will I need?
- If I have trouble making my mortgage repayments what should I do?

SHOULD I BUY OR RENT?

Ireland is one of the few countries in Europe where buying one's home is the norm. Broadly speaking, at present the cost of buying a home is the same as – or in many cases less than – renting the same property. This is linked to supply and demand, of course, and varies from region to region as well as from property to property. We were in a low-interest environment – and this favoured house purchase – as did the availability of mortgage interest relief. While interest rates are now considered 'high' compared to what they were, consumers are more reticent to borrow, and the relatively meagre tax relief is not an attraction in itself.

If a future government were to introduce greater tenant rights the situation might change but at the moment – if you can raise the sufficient deposit – buying makes better long-term sense. After all, when you give up a rental property you receive nothing back. Whereas when you have paid off your mortgage you will own your home and may have seen a nice, tax-free capital gain as well.

House prices in Ireland have risen at an unprecedented rate in the last ten years and most informed opinion was that as long as we continued in a low-interest environment and our economy remained healthy a sharp fall in house prices seemed unlikely. However, now things have changed even over the last 12 months. Renting is cheaper but as property values fall, you may pick up a bargain from foreclosures or 'distressed sales'.

HOW MUCH CAN I BORROW?

You should always put down as much of a deposit as possible when buying your home. You will need a minimum of 8% of the purchase price (that is to say €24,000 if you are buying a €300,000 property) but it is preferable to have more. Why? Because it makes you less vulnerable to moves in interest rates and property values plus your authorised mortgage intermediary will be able to negotiate a lower interest rate with a lender if you have over 20% deposit – the less the percentage you have to borrrow, the better the interest rate.

Depending on what you earn, lenders will generally give you a mortgage of between three and five times your income. For example:

- If you earn €60,000 a year you may be able to borrow up to €300,000 over 35 years.

- If you and your partner earn a combined income of €80,000 you may be able to borrow between €300,000 and €360,000 over 35 years.

However, it is always worth remembering that interest rates may rise in the future and if possible you should try and avoid borrowing the maximum amount.

For first-time home buyers a 100% mortgage package was available with most lenders, even though it was subject to very stringent income guidelines. Now it has been withdrawn owing to the current economic troubles.

WHAT IS APR?

The initials 'APR' stand for **annual percentage rate** and it is the way in which the cost of your loan is expressed. What makes it different from a straight interest rate is that it takes into account not just the interest rate but also the timing of any interest payments, capital repayments and other charges, arrangement fees and so forth. The APR must, by law, reflect the actual rate of interest charged over the full period of the loan.

IS IT WORTH SWITCHING MY MORTGAGE TO GET A LOWER RATE?

The short answer is: it depends! Many lenders offer all sorts of exciting inducements to new customers at the expense of their existing borrowers who get charged more. There are two things to consider:

- How much can you save by switching lender?
- What is switching lender going to cost you?

The first question is relatively easy to answer. The second question will depend on a variety of factors including:

- whether you are on a fixed interest rate – in which case there may be a penalty for switching
- how much – if anything – the new lender is going to charge you by way of legal and other costs.

If you can save 0.25% a year interest – or more – it could well be worth the switch. If in doubt, consult an authorised mortgage intermediary or accountant and ask them to do the figures for you.

HELP! I'M SELF-EMPLOYED

Most financial institutions are pleased to lend to someone who is self-employed – though if you have less than three years' sets of accounts it may be harder. This is another instance where a professional authorised mortgage intermediary will help. He or she will know which lenders are keen for your business and willing to offer you the lowest rates.

Note: it is no longer possible to get a mortgage in Ireland without a statement from your accountant to the effect that your tax affairs are completely up to date.

WHAT WILL IT COST FOR ME TO BUY MY HOME?

There are various expenses in buying a home:

Survey fees. No lender will let you have a mortgage without a proper survey and valuation. The price of this will vary but is likely to be in the region of €130. You may like to ask an architect or some other type of professional property adviser to survey the building for you to check its condition and the likely cost of repairs. The fee for this will be linked to the amount of work required and could run to several hundred Euros or more for a large house.

Legal fees. This is primarily the cost of employing a solicitor to look after the whole transaction for you. The normal cost is in the region of 1% of the total price plus VAT at 21% and outlay. So for a €200,000 house you will have to find in the region of €2,400. Your lender may also charge you a certain amount to cover their legal fees if it is a commercial transaction. Negotiation over legal fees is possible and you should ask for a reduction, especially if you are a first-time buyer.

Land registry fees. On a €200,000 property these would be up to €750.00. The fee is to cover registering the property in your name.

Stamp duty. You have to pay two lots of stamp duty. Firstly, on the value of the house. If you are a first-time buyer then the duty is waived. Otherwise, it will be from between 3 and 9% (on a sliding scale) depending on the price. There is also stamp duty at 0.1% on your mortgage if it is over €254,000.

Stamp duty*

Residential property Consideration	Standard	First-time buyer	Investors
Up to €125,000	Exempt	Exempt	Exempt
Next €875,500	7%	Exempt	7%
Balance	9%	Exempt	9%
Commercial stamp duty rates	For any property over €150,000, stamp duty is chargeable at 9%		

*No stamp duty payable by owner-occupiers or first-time buyers on purchase of homes up to 125 square metres. On new houses/apartments above this limit, duty is charged on ssite value or a quarter of the value, whichever is greater.

(Source: Matrix courtesy of www.moneydoctor.ie)

Search fees. This is to check that the property has planning permission, isn't located on the site of a proposed development and so forth. Usually around €150.

Indemnity bond. Borrowing over 80% of the property price? The lender will almost certainly want to take out insurance in case they ever have to re-possess the property and sell it for less than 92% of the purchase price. The insurance, known as an indemnity bond, makes up any loss they may experience. Some lenders pass this cost on to the borrower; others absorb it.

Arrangement fees. Some lenders charge application and arrangement fees. These could amount to between €100 and €300 but generally only apply to non-home loans.

If you would like to know exactly what your home loan is going to cost you to buy visit my website – www.moneydoctor.ie – where you'll find a calculator that will work it out for you.

To give you a typical example, for a first-time buyer purchasing a house for €200,000 with an 80% mortgage (€160,000) the total fees will be in the order of €2,000 excluding the indemnity bond and the deposit.

WHAT TAX RELIEF WILL I RECEIVE ON MY HOME LOAN?

You will be entitled to **mortgage interest relief**, which will be given to you automatically 'at source':

Mortage interest relief

First mortgage	Single(€)	Widowed(€)	Married(€)
Ceiling	10,000	20,000	20,000
Tax credit (First 7 years)	2,000	4,000	4,000
Others			
Ceiling	3,000	6,000	6,000
Tax credit (First 7 years)	600	1,200	1,200

DOES IT MAKE SENSE TO BUY A SECOND PROPERTY AS AN INVESTMENT?

Buying property and renting it out has become an increasingly popular investment over the last few years. There are various reasons for this including:

- tax incentives – you can claim any loan interest you pay on borrowings to acquire and/or improve the property, against any rental income you receive, plus if you buy certain types of property or property in particular areas you will receive additional tax breaks
- rapid increases in property values
- high yields in relation to other investments
- low cost of borrowing money.

In general, the only investors who don't make money from renting out property are those who have over-estimated the return they'll receive, haven't allowed for all the likely costs and lack the patience to wait out any market downturns. The secret to success is undoubtedly:

- Allow for periods without tenants (known as 'voids').
- Make sure you have calculated all the costs including loan repayments, redecoration, maintenance and repair.
- Don't view it as a short-term investment.

WHAT ARE THE BENEFITS OF OWNING A HOME IN A DESIGNATED AREA?

If you buy, build or restore a house in particular areas of the country – called 'designated' areas – you are entitled to tax relief on part of the expense. This tax relief is quite generous and well worth claiming.

WHAT'S THE STORY WITH LOCAL AUTHORITY LOANS?

County councils and city corporations both provide financial support to anyone on relatively low incomes so that they can afford to buy their own home but you can be waiting a long time to be facilitated.

If you cannot get a loan from a building society or bank, you may be eligible for a local authority mortgage. The amount borrowed can be up to 97% of the cost of the house subject to a maximum loan of €165,000 and subject to repayments which cannot exceed 35% of the household net income (i.e. income after tax and PRSI).

WHAT OTHER STATE HOUSING GRANTS MIGHT BE AVAILABLE TO ME?

There are various other grants and available from the state including:

Affordable housing. Many new developments now include a percentage of what is referred to as 'affordable housing'. These are houses, flats or building sites that must be sold at well below market price to people who would not otherwise be able to afford to buy their own home. The affordable housing scheme allows lower-income house buyers the chance to buy newly constructed homes and apartments in areas where property prices have created an affordability gap for lower-income house buyers. There are of course conditions that preclude the buyer from making a 'quick kill'.

Improvement grants. A range of loans will be available from your local authority so that you can improve or extend your home.

Mortgage subsidy. If you are a local authority tenant and you give up your home to buy a property on the open market you may be entitled to financial support for up to five years. The **mortgage allowance scheme** is an allowance of up to a maximum of €11,450 payable over a five-year period to local authority tenants. The allowance is paid directly to the lender and your repayments are reduced accordingly for the first five years of the mortgage. The allowance paid in any year cannot exceed the amount of the mortgage repayments.

Shared ownership. The **shared ownership scheme** is aimed at those who cannot afford to purchase an entire home in one transaction. It allows you to buy a proportion of your home initially and to increase that proportion in steps until you own the whole house. During this stage, ownership is shared between you and the local authority and you make payments on a mortgage for the part you own and pay rent to the local authority for the other part at a rate of 4.3%.

Disabled persons grant. Given to cover the cost of adapting a private home for the needs of someone who is disabled.

Thatching grant. Available towards the cost of renewing or repairing thatched roofs on houses. Thatchers are a dying breed but it is important to reward and help those who are maintaining our heritage.

IS IT WORTH REPAYING MY MORTGAGE EARLY?

Should you overpay your mortgage each month? Should you use all your available cash to reduce your mortgage? Should you use a lump sum of cash to reduce or pay off your mortgage? The answer is *probably* yes if the following applies to you:

- You don't have any other – more expensive – debts. (If you do, these should be paid off first.)
- It won't leave you without some savings tucked away against a rainy day.
- There aren't other investment opportunities that might be worth more to you in cash terms.

If you were thinking of paying off some or all of your mortgage, I would strongly advise consulting an authorised adviser or mortgage intermediary first. He or she will be able to work out the figures for you.

WHAT DIFFERENT TYPES OF HOME INSURANCE WILL I NEED?

This is covered in greater detail in Chapter 12 on insurance. In summary, homeowners should take out the following cover:

Building insurance. This will be compulsory if you have a mortgage. Basically, it means that if some damage is done to the fabric of your home (by a fire or flood, for instance) then money is available to repair or rebuild as necessary.

Contents insurance. This protects you against loss or damage to your home contents.

Mortgage repayment insurance. This cover is optional but means that if you are ill or made redundant your mortgage repayments would be paid for you. Payments usually last for up to a year.

IF I HAVE TROUBLE MAKING MY MORTGAGE REPAYMENTS WHAT SHOULD I DO?

Contact your lender immediately. The worst thing you can do is keep them in the dark about any financial problems you may be encountering. If you need help with your finances you could contact:

- Your local St Vincent de Paul Society who run a special advice scheme.
- The Department of Social Welfare – who also run a free advice scheme called MABS (Money and Budgeting Advice Service). You can obtain details from your local social welfare office or public library.

THE MONEY DOCTOR SAYS...

- If you have any questions about property or mortgages not answered in this book then please do email me (jlowe@moneydoctor.ie) or a Money Doctor adviser and we will be delighted to help.

PART 6
GUARANTEED SAVINGS
AND INVESTMENT SUCCESS

My favourite quote about wealth is Ernest Hemingway's, who in response to F. Scott Fitzgerald's comment that the rich are different, replied: 'Yes, they have more money.'

And getting yourself into a position where you have 'more money' is what this section of the book is all about for, as the entertainer, Sophie Tucker observed, 'I've been rich, and I've been poor: rich is better.' Not, I hasten to add, that I am suggesting you get rich for the sake of it. My interest is in making sure you have sufficient money to be free – free from the worry of not having enough and free to choose how you spend your time.

There are some widely held misconceptions about how to get rich. Some people think the only way they will manage it is by owning their own businesses; others feel the Lotto offers them their best chance; a third group seem to imagine it will happen all by itself.

In my experience, the only way to get rich is to take it slowly *and* steadily. *Set aside part of your income every month and invest it wisely and you will be amazed at how – over the years – it grows.*

Many people feel that there is not much difference between savings and investment, but to my mind there is a clear distinction:

- *Saving is all about short-term goals. It's the money you tuck away on a regular basis to pay for your holidays, or in case of emergency. Because it's money that needs to be available to you it can't be tied up where you can't get your hands on it.*

- *Investment, on the other hand, is all about medium- to long-term goals. You invest to ensure yourself a more prosperous and secure future. You may invest a lump sum, or on a regular basis, but the real thing is (barring an unforeseen crisis) you should be able to leave your money to work for you undisturbed for a reasonable period of time.*

Accordingly, this section is divided into two chapters. In the first you'll discover the best possible way to save your money with a view to building your own emergency fund. In the second, you'll learn how to invest your money in such a way as to build your wealth. Between the two you'll have all the tools you need to make your money grow, and grow and grow…

17

SAVING FOR A RAINY DAY

THE QUICKEST, MOST EFFICIENT WAY TO BUILD UP AN EMERGENCY FUND

One of your key financial objectives should be to have some easily accessible cash savings to pay for larger expenses or simply in case of a 'rainy day'. In this chapter you will discover:

- why it is so important to have cash savings
- how much savings you should build up
- the best way to make your savings grow.

GOOD, OLD-FASHIONED SAVINGS

We are lucky enough to live in a country where the state will provide a safety net for widows, those who are seriously ill or disabled, pensioners and others in dire financial straits. However, the amount on offer is

relatively meagre and won't cover most of the day-to-day financial crises ordinary people face. For instance, the state isn't going to help you with an unexpected bill for repairs to your home or car. Nor will they pay all your regular bills if you find yourself without an income for any reason. The fact is you should have a bit of cash tucked away – good, old-fashioned savings – just in case you ever need it. You should probably also have some extra cash to hand so that you can take advantage of an unexpected investment opportunity, for capital expenditure or just in case you see something you want to buy.

Saving up money to create a safety net requires a degree of commitment. It is in our nature, after all, to spend rather than to save. But if you can motivate yourself to tuck a little bit away each month I promise you'll never regret it!

SAVING MADE SIMPLE

It is one thing to think 'I must build up my savings' but often quite another thing to actually do so. Saving can only be achieved by conscious effort. Ideally, you should open your savings account somewhere convenient and arrange to make regular payments into it. For instance, you might set up a standing order to transfer a regular amount each month from your bank current account to a deposit account. Some employers offer 'payroll deduction' schemes where the money goes straight from your salary to a savings account. Also, if you are entitled to receive a child allowance from the state you could consider saving all of this on an automatic basis. The real thing to remember is that a savings plan should be regular, and sacrosanct.

HOW MUCH IS ENOUGH?

Just how much savings you should aim to accumulate will be determined by your personal circumstances.

- A single person in his or her 20s without any responsibilities and low overheads probably only needs to have enough cash to cover – say – three months' worth of expenditure.

- A couple with children, a mortgage and a car to run should probably aim to build up as much as six months' expenditure.

If you aren't already lucky enough to have a lump sum available to form your safety net, then the best way to build it up is to establish a pattern of regular saving each week or each month. Remember, something is better than nothing – even if it is a relatively small amount, it will soon add up.

YOUR SAVINGS STRATEGY

If you have – say – six months' worth of expenditure saved up and you don't need instant access to all of it, my advice is to keep about a third where it is readily available and the rest where you can access it by giving notice. This strategy will allow you to earn extra interest.

Incidentally, if you are in a permanent relationship then ideally you should both have access to the emergency fund. In the event of some problem affecting one of you, the other may need to use this money.

EMERGENCY FUND: THREE BASIC REQUIREMENTS

An emergency fund should meet three basic requirements:

1 It should provide you with total security. Your savings must not be at risk.

2 It must earn as much interest as possible under the circumstances.

3 It must provide you with the level of access you need.

For these reasons the number of options available to you are limited pretty much to those listed below:

Deposit accounts

If you leave money on **deposit** with a bank, building society or credit union they will pay you interest. How much interest you earn can vary according to:

- how much money you have on deposit
- the length of notice you have to give before you can make a withdrawal (notice accounts/fixed rate accounts)
- the commitment to saving regularly (check out Regular Saver Accounts).

Rates can vary substantially and change all the time. Shop around and don't be afraid to move your money to where it can be earning more for you. Remember, currently the Investor Compensation Scheme will guarantee €100,000 of your savings plus the government now guarantees the six Irish-owned banks and building societies and five non-Irish-owned banks for all deposits and no limits, so it may still pay you to spread your savings around the various deposit takers.

An Post accounts

An Post offers a good range of savings products, all of which offer competitive returns and some of which are tax free. If you want to build up an emergency fund the two most appropriate accounts to consider are the **Instalment Savings** scheme or the **Instant Access** deposit account. An Post's Instalment Savings scheme requires you to make regular monthly payments for at least one year of between €25 and €500. In exchange, you will enjoy tax-free growth. An Post's Instant Access deposit account is very similar to a bank or building society deposit account. The interest rate isn't high, but it is competitive and you do have instant access. Once you've built up your emergency fund you may like to consider transferring your money into either an An Post **savings bond** or An Post **savings certificates**. Both are designed for medium- to long-term growth (at least three years), but you can get your money quickly if you need to. In addition, it's worth keeping in mind that savings certificates are tax free.

Membership of a credit union

As a member of a credit union you will earn an attractive return on the 'shares' you hold. This return is in the form of a dividend and will vary from year to year and from union to union. However, it is usually well above the rate offered by ordinary deposit accounts.

Note that if your local credit union offers a **Special Term Share** account, the return should be tax free, providing the amount of interest you've earned is less than €476 a year.

SAVINGS AND TAX

On deposit accounts, deposit interest retention tax (**DIRT**) is levied at source on your interest at a standard rate of 20%. However, if you are not liable for income tax, or you or your spouse are over 65 years of age or you are permanently incapacitated then you are entitled to claim back any DIRT deducted from your interest. You can make a back claim for DIRT tax for up to six years. Send a DE1 form to your deposit taker to reclaim the tax. The institutions will then pay you a gross return. Otherwise, use the 'old system' for back claims.

MONEY DOCTOR WEALTH CHECK

How to reclaim DIRT

Nothing could be easier than reclaiming DIRT. All you do is complete a short form available from any larger post office, bank, building society or tax office. You'll need to attach evidence of the DIRT that you have paid. This is done by asking the financial institution (or institutions) concerned to provide you with a special certificate. The DE1 leaflet is available at www.revenue.ie/leaflet/dde1.pdf for those who wish to claim exemption from paying DIRT.

THE MONEY DOCTOR SAYS...

- Saving on a regular basis may not always be easy but it will bring you real peace of mind.
- You should have an emergency fund in place sufficient to cover all your bills for between three and six months.
- As with everything: shop around. You could earn a considerably greater return by moving your money to where the best rates are.
- Watch out for Regular Saver Accounts – you save from €100 to €1000 per month up to 24 months at *very* attractive rates of up to 8%. E-mail me for details of these deposit takers.

18

INVESTMENT STRATEGIES YOU CAN COUNT ON

HOW TO MAKE YOUR MONEY GROW AND GROW AND GROW

Every investor faces the same conflict: how to balance risk and reward. Should you accept a lower return in exchange for peace of mind? Or should you attempt to make your money grow more quickly and face the possibility of losses? In fact, the best solution to the dilemma is: neither. As this chapter will demonstrate, the optimum way to build up your wealth is to:

- Set clear objectives. Know where you are going and what you want to achieve.
- Diversify. Invest your money in more than one area to combine growth and security.
- Be consistent. Don't chop and change but stick to your strategy.
- Stay on top of it. Keep an eye on performance all the time.
- Avoid unnecessary expenses and charges.

In addition to outlining a proven method of making your money grow, the chapter summarises all the major investment vehicles you should consider, providing you with 'insider' tips in relation to:

- pooled investments
- stocks and shares
- property
- tax-efficient investment.

BASIC INVESTMENT PLANNING

As discussed in earlier chapters your primary investment priorities should be to:

- build up an emergency fund
- start a pension plan
- buy your own home.

What you should do next will depend on your circumstances. Whether you have a lump sum to invest or simply plan to save on a regular basis, your objectives will basically revolve around the following questions:

- How much money is involved?
- How long can you tie your money up for?
- What type of return are you looking for?
- What risks are you willing to accept?
- To what extent is tax an issue?

Let's look at each of these in turn.

How much money is involved?

If you are saving regularly then you have a choice between investing in a specially designed longer-term plan or building up 'blocks' of capital and investing each one somewhere different.

If you have a lump sum – or as you build up 'blocks' of capital – then the choice of investments available to you opens up. For instance, with some capital available, property investment becomes an option as does buying publicly quoted shares.

You must have a clear idea in your mind about how much you plan to invest and in what form. If you are saving on a regular basis, consider how long this will be for. Bear in mind that regular savings products have advantages and disadvantages. On the one hand, they tie you in and there can be strict penalties for early encashment or withdrawal. On the other, they force you to be disciplined and take away the tricky decision of how to invest your money. You should also think about the cost of such plans.

How long can you tie your money up for?

Is there a date you need your money back? In other words, are you investing for something specific or just to build your overall wealth?

Investments have varying degrees of accessibility or liquidity. An investment that allows you to get at your money immediately is considered 'highly liquid'. Cash in a deposit account or publicly quoted shares, for instance, are both liquid. Property and pension plans are not.

How long you stay with any particular investment will partly be determined by the investment vehicle itself (a ten-year savings plan is – unless you break the terms – a ten-year savings plan) and partly by events (there may be a good reason to sell your investment).

What type of return are you looking for?

Returns vary enormously. The graph below shows how €1,000 would have grown over almost 20 years had you invested it in different ways.

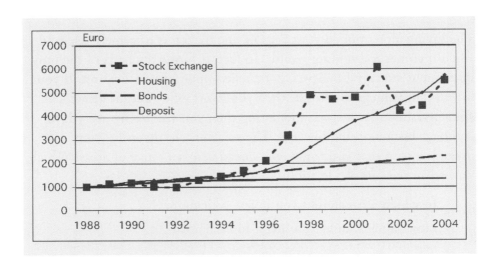

What risks are you willing to accept?

In general, *the higher the return, the greater the risk.* The highest possible returns are to be made from investments such as **commodities** and **spread betting** – but in both cases you can actually lose substantially more than your original investment. The lowest returns are to be made from investments such as bank deposit accounts and An Post savings plans – where your money can be considered 100% secure.

In formulating your overall investment strategy, you need to consider your approach to risk. Are you willing to accept some risk in order to boost your return? How much?

To what extent is tax an issue?

If you are a higher rate taxpayer – or expect to be – then you need to consider to what extent tax saving is an issue for you. Bear in mind that there are a number of highly tax-effective investment options available – though all carry above-average risk. Remember, too, that capital gains are taxed at a much lower level than income – which may make this a more attractive option for you (see Chapter 28).

A proven investment strategy

The saying 'don't put all your eggs in one basket' is extremely relevant when it comes to building wealth. In fact, it forms the basis of the only investment strategy I believe can be relied upon: **diversification**. If your investment strategy is too safe then you won't enjoy decent growth. If your investment strategy is too daring then you risk losing everything you have been working towards. The solution? To diversify your investments so that your money is spread across a range of areas. Which leaves you two simple decisions:

1   In which areas should you invest your money?
2   How much should you invest in each area?

As already mentioned, you should start by diversifying into the three most important areas of investment – your emergency fund, your pension and buying your own home. Having done this I would suggest putting your money into the following five areas:

1 Pooled investments.
2 A 'basket' of directly held stocks and shares.
3 Investment property.
4 Higher risk and tax-efficient investments such as BES schemes.
5 Alternative investments such as art, antiques, gold and other precious metals.

Within each area there is much scope for choice, allowing you to vary the amount you invest, the length of your investment, the degree of risk and so forth. You must decide for yourself what mix of investments best suits your needs.

The information below will give you a feel for the various opportunities available. Your next step will depend largely on how active an involvement you want to play. One option is to investigate each area thoroughly yourself. Another option is to allow an authorised adviser to handle it all for you. My own suggestion would be to go for a combination of the two. Educate yourself, keep yourself informed but let an expert guide and support you.

When long term means long term

One of the biggest mistakes investors make is that they forget their own financial objectives. If you are investing for long-term, capital growth – a good, solid gain over, say, 20 years – then if you change your strategy half way through you must resign yourself to a poor return and even losses. This is true regardless of the investment vehicle you are using.

If a change of strategy is unavoidable, then try and give yourself as long as possible to enact it.

There are various areas where investors seem particularly prone to chopping and changing. Long-term savings plans – such as endowments – is one. The stock market is another. In every case (leaving aside some sort of personal financial crisis) the usual reason is despondency over perceived lack of growth or falling values. If you have chosen your investments well you shouldn't be worrying about the effect of a few lean years or an unexpected dip in values. If you are concerned that you have made a bad investment decision in the first place do take professional advice before acting. The biggest losses come when an investor panics.

POOLED INVESTMENTS

A **pooled investment** – sometimes known as an investment fund – is a way for individual investors to diversify without necessarily needing much money. Your money – along with the money of all the other participants – is pooled and then invested. Each pooled investment fund has different, specified objectives. For instance, one might invest in the largest Irish companies, another in UK companies, a third in US gilts and a fourth in Korean property. In each case the fund managers will indicate the type of risk involved. They will also provide you – on a regular basis – with written reports or statements explaining how your money is performing.

Since it would be impossible for all but the richest of private investors to mimic what these pooled investments do, they are an excellent way to spread your risk. A typical fund will be invested in a minimum of 50 companies and will be managed by a professionally qualified expert.

The fund managers make their money from a combination of commission and fees:

- There is often an entry fee of up to 5% of the amount you are investing.
- There will definitely be an annual management fee – usually 1% of the amount invested.
- If you want to sell your share in a pooled investment you may also be charged a fee.

It is sometimes suggested in the media that fund managers are rewarded too highly. My view is that if a fund is meeting its objectives then it is only fair that the fund managers should recoup their costs and earn a fee for their expertise. I wish journalists would put more effort into reporting performance figures and less on complaining about whether a manager is charging 0.85% a year or 0.93%!

A couple of other points before we look at all the options in a little bit more detail:

1 The funds described below are all medium- to long-term investment vehicles. In other words you should be thinking about leaving your money in them for an absolute minimum of five years – and more like ten years or even longer.

2 Although past performance – as it always says in the small print – can be no guide to future performance *it is still useful to know*. One thing to note is who is making the actual investment decisions and how long they have been doing it for. If the individual manager of a fund has changed recently then the past performance may not be so relevant.

I include several different types of investment in this category:

- tracker bonds
- unit trusts and other managed funds
- with-profits funds
- stock market 'baskets' (or guaranteed stock market active funds).

This is because all of them are what I would describe as 'tailor-made investment vehicles'. That is to say they have been specifically designed to meet the needs of ordinary, private investors. This is in direct contrast to, say, un-tailored opportunities – such as buying a publicly quoted share or an investment property – which aren't aimed at any specific group of investors.

Tracker bonds

This is a fund that guarantees to return your initial investment *plus* a return based on a specific stock market index or indices. For example, it might give you all your money back after five years *plus* 80% of any rise in the FTSE 100.

Unit trusts

Your money is used to purchase 'units' in an investment fund. The price of the units will vary according to the underlying value of the investments. For instance, if the unit trust specialises in European technology shares then it is the value of the shares it holds which will determine the price of the units. You can sell your units at any time but you should be wary of buying and selling too quickly as charges and fees can eat up your profit.

Unit-linked funds

As above, but with the added element of a tiny bit of life insurance so that they can be set up and run by life insurance companies.

Managed funds

Again these are – in essence – unit trusts. The term is used to denote a fund which makes a wide spread of investments – thus theoretically reducing the risk – though you should not assume that this is the case.

Specialised funds

A fund that concentrates on a very specific market opportunity – such as oil shares or companies listed in an emerging market. This is obviously riskier but if the underlying investment performs well then you will make above-average returns.

Indexed funds

This is a fund that aims to match the overall market performance. For instance, you might have a fund that plans to achieve the same return as the UK's leading 100 shares (FTSE 100).

With-profit funds

These funds are run by insurance companies and they guarantee a minimum return *plus* extra bonuses according to how the fund has performed over the longer term. These bonuses might be added annually (annual bonus) or when the fund is closed after the agreed period of time (terminal bonus). The terms, conditions, objectives and charges for these funds vary enormously.

Stock market 'baskets'

Investors or their advisers choose a number of stocks, which can range from blue chip shares (such as the big banks and retail groups) to downright risky stocks. Depending on how risk averse you are, a percentage of your 'basket' will be conservative solid choices while the smaller percentage will be a little bit of a gamble. Diversification is again the buzz word – the greater the spread or choice of stocks, the softer the fall if there is to be a fall.

SPECIALISED STOCK MARKET STRATEGIES

Futures, options, hedge funds, derivatives, contracts for differences (CFDs) and the like all form part of the specialised investment sectors of the stock market. Good solid advice is essential if you wish to participate in this area.

ALTERNATIVE INVESTMENTS

There are a large number of alternative investment options, all of which come with varying amounts of risk. Some, such as gold or other precious metals, are easy to buy and sell. Others, such as art, may have a limited market making them difficult to find a buyer for when you want to dispose of them. Examples of alternative investments include:

- paintings and other art
- antique furniture and other objects
- debentures at Wimbledon
- rock memorabilia
- gold and other precious metals

- diamonds and other precious gems
- wine
- jewellery
- collectibles such as rare stamps, classic cars or watches.

In general, alternative investment is 'direct' – this is to say, you purchase the actual items. Specialist knowledge is vital if this is to be a genuine investment and you should not consider alternative investments until you have a reasonably high net worth and a portfolio of more conventional investments since the risks can be high.

MONEY DOCTOR WEALTH WARNING

Think carefully before you buy an annuity

If you have a lump sum to invest and you are aged at least 65, then one option is to purchase an **annuity**. The key advantage of an annuity is that it guarantees you an income for the rest of your life. The key disadvantage is that, once purchased, you cannot get your lump sum back. Furthermore, when you die the income stops and nothing will normally be returned to your estate.

Annuities are purchased from life assurance companies, and the return is linked to your age. The younger you are, the lower the return you can expect to receive. It's possible to take out a 'joint survivor annuity' if you're married. With these, when either you or your spouse dies the income continues at a reduced rate until the death of the other. Joint survivor annuities produce a lower return – or income – than single life annuities.

At the moment annuity rates, like interest rates, are relatively low. If you were a male, aged 65, and you wanted to generate a guaranteed income of €1,000 a month you would need to invest €190,000. However, if you were aged 75 you would only need to invest €130,000.

Annuity rates differ from insurance company to insurance

company, and from day to day. It is possible to arrange for your annuity rate to be linked to inflation, and some companies will also guarantee you a minimum return if you die within five years of purchasing the annuity. Finally, you should be aware that the income from an annuity is subject to income tax.

If you've got a limited amount of capital and you're worried about supporting yourself through your retirement years, an annuity could well be the perfect solution. However, I would advise getting professional help to make sure that you purchase the best-value annuity for your needs.

A low-risk, medium-term investment option

For a low-risk, medium-term investment option, consider **guaranteed bonds**. These offer above-average returns in exchange for you locking your money in for an agreed period. Some offer limited penalty-free withdrawals or provide a regular income for the term of the bond.

INVESTING IN STOCKS AND SHARES

Direct investment in the stock market is not for everyone. The risk associated with buying individual shares is obviously much greater than when buying into a diversified portfolio of shares – which is essentially what you are doing with a pooled or investment fund. If the share price goes up – yes – you can make a small fortune. But if the price falls or the market crashes then your shares can become worth a fraction of what you paid for them.

For an investor with limited funds, buying shares is probably not a sensible option. However, once you have started to build your capital wealth you should definitely consider adding individual share holdings to your portfolio of investments:

- Over the longer term, the stock market has shown a greater return to investors than any of the alternatives including property.
- Irish investors are not limited to the Irish stock market – may buy shares anywhere in the world.

- The charges for buying and selling shares have dropped dramatically, making it feasible to buy and sell in much smaller quantities.

- There are excellent sources of advice on which shares to buy and sell.

- Shares have widely varying degrees of risk.

- One of the big advantages to share ownership is that you literally own part of the company itself and its assets.

- Share ownership should bring you a regular income in the form of dividends plus capital appreciation (if the company is doing well).

Private investors have a choice of doing their own research and making their own decisions or seeking professional help from a stockbroker. Either way, if you are tempted to start buying and selling you should arm yourself with as much information as possible. Remember, it is ultimately your decision what happens to your portfolio. You should always keep a close watch on what is happening to any company whose shares you have bought, the sector it operates in and the market as a whole. I would particularly recommend the internet for information purposes.

How to read the financial pages

If you do decide to buy stocks and shares, you can keep track of their performance by reading the stock market pages in your daily newspaper. Next to the name of your company you'll find the following information:

High. This is the highest price that your particular company share has reached in the past 12 months.

Low. This is the lowest price that your share has reached in the past 12 months.

Share price. This is the average price paid for your share at close of business on the previous day.

Rise or fall. This is usually represented by a (+) or (-) symbol, and it lets you know how much your share increased or fell by in the previous day's trading.

Dividend yield. The dividend yield is the relationship of a share's annual dividend to its price. The figure will be before tax. For instance, if the dividend yield was 5.8%, and if you'd purchased €100 worth of shares at the current price, you would receive an annual income of €5.80.

P/E. This stands for **price-earnings ratio**, and it is one of the methods experts use to value a share. The price-earnings ratio is calculated by dividing the company's share price by the after-tax earnings due to each share over the company's most recent financial year. A high price-earnings ratio means that the market is confident in the company's future. But, by the same token, it could mean that the shares are over-priced. A low price-earnings ratio implies a lack of market confidence in the shares but the potential for an investor to pick up a bargain.

Dividend payments

When you own shares in a company you are entitled to a share of the profits – pre-supposing there are profits to be shared. This share is referred to as a **dividend**, and it is paid twice a year. The first payment is called an 'interim dividend' and the second payment is called a 'final dividend'. Several weeks before the dividend is due to be paid the company directors will announce how much it is to be. A few weeks after this they will 'close the register of shares'. Although you can still buy and sell the shares, if you do so while the register is closed you won't be entitled to the forthcoming dividend. During this period the company shares will be marked XD – which is short for ex-dividend – in the newspapers.

Shares and tax

Irish shares are liable to two different types of tax. First, you'll have to pay **income tax** on any profits (in other words, 'dividends') you receive. In fact, when you receive a dividend from an Irish company they will have already withheld tax at the standard rate of 20%. If the amount of tax withheld exceeds your liability for that particular year you can claim a refund. However, if you are in fact a higher-rate taxpayer you'll have to pay the difference between the standard rate and the higher rate when completing your annual tax returns. Second, when you sell your shares, if you've made a gain, you'll be liable for **capital gains tax** at 20%.

Choosing a stockbroker

The only way to buy and sell shares is through a **registered stockbroker**. When you do this, you will either pay a flat fee or commission, depending on whether the stockbroker is also advising you and/or the size of the transaction.

If you don't need advice when buying or selling, then you will require an **execution only** service. In this instance your main concern should be to keep the costs down to a bare minimum. Online services tend to be the cheapest, but it is well worth checking with your bank and the leading stockbrokers just to make sure.

Stockbrokers will be happy to provide you with an advisory service. You'll pay a higher level of commission for this (up to an average of 1.25%) but – of course – you'll benefit from your stockbroker's knowledge of the market.

There is no official minimum value regarding the volume of shares you can purchase. However, there's the minimum level of charges, usually around €25, so it probably doesn't make much sense to buy less than €1,000 worth of shares at a time.

If you want a list of Irish stockbrokers, then contact:

The Irish Stock Exchange
Anglesea Street
Dublin 2
Tel. (01) 617 4200.

MONEY DOCTOR WEALTH CHECK

Why not start an investment club?

If you'd like to dabble in the stock market but only have a relatively small amount of money to invest, why not start an investment club? An investment club is when a group of friends or work colleagues pool their resources and make buy-and-sell decisions together. My own experience of investment clubs is that they regularly out-perform the stock market because those involved take a real and detailed interest in every investment decision. However, you need time and patience.

Bonds

A bond is a long-term, fixed interest investment. Bonds are issued by public companies and also by governments as a way of raising money and are, in effect, a loan by you to a company or the government. Government bonds are usually referred to as gilt-edged securities or, for short, 'gilts' (see below).

Bonds have a face value and term – expressed as a maturity date.

For instance, if you had purchased a 15-year €100 bond in a Dutch health insurer in 2002 for a face value of €99.10 – the discount is 90c – at a yield of 6.375% (the coupon) you would receive an annual income of €6.38 until the bond reaches its maturity date in 2017 if it is not 'called in' beforehand. On maturity, you are guaranteed to receive €100.

What if you want to cash in your bond sooner? There is a thriving market for second-hand bonds. For instance, the example I mentioned above is currently worth €122.37 with a yield of 3.925%. The second-hand value of a bond will be linked to the underlying security, the rate of interest, and the length of time until it matures.

Gilts

Gilts are the name given to government stock. Governments over the years use 'stock' (rather like an IOU) to raise money to fund their spending. They offer investors a fixed rate of interest for a set period of time in exchange for the use of their savings. The interest is paid without DIRT being deducted – making them very tax-efficient for some non-taxpayers. As interest rates in general fall, government stock tends to rise in value. Gilts are a totally secure and inexpensive way to invest. The returns are usually above average and the cost of buying stock is low – normally a one-off charge of 1%.

PROPERTY

It is easy to understand why so many private investors are attracted to residential and even commercial property:

- Property values have risen dramatically over the last 30 years.
- It is possible to fund up to 90% of the purchase price with inexpensive loans.
- Rental income from property can cover all the expenses – interest, maintenance, tax and so forth.
- Your investment is in bricks and mortar – something solid – that you can actually see.
- If you make a gain when you sell the property you will pay substantially less tax – because it is not 'income' but a capital gain and thus taxed at a lower level – currently 20%.

Looking at how property prices have increased over the last 20 years: if you had borrowed €180,000 to buy a €200,000 property some 20 years ago you would have seen your €20,000 deposit turn into €341,200 profit!

Furthermore, in the current climate it is possible to take out interest-only mortgages that ensure your rent more than covers the cost of the loan and other overheads.

Clearly, property prices rise and fall so you would be unwise to assume that this is a one-way bet. If the market does fall you may find it hard to sell the property and take out your money. Also, the supply of property to rent has risen so much that in some areas it is now harder to find and keep tenants.

On the other hand, as the old saying goes 'they aren't making any more of it' and as planning restrictions become tighter there is every reason to believe that property will continue to be a highly attractive investment. The golden rule, in my opinion, is to pick a location and type of property that is always easy to rent.

Money Doctor Wealth Check

Tax treatment of rental income

Basically, your rental income will be treated the same way as if it was income you had earned by self-employment. You will be allowed all your expenses including:

- wear and tear on furniture, currently an eighth of the cost for each of the following eight years
- any charges made by a management company or letting agent
- maintenance, repairs, insurance, ground rent, rates and so forth
- the cost of any other goods or services you supply to your tenants (such as cleaning).

With regard to relief on interest payable on loans borrowed to purchase, improve or repair a rented property this is allowable except – roughly – from the period 23 April 1998 to 1 January 2002. If you bought rental property during this period you should seek professional advice or contact the Revenue Commissioners to clarify your position. Do note that not all your property expenses will be allowable for tax relief in the year in which they are incurred. For instance, the cost of 'wear and tear' will be spread over several years. For more information about tax treatment of property see Chapter 26.

TAX-EFFICIENT INVESTMENT OPTIONS

Financial experts often comment that 'you should never let the tax saving tail wag the investment dog'. In other words, you shouldn't invest in anything simply to enjoy the tax savings but should always consider the underlying value of the opportunity.

When it comes to **property investment** there are a number of tax incentives designed to make certain types of property more attractive. Basically, these can be summarised as:

- **Capital allowances** when you buy, repair and improve certain sorts of industrial buildings.
- A range of allowances available to owner occupiers and investors in various urban, town and rural renewal schemes – including Section 23 (allowable against all rental income and not just for the property itself) and Section 50 (student accommodation property) investments. We are now in the last throes of these reliefs.
- It is also possible to get substantial tax rebates by investing in BES (Business Expansion Scheme) schemes. These schemes require you to lock into a five-year, higher-risk investment and are only suitable for those with a relatively high income and/or substantial other assets.

THE MONEY DOCTOR SAYS...

- Don't put all your eggs in one basket. Divide your savings and investments into different parts so that if one area doesn't perform as hoped your overall financial objectives can still be met.

- Remember, the stock market has outperformed all other investments over the long term. You can take advantage of this by investing in a pooled fund such as a unit trust or directly in shares.

- You must keep reviewing your investment decisions even if you get a professional to help and advise you.

- Investment is for the long term – anything from five years upwards. Don't allow short-term rises and falls to distract you from your long-term strategy.

MONEY DOCTOR WEALTH WARNING

As with everything, if you get professional help make sure that they are unbiased and don't only represent one or two firms. Some so-called experts will sell you their solution without listening to your objectives. Choose an authorised adviser as described in Chapter 4.

MONEY DOCTOR WEALTH CHECK

If you want more information about investment options...

I regularly update the www.moneydoctor.ie website with details of investment opportunities as well as general advice and information. Or you can always write to me jlowe@moneydoctor.ie.

PART 7

PLANNING FOR A RICHER RETIREMENT

Until twenty or thirty years ago the word 'retirement' was associated with a certain age. Women, if they worked, retired at 60 and men at 65. Life expectancy was shorter and money was scarcer.

Today, retirement has taken on a whole different meaning. With a bit of careful planning it is now common for people to give up work and 'retire' from their late 40s onwards. There is also a strong trend towards second and even third careers.

So when we talk of retiring – yes – we mean giving up work, but we also mean having enough money to do what we want.

Thankfully, successive governments have encouraged the trends I am describing and have rewarded those who save for their retirement with very, very, very tasty tax breaks. Also, there are some relatively new pension structures that offer incredible flexibility.

Anyway, in this section you will learn how it is possible to ensure that when you retire (whenever it may be), you have sufficient wealth to lead a comfortable life. Specifically, you will discover how to:

- *decide what sort of pension you will need*
- *assess your current pension prospects*
- *understand all the various options open to you*
- *arrange a pension that will ensure a comfortable retirement for you*
- *retire early and*
- *find someone you can trust to steer you through the pensions minefield.*

I must emphasise that no one should be complacent about retirement planning. Even if you have a pension, you must review it on a regular basis. You could be a long time retired, anything from 20 to 40 years, so you need to get it right.

19

RETIREMENT BASICS

HOW TO TAKE ADVANTAGE OF THE PENSION OPTIONS OPEN TO YOU

In this chapter we will look at why pension planning is so important and also learn about what I call 'retirement basics' – such as understanding what your existing entitlement (if any) is – together with general planning advice.

WHY YOU SHOULD MAKE PENSION PLANNING YOUR NUMBER ONE PRIORITY

The only people who don't have to worry about retirement planning are those lucky enough to belong to a really first-class pension scheme (one with generous, cast-iron benefits) or who are so rich that money will never be a problem.

For the rest of us, pension planning should be a top priority – more of a priority, in fact, than almost any other financial decision we take. Frankly, it doesn't matter if you haven't bought your own home or invested a single penny of your money providing you have a good pension plan. I say this because, thanks to longer life expectancy, many people will spend anything from 20 to 40 years in retirement.

Typically, as we get older and progress in our careers we earn more money. However, on retirement we are no longer able to earn an income and must rely on either our savings or state benefits. Our earnings are therefore usually at their highest just before we retire. And unless we have made proper provision they will be at their lowest just after we retire. This can result in a massive drop in lifestyle at the point of retirement.

This is where the concept of **income equalisation** comes in – that is, reducing your disposable income when you are earning good money to help increase your income when you are not able to earn. We reduce our disposable income now by putting money into a pension scheme that can be used to increase our retirement income. It is still likely that when we retire our income will fall, but with this type of planning the transition will be far less of a shock to the system.

MONEY DOCTOR WEALTH WARNING

Is your company or government pension going to let you down?

Are you in a company or government pension scheme – outside the state pension which you would be entitled to at age 66? You should check on a regular basis, certainly every other year, that it is actually going to meet your needs on retirement. A growing number of pension schemes are producing disappointing returns and you should not be complacent. Very few company schemes provide enough money to ensure a comfortable old-age income. Get expert help too, because whereas companies are obliged to give you details of your benefits (and losses), you might not necessarily understand them. You can't rely on whoever is operating the scheme to provide you with the information you need.

IT IS NEVER TOO EARLY OR LATE TO BEGIN

Given that it is not impossible that your retirement may turn out to be a longer period than that of your working life, it isn't surprising that pension experts stress the importance of starting to plan early.

Nevertheless, if the number of men and women in their 40s, 50s and even their 60s consulting the Money Doctor on pension planning is anything to go by, a huge percentage of the population don't start thinking about their retirement until it isn't that far away.

Obviously, the later you leave it, the more of your income you will have to devote to building up a decent pension fund and the less well off you can expect to be once you stop work. But just because it is never too late to begin, it doesn't mean you should go to the wire. Every single day counts.

Start by taking stock

The first step towards a comfortable retirement is to take stock of where you are now in pension terms:

- Are you part of one or more companies or occupational pension schemes already?
- Are you entitled to a state pension by virtue of your employment?
- Are you entitled to a non-contributory old age pension?
- Could you live on a quarter of the average industrial wage – because that is roughly what the state pension will give you!
- Have you started a pension plan in the past?

If you answer 'yes' to any of these questions then you need to find out what your existing pension is going to be worth to you.

You also need to consider what other assets you have. Will your home be paid for by the time you retire? Have you any other savings or investments? By the same token, are there any other debts that you will need to discharge before retirement?

Where do you go for the answers to all these questions?

The easiest thing to do is to get a qualified professional to do the work for you, in other words either an accountant (if they specialise in this area) or an authorised adviser. The alternative is to approach all the relevant parties yourself. That is to say:

- your current employer and any past employers

- the managers of any pension scheme you may have started in the past
- the Department of Community, Family & Social Affairs (check your telephone directory for the relevant department or Chapter 5)
- the Pensions Board (**Verschoyle House, Mount Street, Dublin 2**).

If you are unhappy with any aspect of the way a non-government pension scheme has been administered, then you should contact the:

Pensions Ombudsman
36 Upper Mount Street
Dublin 2.

THE MONEY DOCTOR SAYS...

If you are self-employed or you are not in an employer-sponsored pension scheme then, unless you take action, you'll have to rely on the state. You can guess how well off that will leave you.

HOW MUCH WILL YOU NEED WHEN YOU RETIRE?

The whole concept of retirement has been turned on its head in recent years. As a population we are:

- giving up work sooner – often in our late 40s or 50s
- living longer and healthier lives
- leading more active lives in retirement.

We also expect a much higher standard of living. As a result we need more money in retirement than our predecessors. Here are some things you will need to consider:

- Will you need a lump sum on retirement, to pay off debts or to invest for a regular income?
- Will you still have unavoidable expenses (such as children's education) to pay for?
- How much of an income will you need? Could you manage on half of what you earn now? Could you manage on a quarter?

What changes would you have to make in your lifestyle if the only money you had coming in after retirement was the state pension?

Do you have anyone else to provide for? Your spouse, for instance? What will happen if you die before they do?

Our civil servants receive an index-linked income of up to two-thirds of their final pay, a tax-free sum of up to one-and-a-half year's salary, and a half-pension for their spouses after they die. Only a very tiny percentage of private-sector schemes offer this type of benefit.

What's more, if you work in the private sector and wanted to receive the same sort of benefit from the age of 65 you would have to put about 15% of your income into a pension fund from the age of 20 and even 40% when aged over 60.

THE GOOD NEWS

There are three excellent reasons why you shouldn't despair, regardless of whether or not you have any sort of pension in place already:

1 The government realises that it is vital to encourage you to save for your retirement so they will give you *huge* tax incentives to do so. For every €1 invested in a pension, you will receive 20c or 41c back depending on your tax margin.

2 Good planning at any age can optimise your retirement income.

3 By taking action now, you can alter your position dramatically. It is only people who continue to ignore the risks they are running who face the risk (one might say certainty) of an impoverished retirement.

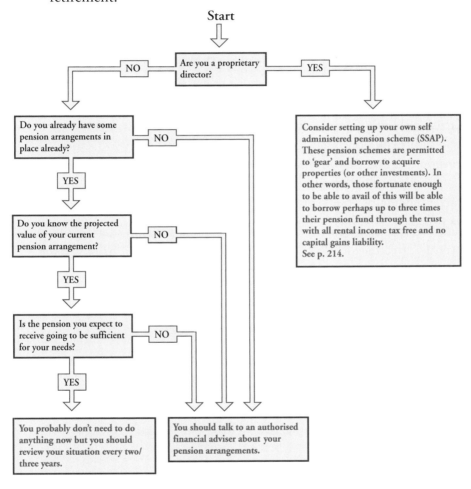

WHAT TO DO IF YOU WORK IN THE PRIVATE SECTOR

If you work for someone else you will be in one of two situations:

• either you will be in a company or occupational scheme or

• you won't be in any scheme at all.

If you are in a company or occupational pension scheme, then you will need to ascertain how good the scheme is, the sort of pension you can expect, what other benefits you may be entitled to and whether it is possible to increase your pension by making **additional voluntary contributions** (AVCs). If, on taking expert advice, the existing pension scheme doesn't appear to be that good, then concentrate on those AVCs.

Don't forget any schemes you may have been in during your previous employment.

If you aren't in your employer's scheme (and all employers are now obliged to operate a scheme under recent legislation – **personal retirement savings accounts** or PRSAs – or at least have a direct debit provision from your salary to such an investment) then you should consider joining. If you have no pension arrangements at all (and you don't want to do something through your employer) then you need to start a scheme of your own.

Your own pension scheme might be a personal pension plan or the more recently introduced PRSAs. I'll be looking at these options in greater detail in the next chapter.

WHAT TO DO IF YOU WORK FOR YOURSELF

If you work for yourself you are going to have to provide your own pension. The big advantage to this is that you can design a pension plan that matches your needs perfectly:

- It will be flexible, allowing you to invest on a regular basis or with lump sums.
- You'll have the choice of investing your money in an established fund or starting your own if you are a company owner, proprietary director (i.e. have at least a 5% shareholding in your company) or a senior company employee (e.g. a small self-administered pension scheme – SSAPs) or self-directed trusts.
- If you own your own company you could even consider setting up a company scheme.

THE MONEY DOCTOR SAYS...

- You are probably, to quote a line from the TV programme *Black Adder*, 'perfectly happy to wear cotton without understanding how the weaving process works'. By the same token, you shouldn't feel that you need to understand pensions legislation in its entirety to make your retirement plans!

- Action is imperative. If you have a really good pension plan, allowing you to retire early, you don't need any other investments (not even a house).

- The sooner you act, the better it will be but it is never too late to start. Extra tax benefits may apply the older you are.

20

PENSIONS MADE EASY

STEP-BY-STEP INSTRUCTIONS ON HOW TO MAKE
YOUR RETIREMENT DREAMS COME TRUE

This chapter contains detailed instructions on retirement planning – all
the information, advice and tips you need to make your own decisions
about what you need and want.

A QUICK GUIDE TO PENSION SCHEMES

One of my teenage daughter's favourite expressions is 'too much
information'. This may be the reaction many of you have when trying to
understand the pension system. Nor is it any wonder when you consider
how complicated the various options are. Opening a book on the subject
at random (a book aimed at ordinary consumers, by the way), my eyes
fell immediately on the following sentence:

Where a 5% Director chooses
the New Retirement Options,
they must first ensure that the
total fund accumulated would
not result in a situation where
the maximum benefits would
be excluded had they gone
down the traditional annuity
purchase route.

My own view is that you should
inform yourself, in the same
way that you would inform
yourself before making any
major purchase, but that unless
you find the topic fascinating

don't waste your time grappling with the minutiae. Instead, let an independent and authorised expert advise you. Here, then, is my quick guide to pension schemes.

LET'S BEGIN AT THE VERY BEGINNING...

Basically, a pension scheme, or a retirement plan, or whatever you want to call it, is a way of saving money specifically for **your retirement**. What differentiates it from an ordinary savings plan is that you will receive substantial help from the Revenue and, in exchange, access to your savings will be restricted. How restricted? Well, it will vary but typically you won't be able to touch any of the money you have saved until you reach a minimum age (this will vary according to the scheme and even the sort of job you have) and even then you won't be able to get your hands on all of it as a tax-free lump sum.

The choices available to you

There are three basic employment categories and the pension options can be defined as follows:

- employee
- self-employed
- directors.

Employee

Occupational pension schemes. Money invested in these schemes is locked away until you actually retire. At this point there will be restrictions on how you take the benefits. For instance, you'll only be allowed a limited amount as a lump sum – tax free – and the rest will have to be taken as an income.

Defined benefits. This is the Rolls Royce of schemes and extremely valuable. It can be either a contributory or non-contributory scheme – invariably, the employer will make contributions to the scheme. With this type of pension the employer guarantees you a certain percentage of your final salary, as a pension for life, for every year you have been working for them. Depending on the particular scheme, this can be up to 66% of the annual average of your last three years' income. You can also elect to take part of your benefits as a tax-free lump sum of up to one-and-a-half times your salary. The beauty of defined benefit schemes is that, irrespective of fund performance, you are guaranteed to receive the promised pension. It is the trustees of the scheme who have to worry about how they are going to fund what could be a very expensive company cost. More and more employers are opting out of the defined benefit pension because of cost, a trend exacerbated by the poor pension fund performances of the late 1990s and first part of the new century. Defined benefit schemes undoubtedly provide the best pension benefits. However, you should note that benefits are based on how long you have been working for that company. If you have a relatively short number of years service you can still top up your pension benefits by making some contributions through additional voluntary contributions (AVCs).

Defined contributions. Your pension is based on the growth of your monthly contributions (again the employer will usually also make contributions to your pension) up to maturity on retirement age. Unfortunately, there is no guarantee of how much you will receive on retirement as values may fall as well as rise. Your fund is purely down to how fund managers perform and how much you have invested. It is vital therefore that you are fully briefed and communicated with on a regular basis so that you can take corrective action if necessary. That corrective action may be an AVC.

Additional voluntary contributions (AVCs). Depending on your own existing pension contributions and your age, you could put up to 40% of your annual income into an AVC. You can offset the entire 40% against your income tax liability, making this procedure a very tax-efficient one. Furthermore, most employers will deduct your AVCs directly from your wages. If they do this you will also benefit from PRSI relief on your AVC. There is also greater flexibility about how and when you take the benefits and you won't have to pay for setting up a scheme of your own. If your employer's pension scheme has a good investment performance or guaranteed benefits, then putting more money into it via an AVC can make excellent financial sense.

Check with an authorised adviser for specific details, as there are so many regulations and you want to ensure you're making the right decision.

> **No occupational pension scheme is available to you.** If your employer does not offer an occupational pension scheme you have the same options as someone who is self-employed (see below). The one exception is that your employer is required, by law, to provide you with a payroll deduction facility to a nominated PRSA provider.

Self-employed

PRSA/personal pensions – with the recent introduction of PRSAs, pensions became more accessible and less expensive to start. PRSAs have maximum charges of 5% of each premium paid plus 1% a year, of the accumulated fund. The affordable pension is here to stay. It includes:

- low cost
- generous tax relief at your marginal rate. Depending on your age this can be on contributions of up to 40% of your income
- easy to understand – you decide how much you want to invest and where you want the money invested
- portable in that you can bring the pension with you from employment to employment together with flexibility in being able to adjust your annual contributions depending on your circumstances, and flexible about how you use the fund on retirement
- when you retire, you can have up to 25% of the fund as a tax-free lump sum (useful for paying off a mortgage) and
- suitable for people who work for themselves, have no company scheme or change their employment frequently.

In theory, a PRSA is a simplified version of a personal pension plan. In practice, the rules governing PRSAs are just as complicated. You should seek independent advice.

Directors

If you are a director, you can avail of a **director's executive pension** (if you have 5% or more shareholding in your company). In fact, the advantages offered by company schemes are so good that if you are self-employed (a sole trader), it may be worth your while to form a limited company in order to take advantage of them yourself. If you do own your own company, then setting up a company pension scheme will probably be the best route for you. The main reason for this is that the limits for which the Revenue will give tax relief on pension contributions are significantly higher for a company investing in a company pension scheme than for an individual investing in a corresponding PRSA or personal pension.

Company schemes can be arranged to benefit as many employees as you want, just you, or selected members of your staff, as you prefer. Note that this route is particularly good for anyone who has left it late in life to plan for his or her retirement.

- As there is no benefit-in-kind on contributions to a company pension scheme, your company will be able to put substantial tax-free money into your pension.
- There is greater flexibility with regard to your retirement date.
- You have more control over where your contributions are invested.
- You can take a portion of your fund tax free – so tax breaks on the way in and the way out!

MORE ON PRSAs/PERSONAL PENSIONS

Small self-administered pension schemes (SSAP) or self-directed trusts

Under most pension arrangements it is left up to fund managers to determine what the pension funds actually invest in. However, if you want more direct control on the actual assets that make up your pension fund you can always set up an SSAP. Here you appoint a **pensioner trustee** to run your pension but you dictate what it invests in. For example, if you want to invest in shares you can pick the individual shares as opposed to just a managed fund.

Recent legislative changes have also brought in for the first time a provision which allows pension funds to borrow for **property acquisition**. This effectively means that you could borrow within your pension fund to buy an investment property (at arm's length – not your own company's offices, your holiday hot spot or your granny's flat) and both the rental income contributions and your own monthly contributions will be paid into your pension fund tax free, while all along your fund (i.e. your property) should be appreciating as you are making those contributions. There is also the added benefit that no capital gains liability is incurred and your estate keeps the asset (i.e. your property) after you die.

I think that for the company executive the SSAPs/self-directed trusts will grow considerably over the coming years as a result of the introduction of that one provision, allowing pension funds to borrow or gear perhaps up to four times the fund value to buy investment property. SSAPs are not just confined to property. Shares, investments and even complex financial instruments (e.g. hedge funds) can be incorporated into SSAPs.

BIG TAX RELIEF – THE REVENUE COMMISSIONERS ARE ON YOUR SIDE

I have made repeated mention of the huge tax incentives offered to those who invest in a pension. These include:

- Tax relief at your marginal rate of tax. So if you are paying tax at 41% when you put €100 into your pension fund it will only cost you €59. Put another way, pension funds almost double the value of your savings before the money has been invested in anything.

- Investments grow tax free. If you put money into your own company scheme it is a legitimate business expense for tax purposes.

- It can be possible to save PRSI (including the health levy of 2%), which represents a further saving of 9% on the annual premiums for those paying at the top tax rate or a total saving of 50% when income tax is included. Put another way, if a gross premium of €5,000 were paid for 20 years, the value of the premiums would be €100,000 at the end of the period. Thanks to the tax element, the net cost **from after-tax income**, is €50,000. To achieve the same return on investing, the net income would need an annual compound return of 7%! This is the value of the government's contribution and is given *for free*.

- While it is in a pension fund, no income tax or capital gains tax is payable on your investment.

- All pension schemes allow you to take out a certain portion of your fund tax free when you come to retire.

- PRSI is not payable once you are 66, excluding the 2% health levy portion, which ceases to be payable at age 70.

There are limits on the amount you can invest into a pension fund and still get the tax relief. Check with your authorised adviser for details.

WHAT HAPPENS TO YOUR PENSION CONTRIBUTIONS?

If you are part of an occupational pension scheme then your money will be invested by the scheme's managers. If it is a big scheme they may invest it directly themselves. Most companies, however, use the services of professional fund managers who invest in everything from stocks and shares to property and commodities. Performance will be determined by how well the scheme is managed and if you are in a 'defined contribution' scheme you need to pay close attention to this. For employer-sponsored schemes (e.g. occupational pension schemes) trustees play an important role as they look after the investment decisions on advice from fund managers.

If you set up your own personal pension plan or your own company sets up a company scheme, then you have much more control over how your contributions are invested while you have to make the investment choices. Most opt for equity funds – where your money is pooled and invested in stocks and shares. Such funds will have varying returns and different levels of risk. As you near retirement you will be less likely to place your fund in a higher-risk investment than you would if you were in your early 30s.

MONEY DOCTOR WEALTH WARNING

Don't buy a pension from someone who can't offer you choice

All the financial institutions involved in the retirement market, and I'm speaking chiefly about life insurance companies and banks, employ salespeople whose job it is to promote their own company's pension products.

One such example is that of a young female solicitor who was persuaded to take out a bank assurance pension plan at a premium of more than €500 per month, based on her expectation of a certain income on retirement in keeping with her current levels of salary. After a couple of months she cancelled the policy because she wasn't asked one of the most important questions: 'Can you afford to pay this amount each month into a pension scheme?'

While it is important to aim for a similar level of income to retire on, it is equally important to be able to afford it and have a life in the meantime. Ideally you should not choose a pension from someone who only represents one company. You should always deal with someone independent who is authorised to tell you about every single option available to you. Pension fund performance and management fees vary enormously. Buying without comparing the whole market could cost you a great deal of money.

WHAT IS IT GOING TO COST?

Almost without exception, the pension industry gets paid on **commission**. This commission comes out of your monthly payments. The amount will vary according to the type of pension scheme you join or set up. Many schemes (but not all) will involve an initial, one-off fee followed by an **annual management charge**. To give you an example, for a standard PRSA the maximum annual management charge is 1% of the accumulated fund, whilst the initial set-up fee is capped at 5% of the premiums. When you take out a pension your authorised adviser will explain, in full, what charges you are paying. Remember, however, the charges are one thing, but what is it going to cost to provide an income?

Having a pension is one thing, but having a pension which is going to provide you with the income you think you will need is another. One example of this was a shop-owner who sought advice on investing a lump sum. One suggestion was to look at investing this in a pension. However, he indicated that he was alright here as he had already put a pension in place. It transpired that this 45-year-old shop-owner was currently earning €50,000 a year and had just taken out a pension plan for €400 a month. He was shocked to learn that if he kept contributions at this level, and took the state contributory pension into account, he could expect to have a total after-tax retirement income of around €750 a month (in today's terms) at age 65 – a fraction of what he currently earned.

You get what you pay for. One way of looking at it is to look at what level of income you think you need and finding out how much it would cost to provide this. You may not be able to afford the cost now but at least you will know what to expect.

Below is a table showing the approximate costs of funding a total after-tax income of €1,250 a month and €2,500 a month in today's terms should you retire at 65. They assume that you will be entitled to the state contributory pension. These figures are meant as a guide only, and make a number of assumptions. You should discuss your own particular circumstances with a qualified authorised adviser.

	Aged 25	Aged 30	Aged 35	Aged 40	Aged 45	Aged 50	Aged 55
€1,250pm	€191pm	€255pm	€347pm	€482pm	€673pm	€1.001pm	€1,681pm
€2,400pm	€341pm	€457pm	€623pm	€864pm	€1,207pm	€1,790pm	€3,019pm

The above figures are before tax relief and assume that contributions are increased by 5% a year, inflation is 5% a year and the state pension increases by 5% a year. It also assumes that the funds the pension is invested in increase by 6% a year and that the tax rates on retirement are similar to today.

WHAT BENEFITS SHOULD YOU BE LOOKING FOR?

How do you judge a pension scheme? Here are some tips:

- If it is a defined benefit scheme, then you should judge it primarily on what percentage of your salary you'll receive once you retire. Remember, these are the only schemes where the benefit is guaranteed based on service and salary.
- Depending on the type of pension plan you have you will be given a certain portion, by way of a tax-free lump sum, of the fund's value. Establish how much.
- Death-in-service benefit. Essentially, this is life cover giving your beneficiaries a lump sum and/or income should you die before retirement age.
- Death-in-retirement benefit. This gives your beneficiaries a lump sum and/or an income if you die after you have retired.
- The minimum retirement age (for occupational pension schemes it is 60, but if you own your company you can take a well-earned rest at age 50).
- How much your pension income will increase each year after you have started claiming it? Will it increase in line with the cost of living? More than the cost of living?
- Any special benefits offered to your spouse or other dependants.

WHAT HAPPENS WHEN YOU RETIRE?

This will depend on your employment status and scheme.

For **defined benefit schemes**, you will receive a tax-free lump sum and a guaranteed annual income, usually index linked and based on your service.

For **defined contribution** schemes, the accumulated fund on retirement is used to buy annuity income based on how much is in the fund after taking out an allowable portion by way of a tax-free lump sum.

For funds accumulated through **director schemes, AVCs, PRSAs** or **personal pensions**, the choices are greater as recent legislation brought in new options – **approved retirement funds** (ARFs) and **approved minimum retirement funds** (AMRFs) – allowing pension funds to be held outside of annuities (see p. 330 for an explanation of annuities) and effectively kept within your estate when you pass on. The taxable benefits can be taken as needed. If you have an annuity, the insurance company keeps the money when you die and your dependants lose out.

THE MONEY DOCTOR SAYS ...

- The tax benefits are enormous. For a taxpayer on the higher rate of tax, €100 into a pension will currently only cost €59 (less if PRSI is taken into acccount). This is a bargain by anyone's standards.

- If your pension incorporates life cover you may receive extra tax relief.

- Please, please take independent professional advice. I am repeating myself, I know. But only someone who is authorised to advise you on every pension available is going to guarantee you the most appropriate pension for your needs.

PART 8

Would you like to slash your 2009 tax bill quickly, easily and without having to plough through a lot of incomprehensible jargon? Then this section is for you. Because in plain English – using plenty of examples and case histories – I am going to explain how, as a taxpayer, you can:

- *make certain that you don't pay a single cent more tax this year than you have to*

- *reclaim any tax you may have overpaid in previous years*

- *plan your finances so that future tax bills are kept to a bare minimum.*

MONEY DOCTOR WEALTH CHECK

*For the hottest tax tips check out **www.moneydoctor.ie***

*Because tax rules sometimes change during the year and because the Money Doctor's team of tax advisers are always searching for new ways to save you tax our website contains a special tax-saving section. So for the hottest tax tips visit **www.moneydoctor.ie** today.*

To make it as easy as possible to find the tax-saving information you require I've divided this section up into lots of short chapters. From the list below you can check which chapters are relevant to your circumstances:

Chapter 21: *Tax basics. An overview of how the Irish tax system works – and your part in it!*

Chapter 22: *Income tax basics. The first steps towards reducing your income tax bill.*

Chapter 23: *All about income tax credits. How tax 'credits' and 'allowances' can help you save money.*

Chapter 24: *PAYE. How to make the Pay As You Earn (PAYE) tax system work in your favour.*

Chapter 25: *Income tax for the self-employed. How to reduce your income tax bill if you work for yourself.*

Chapter 26: *Tax and property. Property investor? How to ensure you keep your tax bill to a minimum.*

Chapter 27: *Tax and the company car. How motorists can drive down their tax bill.*

Chapter 28: *Capital gains tax. Lots of useful tips on how to reduce, delay and avoid capital gains tax. If you think you may be selling any of your assets (including a property) during 2009 or in the foreseeable future then you need to read this chapter.*

Chapter 29: *Capital acquisition tax. The purpose of capital acquisition tax is to tax gifts and inheritances – and the purpose of this chapter is to make sure that your gifts and inheritances aren't taxed!*

Chapter 30: *Love, marriage and lower taxes. Extra tax benefits for those who are married.*

Chapter 31: *Tax for the ex-pat. Tax planning tips for those living and working abroad.*

Chapter 32: *Tax advice for farmers. Special tax tips for farmers and farming businesses.*

MONEY DOCTOR WEALTH CHECK

Could you take advantage of the seed capital scheme?

If you're thinking of starting your own business – and you've never been in business before – then you may be able to take advantage of something called the seed capital scheme. *To be eligible you have to have been employed on a PAYE basis and you have to have capital of your own (or be able to borrow capital elsewhere) to invest in the new venture. Under these circumstances the government will give you an income tax rebate of up to €100,000 (relating to the PAYE paid in the six years preceding cessation of your employment) to help you get your new business off the ground. Because the seed capital scheme is essentially returning or rebating tax you've paid in the past, it doesn't stop you from taking advantage of other government incentives such as grants and employment incentives. Furthermore, you can claim this rebate pretty much regardless of the sort of business you are establishing.*

21

TAX BASICS

GETTING TO GRIPS WITH THE TAX SYSTEM

There are really only two things you need to know about Irish tax to start beating the system. Firstly, most people are hit hardest by just three taxes and it is these that you want to concentrate on reducing or – better still – avoiding completely. They are:

- income tax
- capital gains tax (CGT)
- capital acquisition tax (CAT).

(Of course, there are many other taxes, such as stamp duty and deposit interest retention tax [DIRT], and, believe me, I am not going to ignore them. But it is the first three that will probably offer you the biggest scope for juicy savings.)

Secondly, the beauty of the Irish tax system is that it consists almost entirely of exceptions. There are, literally, hundreds of different reasons why you might not have to pay a particular tax. So, cutting your tax bill is simply a matter of either:

- studying these reasons to see which ones apply (or could be made to apply) to your own circumstances so as to save you tax
- looking at your circumstances and seeing how they might be altered to give you a tax advantage.

Let me give you a quick example. In theory, if you are single the first €35,400 of your 2009 income should be taxed at 20%, and anything over this sum should be taxed at 41%. In practice, there is a minimum income (income exemption limit) you have to receive before you pay any tax at all (this could be as high as €40,000 depending on your age and circumstances) and once your income exceeds this level there are all sorts of allowances, credits and other ways to reduce the amount you actually have to part with.

How old you are, where you live, your marital status, the source of your income, any borrowings you may have, your health, the health of your family … all these factors and many, many others can be used to slash your tax bill.

It is not inconceivable that you could have an income of as high as €75,000 and not actually have to pay a single cent in tax!

Keeping it legal

The difference between legal tax saving – which is called tax avoidance – and illegal tax saving – which is called tax evasion – was once described as being 'the thickness of a prison wall'. It is perfectly legal to use our tax laws in any way you can to reduce the amount of tax you pay. Naturally, all the tax-saving suggestions in this book are 100% legal.

Get to know your tax liabilities and the Revenue Commissioners in the process

Here is a list and brief description of taxes affecting individuals:

Income tax

This, as its name implies, is a tax on annual income. How much you have to pay is linked to:

- how much you earn
- your personal circumstances
- what tax credits and allowances you are entitled to.

If you are an employee you pay your income tax monthly but if you are self-employed you pay it annually. Either way, there are dozens of income tax-saving tactics available.

Capital gains tax

If you buy something at one price and either sell it later for a higher price or give it away when it is worth more than you paid for it then you will have made a capital gain. This gain may be taxed – depending on all sorts of factors including:

- how big the gain is
- what sort of gain it is
- the rate of inflation
- allowable expenses.

It is paid annually. As with income tax there are plenty of ways in which to reduce your liability to capital gains tax. See Chapter 28.

Capital acquisition tax

This is a tax on gifts and on inheritances. The person *receiving* the gift or inheritance pays it. Whether tax has to be paid will depend on a variety of factors including:

- the amount of money or the value of the property involved
- the relationship between the parties involved
- the nature of the gift or inheritance.

Once again, it is paid annually and there are any number of ways in which it is possible to avoid and/or reduce this tax. See Chapter 29.

Stamp duty

If you are buying a property you will be liable for **stamp duty** – which is a one-off tax. You'll also have to pay stamp duty – at a considerably lower level – on your mortgage deed. For individuals, it is very hard to legally reduce or avoid this form of taxation. See p. 164 for matrix.

Pay Related Social Insurance (PRSI)

If you are employed or self-employed you will have to pay health, employment and training levies – which are usually all lumped together and referred to as PRSI. There is little scope for legally avoiding PRSI.

However, PRSI is no longer payable once you reach the age of 66, with the exception of the health levy portion (2%) which is no longer payable at age 70.

Value Added Tax (VAT)

This is a tax on your spending. It is charged at different rates from 0% to 21% – depending on what you are buying. Businesses and the self-employed have some opportunities for avoiding or reducing their VAT liability – individuals are limited in their options.

DO YOU HAVE TO FILL IN A TAX RETURN?

One question I frequently get asked – especially by those in retirement, regular employment, or receiving welfare payments – is whether or not they are legally obliged to complete an annual tax return. Let us start by considering who must fill out that dreaded form whether they want to or not. Into this category falls:

- anybody who works for themselves – full or part time
- anyone with a second income, even if it's from casual work like cleaning or baby-sitting
- all company directors
- anyone in receipt of income that hasn't already been taxed – for instance, a private pension or dividends from an overseas investment
- anyone who has made a capital gain
- anyone with rental income from a property
- anyone who has received or made a gift
- anyone who has received money of any sort that may be liable to tax here in Ireland.

The fact that you may be paying PAYE does not exclude you from having to complete a tax return. Indeed, even if you're on PAYE it may be to your advantage to complete a tax return as it could reduce your tax bill for the year.

So who *definitely* doesn't have to complete a tax return? If you fall into any of the following categories, you are off the hook:

- You have a relatively low income. See p. 230 for details.
- You have absolutely no income.
- You pay your tax through the PAYE system, and haven't received any other money that might be liable to tax.

MONEY DOCTOR WEALTH CHECK

Take advantage of the taxperson

Many people forget that the Revenue Commissioners are there to serve you. They publish a wide range of brochures designed to assist taxpayers, and you'll also find an enormous amount of information online at their website (www.revenue.ie). Your local tax office will be delighted to answer questions for you, and you can also telephone them on their information helpline, details of which you'll find in the 'Useful Contacts' section (Appendix 9). The Revenue Commissioners also have a highly efficient online service called, oddly enough, the Revenue Online Service or ROS. This internet facility allows you to file your tax returns, make payments, and access your personal revenue data any time, night or day. Registering is a simple process, and the software is easy to use and compatible with every type of computer. When completing a tax return you will also find that it saves you a vast amount of time since you won't have to wade through all the relevant sections looking for the questions you need to answer. However, it is not yet available to everyone.

22

INCOME TAX BASICS
THE FIRST STEPS TOWARDS
REDUCING YOUR INCOME TAX BILL

'Income tax', claimed Will Rogers, 'has made more liars out of the American people than golf.' Being a patriotic soul I like to think that we Irish people are above such deceit. Not that we mightn't be tempted when it comes to income tax – if only because the thing is so wretchedly confusing.

The Revenue Commissioners (who appear to be allergic to plain English) hardly help by defining income tax as being the tax:

> payable on your taxable income, i.e. your total assessable income tax for a tax year, less deductions for any non-standard rate allowances (not tax credits) to which you may be entitled.

Then, as if this wasn't sufficiently obtuse, they divide 'income' into several different categories which they call – unhelpfully – schedules. The schedules are then divided into 'cases'. And so it goes on.

Unfortunately, if you are going to make a serious attempt to reduce your income tax bill you really need to understand how the Revenue Commissioners are actually taxing you. Therefore, the first part of this chapter is devoted to a basic, jargon-free guide to income tax. However, once the terms of engagement, as it were, have been explained we will get straight down to all the different ways in which you might cut – or even avoid altogether – your income tax liability.

WHAT SORT OF INCOME DO YOU HAVE?

In order to differentiate between the different types of income people receive, the Revenue Commissioners classify income under a number of different headings or 'schedules'. Since accountants and other financial professionals refer to these schedules all the time, it's quite useful to know what they are:

Schedule C relates to organisations like banks that have deducted income tax from certain payments. You almost certainly won't have to worry about this.

Schedule D is divided into five separate classes referred to as 'cases'.

- Case I relates to profit from a trade.

- Case II relates to profits from a profession.

- Case III refers to interest not taxed at source, and all foreign income.

- Case IV refers to taxed interest income not falling under any case schedule.

- Case V refers to rental income from properties in Ireland.

Schedule E basically covers all the money earned from regular employment, and is technically defined as 'income from offices or employments, together with pensions, benefits in kind, and certain lump sum payments arising from an office or employment'.

Schedule F covers dividends and other distributions from Irish-resident companies.

Whenever you deal with the Revenue Commissioners in relation to income tax you'll find that they make reference to the above schedules and cases. It is always worth checking that they have your income correctly classified as – if they don't – it could help to reduce your tax bill.

A QUICK EXPLANATION OF INCOME TAX RATES

For many years, income tax has been levied at a different rate according to the amount of income involved. There are currently two different rates in Ireland – 20% and 41%. Which rate of tax you'll pay will depend on your circumstances and income. For instance, for 2009 if you are a single person the **first €35,400** of your income will be taxed at 20% and the balance would be taxed at 41%. It is worth remembering that these tax rates can change from year to year.

The table below shows the different tax bands and rates for 2009. As you will see, taxpayers are divided into four different groups. These are:

- single people and widow(er)s
- one-parent families
- married couples where only one spouse is working
- married couples – where both spouses are working.

Rates of income tax

Single/widowed without dependent children	35,400 @ 20% Balance @ 41%
Single/widowed qualifying for one-parent family tax credit	39,400 @ 20% Balance @ 41%
Married couple (one spouse with income)	44,400 @ 20% Balance @ 41%
Married couple (both spouses with income)	44,400 @ 20% (with increase of 26,400 max.) Balance @ 41%

Some good news for anyone on a low income

If your income falls below a certain level, you are completely exempt from income tax. The chart below sets out the maximum amount of income you can receive – according to your circumstances – this year without paying a single cent in tax. It's worth noting that if you earn income over the amounts set out below, you will be eligible for something called 'marginal relief', which is explained below.

Low income exemption limits

Single/widowed	Exemption limits for 2008
Under 65	€5,210
65 or over	€20,000
Married	
Under 65	€10,420
65 or over	€40,000
Additions to exemptions limit for dependent children (€)	
1st and 2nd child (per child)	€575
Each subsequent child	€830
Marginal relief tax rate	40% of the amount by which the total income exceeds the exemption limit.

Taking advantage of marginal relief

Supposing you are on a relatively low income, but you earn slightly more than the amount necessary to avoid tax completely? Recognising that it would be unfair to tax you too heavily, something called **marginal relief** exists. Any individual/married couple whose total income from all sources is slightly over the exemption limit may qualify for marginal relief but it will only be granted if it is more beneficial to the claimant than their tax credits. It restricts the tax payable to 40% of the difference between your income and the appropriate exemption limit. The exemption limits vary depending on age, marital status and the number of qualifying dependent children. As this is quite complicated, let me explain it with an example:

Marginal relief advantageous

Over 65 married with two children				
	€			€
Total income	40,000	Total income		40,000
Tax @ 20%	8,000	Less: Exemption		40,000
Less: Tax credits	5,830	Excess		nil
Tax due	2,170	Tax @ 40%		nil

Marginal relief not advantageous

Under 65 single with no children			
	€		€
Total income	18,000	Total income	18,000
Tax @ 20%	3,600	Less: Exemption	5,210
Less: Tax credits	3,520	Excess	12,790
Tax due	80	Tax @ 40%	5,116

PERSONAL CREDITS AND TAX ALLOWANCES

Although you are liable to pay income tax at the rates outlined above, you are entitled to claim all sorts of personal tax credits and allowances which will help you to reduce this bill by a fairly substantial amount. You'll find a complete guide to all the income tax credits and allowances in the next chapter.

PRSI – another form of income tax

The initials PRSI stand for pay related social insurance. Because it is calculated as a percentage of your income it is, effectively a form of income tax. In fact, PRSI incorporates two other taxes: the health levy, and the employment and training levies.

The purpose of PRSI is to raise money to provide all sorts of social welfare benefits – these range from invalidity pensions to redundancy pay, and from a bereavement grant to a maternity benefit. Your ability to claim social welfare benefits is linked to your having paid your PRSI. It is, therefore, worth remembering the following points:

- How much PRSI you have to pay will depend on your job. There are three key categories: private sector employees, public sector employees, and the self-employed.

- Your entitlement to benefits is normally based on your contributions made two years before the benefit year in which you claim! In other words, what you paid in 2007 will determine what you can claim in 2009.

- The level of PRSI you have to pay is calculated as a percentage of your gross income, less any payments to an approved pension scheme or certain other health schemes.

- If you earn less than €127 a week, you don't have to pay any PRSI at all. If you earn less than €500 in a particular week, you won't have to pay the health levy.

- You can volunteer to pay PRSI, or pay it at a higher level, if this is to your advantage.

The PRSI health levy rates are set every year in the Budget. It's worth noting that the employee and employer normally share PRSI contribution costs. Most employees, of course, pay their PRSI through the PAYE tax system.

A summary of the benefits to which you are entitled under PRSI is to be found in Chapter 5. It is, perhaps, worth mentioning here that to claim a **social insurance benefit** it is necessary to have a minimum number of PRSI contributions. Confusingly, the word 'contribution' means not just the PRSI you've paid, but also your PRSI credits. PRSI credits are awarded to someone who would normally have been making a contribution but for various reasons did not do so. For instance, you would receive PRSI credits during any weeks when you received a disability benefit or unemployment benefit. You also receive credits when you first start working.

If there was an Olympic category for the 'most complicated tax in the world', then PRSI would probably win a gold. If you need help with your PRSI then I would suggest either talking to an accountant or else contacting the Department of Social & Family Affairs or – alternatively – the Revenue Commissioners.

23

ALL ABOUT INCOME TAX CREDITS

HOW TAX 'CREDITS' AND 'ALLOWANCES' CAN HELP YOU SAVE MONEY

Depending on your circumstances, you can reduce your income tax bill by claiming certain **tax credits** and **allowances**. A great deal of confusion exists over the difference between 'credits' and 'allowances'. The key points to remember are:

- A tax credit is money off your actual tax bill. So, if you have a tax bill of €1,000 and tax credits of €800, you only pay €200 in tax.

- A tax allowance reduces the amount of income on which tax is payable. How much it will be worth to you will depend on the rate of tax you pay. For instance, if you pay income tax at 20% then a €1,000 tax allowance will save you €200 of tax.

The old system of tax allowances has largely been replaced by tax credits.

Every year you are sent an annual **tax certificate** referred to, somewhat long-windedly, as the 'notification of determination of Tax Credits and standard rate cut-off point', which sets out full details of all your tax credits together with the income level at which you will start to pay the higher rate tax.

HOW TAX CREDITS WORK IN PRACTICE

Before going into detail about all the different personal tax credits that exist, let's just look at how they work in practice. In 2008, John O'Brien, a single taxpayer on PAYE, pays tax at 20% on the first €35,400 of income and 41% on anything above this sum. His tax credits amount to some €3,660. Below, I've shown how his tax credits reduce his tax liability on an assumed income of €40,000.

Income	€40,000	
Tax €34,000 @ 20 %		€7,080
Tax €4,600* @ 41%		€1,886
Total tax before tax credits		€8,966
Deduct tax credits		
Single tax credit	€1,830	
PAYE tax credit	€1,830	€3,660
Tax payable		€5,306
*€40,000 less €35,400		

CHECK YOUR TAX CREDITS EVERY YEAR

Do remember to check that you're claiming all your tax credits every year. It's also worth bearing in mind that you can go back to the Revenue Commissioners and claim tax credits that you failed to take advantage of for the previous four tax years.

A COMPLETE GUIDE TO PERSONAL TAX CREDITS AND ALLOWANCES FOR 2009

Over the next few pages you'll find brief details of all the different tax credits and allowances for which you may be eligible.

Single person's credit

You can claim this if you're single; if you're married but decide to opt for single/separate assessment or if you're separated and you and your former partner have not opted for joint assessment. It is worth €1,830 for 2009.

Married person's credit

This is double the single credit, and it's granted to married couples who have opted to be assessed together. It can also be claimed by separated couples where one partner is maintaining the other and is not entitled to claim tax relief on the maintenance being paid. For more details on tax relief for separated and divorced couples see Chapters 34 and 35. The married person's credit is worth €3,660.

One-parent family credit

If you're a parent (or guardian) and, for whatever reason, you are not entitled to the married person's credit, then you're entitled to a personal credit of €1,830.

Widowed parent credit

A special credit is granted to widowed parents for the first five years following the year of bereavement. For the year 2008 the credit is: €4,000 in the first year; €3,500 in the second year; €3,000 in the third year; €2,500 in the fourth year; and €2,000 in the fifth year.

Special age credits

If you are over 65 – or if your spouse is over 65 – then you receive an extra credit. If you're single or widowed this is worth €325. For a married couple it is worth €650.

The home carer's credit

If you care for someone who's elderly (defined as being over 65) or incapacitated, you may be eligible to claim an additional credit of up to €900. The home carer credit is only available to married couples where one spouse cares for one or more dependent people. You can't claim if you are looking after your own spouse. The maximum income of the home carer to claim maximum relief is €5,080. A reduced tax credit applies where the income is between €5,080 and €6,750.

A new childminding relief was introduced in 2006. Where an individual minds up to three children (other than their own children) in the minder's own home, no tax will be payable on the childminding earnings received provided the amount is less than €15,000 per annum. If the childminding income exceeds this amount, the total amount will be taxable, as normal, under self-assessment. An individual will be obliged to return their childminding income in their annual tax return.

Incapacitated child credit

If you are looking after an incapacitated child then you're entitled to claim a tax credit of €3,660. Note that the child must be under the age of 18 or, if over the age of 18, must have been incapacitated before reaching 21 years of age or whilst still receiving full-time education.

Dependent relative credit

If you can prove that you maintain, at your own expense, a relative who cannot live independently (or a widowed mother whether incapacitated or not), you can claim a tax credit of €80 per year provided the relative's income does not exceed €12,745 per year.

Incapacitated person's allowance

An allowance of €50,000 is available to any taxpayer who is incapacitated and has to employ someone to look after them. The same allowance is available to any taxpayer who is employing someone to look after an incapacitated spouse. In fact, the allowance is available where a family employs a carer to look after a totally incapacitated person. Clearly, to take advantage of this allowance you need to have an income, and because it's an allowance (as opposed to a tax credit) the value of the benefit will be determined by your marginal – or top – rate of tax.

Blind person's credit

If you are blind, you can claim a tax credit of €1,830. If both you and your spouse are blind then you may both claim, bringing the total credit up to €3,660. An additional allowance of €825 is available to any blind person who uses a guide dog. This allowance is at marginal rate (up to 41%).

PAYE credit

If you pay tax by the PAYE system you're entitled to a PAYE credit of €1,830. If you're married, and both you and your spouse are on PAYE, then there is a doubled credit. However, you should bear in mind that you cannot claim the PAYE credit if you are the director of a company and control, either directly or indirectly, 15% or more of the shares. You can't claim it, either, if you employ (either as an individual or as a partner in a firm) your spouse.

Medical insurance

If you take out medical insurance, the premium you pay will already have been discounted by the standard rate of tax (currently 20%). The insurance company will receive this tax relief directly from the government so there is no need for you to make a separate claim. It is worth noting that you can enjoy this tax relief even if you don't pay tax!

Permanent health insurance

If you are worried about a drop in your income as a result of an accident or illness, and you take out permanent health insurance to protect you against this eventuality, your contributions will be tax deductible. Do note, however, that the amount of relief you can claim must not be more than 10% of your total income for the year of assessment. Do remember that any benefit you claim under a permanent health insurance policy will be liable to income tax.

Medical expenses relief

If you have to spend money on medical care, dental treatment or nursing, then you can claim tax relief at your marginal or top rate. You should note that:

- You can claim for yourself, your spouse or any other person for who you claim tax allowances.
- The allowance can be shared among a number of people so that if, for example, several children are paying for their parent to receive treatment, each can claim.
- You may even be able to claim the cost of travelling to and from the hospital or other treatment centre.
- When it comes to medical expenses most things are eligible for tax relief, from an ordinary visit to a doctor to hearing aids, and from physiotherapy to the cost of gluten-free food for cœliacs.
- Note that all expenses in relation to maternity care are fully allowable.

There are a few exceptions you should be aware of including routine dental treatment, having your eyes tested, and the purchase of spectacles or contact lenses.

Rent relief

If you're single and are a tenant paying rent for private rental accommodation, then you can claim a tax credit of €400. A married couple can claim €800 and a widowed person can also claim €800. If you are aged 55 or over then the amount of the credit increases to €800 for a single person and €1,600 for a married couple or a widowed person.

Relief for long-term unemployed people

If you have been unemployed for at least 12 months, and you then return to work, you will receive an additional personal allowance as well as a child tax allowance if, of course, you have one or more children.

The allowance lasts for three years, and the amounts are set out below:

	Personal tax allowance	Child tax allowance (for each qualifying child)
Year 1	€3,810	€1,270
Year 2	€2,540	€850
Year 3	€1,270	€425

Third-level college fees

The government give a very generous €3,175 of tax relief in respect of tuition fees paid either for yourself or for a dependent relative. The relief applies to tuition fees for full- and part-time undergraduate courses, a wide range of training courses, and many post-graduate courses. This relief is given at the standard rate and cannot be recouped by grants or scholarships. Whilst you can claim relief up to €5,000 the relief itself may not exceed the liability of the taxpayer.

Charitable donations

If you are self-employed (but not if you pay tax through the PAYE system) tax relief is available for any donations or gifts (minimum €250) made to charities or a wide range of not-for-profit organisations.

Trade union subscriptions

A tax credit at the standard rate of tax (20%) of €70 is available for trade union subscriptions.

Loan interest relief

If you're paying interest on a loan, you may be able to claim tax relief. Various types of loan are eligible, including:

- mortgages in relation to your main home
- bridging loans
- loans taken out for business purposes
- loans borrowed to pay death duties
- borrowings used to acquire shares in your own business.

With regard to mortgage interest relief, this is now granted 'at source' which, in plain English, means that your lender will claim it on your behalf and reduce your monthly payments accordingly. You should be aware that mortgage interest relief is available on money borrowed for the purchase, repair, development or improvement of your sole or main residence situated in Ireland or in the UK. You can also claim the relief if you have to borrow money to 'purchase a residence for a former or separated spouse or a dependent relative where the accommodation is being provided by you rent-free'. The amount of relief you can claim will be determined by your personal circumstances. If you're a first-time mortgage holder then you can claim 100% tax relief at the standard rate of tax (20%) for the first seven years of your mortgage, up to a limit of €20,000 for married couples or widow(er)s or €10,000 for a single person. If you are not a first-time mortgage holder, the amount is reduced to €6,000 for married couples or a widowed person, and €3,000 for a single person. The relief in relation to bridging loan interest comes into play if you buy a new home before you've sold your existing property.

	Single(€)	Widowed(€)	Married(€)
First mortgage			
Ceiling	10,000	20,000	20,000
Tax credit (1st seven years)	2,000	4,000	4,000
Others			
Ceiling	3,000	6,000	6,000
Tax credit (1st seven years)	600	1,200	1,200

Relief on deeds of covenant

If you make a legal commitment – known as a deed of covenant – to pay money for a period of time to someone who is aged 65 or over, or permanently incapacitated (providing the latter isn't to a son or daughter under 18) you will be able to claim the tax relief.

Pension contributions

If you're making payments into an approved personal pension scheme (here the word 'approved' refers to Revenue Commissioners' approval!), then income tax relief will be available to you at your marginal (top) rate of tax. The amount of relief is restricted to a percentage of your income. Unused allowances in any one year can be carried forward to the next. The percentage of your income that you're allowed to put, tax free, into a pension scheme increases as you get older. For 2009 it works as follows:

- If you're under the age of 30 you can put up to 15% of your income into your pension scheme tax free.
- If you're aged between 30 and 39 you can put 20%.
- If you're aged between 40 and 49 you can put 25%.
- If you're aged 50 and over you can put 30%.
- If you're aged 55 and over you can put 35%
- If you're aged 60 and over you can put 40%.

However, there is a cap of €275,239 on the income taken into account.

Service charges

Most of the service charges in relation to your home are eligible for tax relief at standard rate. This includes:

- charges imposed by your local authority for water, rubbish collection and/or sewage disposal
- any money you pay to an independent contractor for refuse collection
- the cost of water when arranged through a group water scheme.

If you're on PAYE, then it should be possible to arrange for your local authority to inform your tax office when they receive payment, so that it can be taken into account when calculating your income tax. If you're not on PAYE – or if your payments aren't being made to a local authority – then you'll have to keep your receipts and make a separate claim.

Investment relief

Two different forms of tax incentive are available to investors. The first is 'relief for investment in corporate trades' – known generally as BES. The second is a relief for investment in the film industry – known as Section 35 Investments. Note that BES relief was extended in the 2007 Budget to 2013, and that film industry relief will cease on 31 December 2012.

Seafarer's allowance

If you are a seafarer and you're away on a voyage for at least 161 days in a tax year, then you are eligible for a special allowance of €6,350. Do note, however, that this allowance can only be offset against seafaring employment.

24

PAYE
HOW TO MAKE THE PAY AS YOU
EARN (PAYE) TAX SYSTEM WORK IN YOUR FAVOUR

Just because you're in salaried employment and have your income tax deducted automatically using the **pay as you earn** (PAYE) system doesn't mean there aren't plenty of things you can do to keep your tax bill to a bare minimum. So, in addition to explaining how PAYE operates, this chapter also examines some of the tax-saving opportunities open to those who pay tax by this method.

THE INS AND OUTS OF **PAYE**

It is easy to understand why the Revenue Commissioners like the PAYE system. It allows them to collect tax as it falls due rather than once a year. But it does have two advantages for the taxpayer as well. Firstly, your employer and the Revenue Commissioners handle all the administration involved with your tax bill. If you were self-employed this could cost you thousands of Euros a year. Secondly, you don't have to worry about being faced with a tax bill every year.

PAYE is operated by employers in conjunction with the Revenue Commissioners. The system is simplicity itself:

- Your employer provides your details to the Revenue Commissioners.
- Before the beginning of each tax year (usually in December), the Revenue Commissioners issue a 'Notification of Determination of Tax Credits and Standard Rate Cut-off Point'. This sets out any tax credits due to you, details your rate or rates of tax, and incorporates something called your **standard rate cut-off point** which I'll explain further in a moment.
- Using the information supplied by the Revenue Commissioners, your

employer calculates how much tax to deduct from your salary.

So what is the standard rate cut-off point? Basically it's the amount of money you can earn at the standard rate – currently 20%. This is determined by your personal circumstances – whether you are married, single or widowed. You may also have allowances that are allowed at the higher rate of tax, such as a contribution to an approved pension scheme. Where this is the case, your standard rate cut-off rate will be higher.

The formula for working out PAYE is:

- The standard rate of tax (currently 20%) is applied to your gross pay up to the standard rate cut-off point for the period in question.
- Any income over and above that amount in the pay period is taxed at the higher rate (currently 41%).
- The tax payable at this point is referred to as the **gross tax payable**.
- Any tax credits you're entitled to are then deducted from the gross tax payable to arrive at the **net tax payable**.

This is probably best explained with a couple of real-life examples.

John earns €53,000 per annum and, being married, takes all the tax credits available as he pays all the bills, the mortgage and the little luxuries. This means that approx. €28,000 is tax free and the balance is at 20% equating to €5,000 tax liability together with PRSI of approx. €4,000 means that John's net income is approx. €44,000.

Patricia, his wife, earns €26,000 and, as she has no credits, has to pay PRSI and the higher tax rate of 41% on her entire salary. Therefore, her net income is approx. €13,000 or half of her salary.

MONEY DOCTOR WEALTH CHECK

It is in your interest to keep the taxperson up to date…

If the Revenue Commissioners don't have all your personal information, they may make a mistake regarding all the different sorts of tax credits and allowances to which you are entitled. You can use the information in the previous chapter to compile a list of credits and allowances that you believe you can claim, and you should then complete a **Form 12A** 'Application for a Certificate of Tax Credits and Standard Rate Cut-off Point' and send it to your tax office. This form is available on request or can be downloaded from www.revenue.ie When you receive your 'Notification of Determination of Tax Credits and Standard Rate Cut-off Point' double-check that it lists all the tax reliefs you wish to claim.

EMERGENCY TAX

If your employer doesn't have the information needed in order to calculate the correct amount of tax to deduct (a 'Notification of Determination of Tax Credits and Standard Rate Cut-off Point') you will automatically be put onto PAYE emergency tax. As emergency tax only incorporates minimal tax credits it is important, from your point of view, to contact your local tax office to resolve the situation.

GETTING YOUR TAX BACK! PAYE REFUNDS

There are various circumstances under which you may be entitled to a PAYE tax refund. For instance:

- If you become unemployed: in this situation you should write to your Inspector of Taxes and ask for a **Form P50**. You should complete and return this, along with Parts 2 and 3 of your **Form P45** (the form your last employer should have given to you prior to you leaving).

- If the Revenue Commissioners have made an error and overtaxed you due to some factor of which they were unaware.

After the end of the tax year (31 December), your employer should give you a **Form P60**, which sets out the amount you earned in that year together with any tax that has been deducted. Check this form in order to make sure that all the allowances, deductions and credits to which you are entitled have been claimed. If you believe there is an error you should advise your employer and your local Inspector of Taxes in order to request a refund.

MONEY DOCTOR WEALTH CHECK

Double-check you are claiming everything

Below is a list of all the tax credits and allowances you may be entitled to (full details are to be found earlier in this chapter). Why not take a moment or two to check through it now to make doubly sure that you aren't paying a cent more tax than you have to?

Tax credit	2008 (€)
Single person	1,830
Married person	3,660
Widowed person (w/o dependent children)	2,430
Widowed person (qualifying for one-parent family tax credit)	1,830
Widowed person (in year of bereavement)	3,660
One-parent family (widowed person)	1,830
One-parent family (other person)	1,830
Age tax credit (65 years plus & single/widowed)	325
Age tax credit (65 years plus & married)	650
Home carer's credit (max.)	900
Incapacitated child (max.)	3,660
Dependent relative (max.)	80
Employee's tax credit	1,830

MAKING SURE YOUR EXPENSES ARE TAX FREE

One of the areas in which the Revenue Commissioners are extremely strict is that of **expenses** paid to employees. What they don't want is a situation where employers are disguising a benefit (effectively extra salary) in the guise of a legitimate expense. The Revenue Commissioners' guidance rules say that any expense 'must have been wholly, exclusively and necessarily incurred for the purpose of performing the duties of your employment'. (What is interesting is that if you're self-employed the 'necessarily' criterion doesn't apply.)

So what is, and isn't, allowable? If you have to buy special equipment or clothing, for instance, it is unlikely that the Revenue will argue with your claim. By the same token, they are unlikely to take issue if you use a company-owned computer at home or claim part of your telephone bill when used for work calls. In general, what you can get away with – I mean, legitimately claim, of course, slip of the pen – will very much depend on the nature of your employment. For instance, if you work in a publishing company, any books you buy will almost certainly be allowable, as might trips to the theatre or cinema. If you're an engineer, this is unlikely to be the case!

If the Revenue Commissioners believe that you are making a claim for something that is not wholly, exclusively and necessarily incurred for the purpose of performing the duties of your employment, they will tax it! This tax is called **benefit in kind**. Your employer will be required to value the benefit and to stop tax and PRSI at source through the PAYE system. So, for example, if your employer were to send you away on a one-week holiday to recuperate from overwork, you would pay tax on the cost of that holiday as if you had been paid the extra salary.

Motor and travelling expenses

If you make a journey in your own car for business purposes, the money paid to you by your employer will not be taxable as a benefit in kind providing it does not exceed something referred to as the **civil service mileage rate**. If you are going to claim motoring expenses from your employer, you should keep a track of the journeys you make and the mileage actually incurred.

Sadly, you cannot claim for journeys between your home and work.

The amount you can claim under the civil service mileage rate rules varies according to whether or not you use your car in the normal course of your duties, or only occasionally. The current rates are set out in the table below:

Civil Service kilometre rates from 1 July 2008

Official Motor Travel in Calendar Year	Engine capacity up to 1,200cc (Cent/km)	Engine capacity 1,200cc to 1,500cc (Cent/km)	Engine capacity 1,501 cc and over (Cent/km)
Up to 6,437 km	52.16	61.67	78.76
6,438 and over	28.29	31.49	37.94

A chance to claim more

Some trade unions and professional bodies have negotiated special, higher, flat-rate motoring allowances for their members. For instance, teachers, nurses, journalists and building workers may all claim their special flat rate allowance tax free – without the Revenue Commissioners questioning it. It's worth checking with your own trade union or professional body to see if such an arrangement is in place.

OTHER TAX-FREE AND TAX-EFFICIENT PERKS

Below is a list of tax-free or tax-efficient benefits that it's possible for an employee to receive.

Daily and overnight allowances

If you're working away from home your employer can pay you a daily and/or an overnight allowance to cover the cost of any expenses you may incur, such as lunch, an evening meal, accommodation, and so forth. The amount you can receive tax free depends on your salary level. The more you earn, the more you can receive tax free. However, the longer you stay away the less you can receive. The current rates are set out in the chart below.

The Civil Service Subsistence Allowances have recently undergone a revision per Department of Finance Circular 27/2002. The revised rates, effective from 1 July 2008, are as follows:

Civil Service domestic subsistence rates from 1 July 2008

	Overnight Rates			Day rates	
Class of Allowances	Normal Rate	Reduced Rate	Detention Rate	10 hours or more	5–10 hours
A Class	€145.32	€133.97	€72.64	€44.81	€18.28
B Class	€143.58	€122.81	€71.82	€44.81	€18.28

Class	Salary
A	Excess €59,956
B	€31,159–€59,956

Free or inexpensive accommodation

If your job necessitates it, your employer can offer you rent-free or subsidised accommodation without any tax being incurred. Naturally, your residence has to be in part of your employer's business premises and there has to be a clear work-related reason for your needing to live there.

Staff entertainment

Your employer is allowed to entertain you at a reasonable cost without you incurring any benefit in kind.

Communal transport to your place of work

For instance, if your employer provides a **company bus** or **shared taxi** to bring you or from your place of employment, this is tax free.

Presents!

Your employer can give you **non-cash personal gifts** providing it isn't for some reason connected with your work. However, it could be because you are retiring.

Meals

Meals, whether free or subsidised, are entirely tax free if they're provided in a staff canteen. However, the facility has to be open to all the employees.

Lump sum payments

Lump sum payments for special reasons – such as redundancy, on account of an injury or disability, or relating to your pension scheme – may be totally exempt from tax depending on the amount and circumstances. Details relating to redundancy payments may be found in Chapter 33.

Educational fees

Any scholarship income or bursaries paid by your employer will be completely free of tax providing that the course is relevant to your employment.

Injury or disability payments

Payment made on account of an injury or disability will also usually be 100% tax free.

Work tools

Equipment, tools, or working clothes, or anything else required to fulfil your employment will not be taxed.

Pension scheme payments

If your employer contributes to an approved or statutory pension scheme, then those contributions are also tax free. For more details on this, see Chapter 20.

Life cover

The cost of providing you with life assurance cover is also tax free provided the amount of cover is no more than eight times your salary.

€250 bonus!

You are entitled to receive an annual, non-cash benefit of up to a value of €250 without paying a cent in tax. Many employers provide this in the form of a gift voucher, which gives the employee flexibility as to how to use it.

Health insurance

If your employer pays the cost of permanent health insurance for you, this is tax free.

Medical cover

Your employer can also pay for your VHI or other medical expenses insurance without you being taxed on the benefit unless you're a higher rate taxpayer (when you will have to pay tax at 41%).

Season tickets

Bus, train and Luas passes are tax free. Furthermore, the only condition is that they are monthly or annual transport passes, so they don't necessarily have to be used for work purposes.

Childcare

Crèche and childcare facilities, provided by your employer on a free or subsidised basis, will not be taxed providing that they are not privately owned.

Relocation expenses

All your home relocation expenses will be tax free providing you are being forced to move as a requirement of your job.

Sports and recreational facilities

Sports and recreational facilities – so long as they are located on an employer's own premises – can be enjoyed tax free by workers. This, of course, can include a company gym or health spa.

Mobile telephones

Your company-provided mobile telephone is tax free providing it can be justified on the basis of business use. This rule also applies to the provision of computers, and even broadband access at home.

Car parking

A free car-parking space will not be taxed either – potentially a very valuable benefit indeed if you happen to work in a city centre.

Exam payments

A cash award given to you in recognition of obtaining a qualification of relevance to your job will also be treated as tax free providing it is roughly equivalent to the expenses incurred in studying for the exam.

Membership fees

If you need to join any professional body by reason of your employment, then your subscription will be tax free.

Health screening

If your employer insists on you having a medical check-up it will be tax free.

Long-service presents

If you work for your company for at least 20 years they can buy you a present costing no more than €50 for each year of service, and it will be completely tax free, a potentially €1,000 tax-free gift.

Has your employer offered you an opportunity to buy shares?

An increasing number of employees are being offered an opportunity to buy shares – directly or indirectly – in their employer's company. The tax treatment of the various different types of share schemes varies. Some offer an opportunity to save tax and others don't. You should also note that some employee share schemes won't cost you anything to participate in, whereas others will require you to make an investment. As this is a complicated area I would always suggest taking professional advice before participating. However, to give you a general idea of the different types of scheme work I have outlined the seven (!) main options below together with a few guidance notes.

Approved profit share scheme. This is probably the most advantageous scheme from an employee's point of view, as it allows you to receive shares tax free up to an annual limit of €12,700 provided certain conditions are met. Basically, providing you hold the shares granted to you for at least three years, they will be entirely tax free.

Employee share ownership trusts (ESOTs). Employee share ownership trusts were created to run alongside company profit-sharing schemes and they work pretty much in the same way so far as the employee is concerned. One additional benefit, however, is that after ten years a one-off additional payment of €38,100 can be made.

Stock options. A stock option allows you the opportunity to purchase shares in your employer's company at a pre-set price, normally within a certain timeframe. The benefit arises if the price at which you can buy the shares is less than their market value. This does, of course, constitute a gain from your point of view, and such a gain would be taxable. Stock options are rarely tax efficient.

Share subscription schemes. If you purchase new shares in your employer's company and hold them for at least three years, then you will achieve a tax benefit. However, there is an upper limit on the amount of tax you can save and you will – of course – incur a risk, since the value of the shares you buy may fall during the period you hold them.

Save as you earn scheme (SAYE). Save as you earn (SAYE) is basically a scheme that allows you to purchase shares in your employer's company over a period of time, with the cost of those shares being deducted from your salary as it's paid. There is the potential for some tax savings here – though they are not enormous.

Share incentive schemes. Share incentive schemes and employee share purchase plans offer you an opportunity to buy shares in your employer's company, but do not normally attract much of a tax benefit.

The free gift of shares. If your employer gives shares to you, without charge, you will be liable to tax on the benefit of receiving them but you should escape PRSI.

All the different schemes outlined above have stringent conditions attached to them by the Revenue Commissioners, and I cannot over-emphasise the need to take professional advice.

REVENUE ONLINE SERVICE (ROS)

Finally, a point to note is that the Revenue in mid-2006 extended their Revenue Online Service (ROS) to be available to PAYE taxpayers. Once you have registered you can avail of a full suite of services, including viewing information on your Revenue record and submitting tax credit claims and incomes information. You can also carry out a range of transactions without the need to fully register for the service. To access the site and register go to http://www.ros.ie.

25

INCOME TAX FOR THE
SELF-EMPLOYED

HOW TO REDUCE YOUR INCOME TAX BILL
IF YOU WORK FOR YOURSELF

If you are self-employed – or thinking of becoming self-employed – then this chapter is essential reading. You will find out:

- how the tax system operates in relation to your earnings
- the different ways in which you can reduce your share of the tax burden
- how to avoid the unwanted attention of the Revenue whilst simultaneously making some worthwhile tax savings.

First things first

Perhaps it would be helpful to start by explaining the basic ground rules. Let's look at what is meant by the self-assessment system and preliminary tax.

SELF-ASSESSMENT SYSTEM

If you are a director in your family company or if you're in salaried employment (in other words on PAYE) but have income from other sources, you'll have to pay tax under the **self-assessment system**. Self-assessment means that you have to complete your own tax return, decide how much tax you owe, and pay it to the Revenue Commissioners at the specified time. You can, of course, get a professional accountant to do all of this for you.

The latest date by which you can complete your income tax return

(**Form 11**) for the Revenue Commissioner is 31 October following the year of assessment. In other words, your 2008 tax return must be submitted no later than 31 October 2009.

PRELIMINARY TAX

When you submit your income tax return you must also pay something called **preliminary tax**. Preliminary tax is the amount of income tax you think you're going to owe for the year in which you pay it. In other words, on 31 October 2009 your preliminary tax will be the amount of tax you think you'll owe for 2009. The amount you'll actually have to pay is the lower of either 90% of your final liability for 2009 or 100% of your liability for 2008. Let me give you an example:

> Supposing you had a good year last year, but are having a bad year this year. Last year you had to pay €10,000 tax, but this year you believe you only expect a liability of €1,000 tax. Your preliminary tax bill would, therefore, be 90% of this year's liability – or €900.

> Since your preliminary tax is only an estimate of the tax you owe you will, naturally, either have to pay the difference or ask for a refund. This is done at the same time. Supposing, for instance, you've paid €1,000 preliminary tax on 31 October 2008. Your final tax bill for the year, however, turned out to be €1,500. The €500 extra will fall due no later than the 31 October 2009.

In other words, on or before 31 October every year you submit a return and pay an amount on account plus the balance of the previous year's income tax. If you're owed money by the Revenue Commissioners from the previous year, then you are allowed to deduct it from the amount you're paying. This is known as **Pay and File**.

THE MYSTERY FACTOR!

As if this isn't all complicated enough, there is an added factor that makes it all even more confusing: *you can choose the dates of your financial year.* The tax year, of course, runs just like the calendar year, from 1 January to 31 December. However, the Revenue Commissioners will allow you to pick your own accounting period. So while your 2008 tax return could refer to the period 1 January 2008 to 31 December 2008, it could actually refer to the 12 months ending on 2 January 2008.

A quick aside about accounting dates

It may seem like a tiny detail to you – considering the enormity of being self-employed and running your own business – but your accounting date can have important implications. For instance, if you run a seasonal business you're unlikely to want your accounting period to end during a busy period. Also, whilst you can choose an accounting period that gives you the longest possible time to pay your tax, if you aren't good at putting money away to meet your tax liabilities all you're doing is postponing your problem and making it worse.

As hardly anyone starts a new business on 1 January, what many self-employed people do is submit their first set of accounts for a period of less than 12 months. For instance, if you started your business on 1 July you might submit your first set of accounts to cover the period 1 July to 31 December. Your second tax return would then run from 1 January the following year.

You are actually entitled to change your accounting period any time you want. However, this can trigger an additional tax charge so you need to think carefully before you do so.

MAKE YOUR PAYMENTS ON TIME... OR ELSE

The Revenue Commissioners do not take kindly to income tax returns being submitted late. They take a similar line if you fail to pay any tax you owe on the date it is due. Indeed, if you don't submit your tax return by 31 October the Revenue Commissioners will add a surcharge to your tax bill:

- a surcharge of 5% of any tax due can be imposed if you are up to two months late

- if you are more than two months late then the surcharge can rise to 10% of the tax due

- in addition to the surcharge, you will be charged interest at the rate of roughly 1% per month on any outstanding tax.

If you are going to have trouble making a tax payment, let the Revenue Commissioners know in good time. Remember, it is almost certainly cheaper to borrow the money from a bank than to suffer heavy late payment surcharges and interest.

Revenue Online Service (ROS)

The Revenue has a service 'Revenue On Line' known as 'ROS' which has been available to self-employed taxpayers for some time. Once registered for this service ROS enables you to view your own current position with Revenue for various taxes and levies, file tax returns and forms and make payments for these taxes online in a variety of ways.

The service is highly efficient and avoids the pitfalls of postal delays when returns are being sent close to the due date.

Furthermore, self-employed taxpayers filing their annual return (Form 11) through ROS are given an extra two weeks approximately after the 31 October deadline to pay and file. To qualify for the extension you must:

- File your return through ROS.

- Pay preliminary tax for the current year.

- Pay income tax balance due for previous year.

- Pay capital gains tax on gains arising from 1 January to 30 September in the current year.

To register for ROS go to http://www.ros.ie

MONEY DOCTOR WEALTH WARNING

Don't get on the wrong side of the Revenue

If you are self-employed or a company director, then the last thing you want is an investigation or audit by the Revenue Commissioners. You'll be pleased to discover, therefore, that it is possible to reduce your chances of being bothered by Revenue dramatically. All you have to do is follow a few very basic rules:

1   If your return is late then this increases the Revenue's interest in you. By the same token, make sure you pay the tax you owe on time.

2   Given that the Revenue Commissioners deal with every business in the country, they have a good idea about the sort of profits that you ought to be making. If you consistently appear to be making less than the industry average, they may decide to take a closer look.

3   A low salary or low drawings may make them suspicious as well. They'll be wondering if you're earning cash and not declaring it.

4   Incomplete returns. If your tax return has not been completed correctly, you are simply asking for trouble.

5   Discrepancies. The Revenue Commissioners are not idiots, and if there is a discrepancy between, say, your VAT return and your annual tax return, eyebrows will be raised and questions will be asked.

6   Erratic turnover figures. If your company or business seems to do well one year, and not the other, your inspector may decide to look a little closer.

7   Ownership by an offshore entity. If the Revenue Commissioners notice that your shareholders are located in a tax haven – or if they see that you are doing a lot of business with a tax haven – this is bound to set off alarm bells.

The basic rules are **stay on top of your paperwork** and **pay your tax on time**, and you are much, much less likely to suffer the bother and expense of a Revenue investigation.

DO YOU NEED TO REGISTER FOR VAT?

You only have to register for value added tax (VAT) if your sales are in excess of certain amounts. The amounts are:

- €37,500 per year if you provide services
- €75,000 per year if you provide goods.

Once you're registered for VAT you must charge it on all your invoices but – looking on the bright side – you can reclaim any VAT you pay out on business expenses (other than those for entertainment or motoring). Once registered, you will need to keep proper VAT records and complete a return every two months.

Don't forget your PRSI

If you are self-employed and your gross income exceeds €3,174 a year, you will have to pay PRSI contributions. For more information about PRSI see Chapter 5.

AND ANOTHER THING

If you are operating your self-employed business from home, remember that it is now also a business premises and that you should advise your insurance company. In most cases, this is unlikely to affect your insurance premium – but it is important that you are covered if equipment is stolen or damaged, or if a business visitor has an accident while on your premises.

Incidentally, if you do use your home as business premises, then you can claim some of the running costs as expenses against your annual tax bill. Do bear in mind, however, that if you pay yourself 'rent' this may have capital gains tax implications when you come to sell your home. This is because although there is no capital gains tax on a principal residence there could well be a liability on a business premises.

Self-employment comes in many forms

The term 'self-employed' refers specifically to people who are:

- in business as a 'sole trader'
- in partnership with one or more other people.

Many people who work for themselves actually do so as a 'contractor' working on a regular basis for someone else. You should be aware that if you work for an employer for more than eight hours a week you are entitled to a contract of employment. Such a contract would give you all sorts of benefits such as the right to holidays, the right not to be dismissed unfairly, minimum notice and so forth. On the other hand, as a contractor, you aren't protected under employment legislation and must – of course – make your own tax arrangements.

Many self-employed people find it is worth their while to form a limited company and to trade in this way. The advantages of running a limited company include:

- limited financial risk
- ability to make more generous pension contributions to your retirement fund
- possible tax benefits.

However, don't rush into forming a company without taking legal and accounting advice.

WORKING OUT YOUR PROFITS

When you are self-employed you pay income tax on what the Revenue Commissioners refer to as **taxable profits**. Your taxable profits are your gross income (the total amount you make) less any expenses which are allowed for income tax purposes. So, if you earn a total of €20,000 a year and have expenses of €5,000, you taxable profits will be €15,000 a year.

EXPENSES

So what expenses are allowable against your profits? In some ways it is actually easier to consider what expenses the Revenue Commissioners will definitely *not* allow:

- any money you spend which is not 'wholly and exclusively' for the purpose of your business. For example, if you buy a suit for work the Revenue Commissioners would say that it isn't 'wholly and exclusively' for business purposes. If you're considering any sort of major expenditure as part of your business, and you're not sure if it will be allowable, it's well worth checking with either the Revenue Commissioners or your accountant first

- entertainment. With the exception of entertaining your staff, the provision of accommodation, meals, or drink for your customers is *not* allowable. Indeed, if you take a client out to dinner not only will the expense be disallowed but you may also suffer benefit in kind tax yourself

- any sort of personal expenses

- money spent on improving your business premises. This said, money spent renewing or repairing your business premises is allowable.

So what *can* you claim? Let me give you an example. Imagine that you are a chef who has opened his or her own restaurant. Here are some of the expenses that you could legitimately claim against your profits:

- rent
- wages paid to employees
- interest paid on business loans
- other property expenses including electricity, gas, water, rubbish disposal, and so on
- furniture
- equipment for the kitchen
- linen, tableware, glasses, and related items
- travel, stationery, telecommunications, postage and advertising
- cookery books

- buying trips overseas to source produce not only for your restaurant but – perhaps – because you plan to go into the import and wholesale business
- ingredients
- uniforms for yourself and staff
- wine
- other beverages.

You might also argue that you needed to eat in your competitors' restaurants for research purposes. The real point is: if you can show you had to spend the money to run your business then it is almost certainly an allowable expense.

A WORD ABOUT CAPITAL EXPENDITURE

Many businesses require special plant, machinery or equipment. When you buy this, it is referred to as **capital expenditure**. Such expenditure will be allowed as a business expense. However, not all at once. Since December 2002, 12.5% of the cost is allowed as an expense each year. So if you spend, say, €1,000 on a photocopier you can claim €125 a year as a cost against your income for the following eight years. This is one of the reasons why many people who are self-employed opt to lease rather than purchase certain items.

OTHER TAX-SAVING POSSIBILITIES

There are a number of different ways in which someone who is self-employed can hope to reap a tax advantage. These include:

- claiming for business expenses that would be disallowed for someone who was employed
- by taking advantage of the special rules regarding pension plans
- by using the self-assessment system to delay the payment of tax.

In Appendix 3 I give 100 updated 'top tax tips', many of which relate to the self-employed and how to minimise your tax liability.

26

TAX AND PROPERTY

PROPERTY INVESTOR? HOW TO ENSURE YOU KEEP YOUR TAX BILL TO A MINIMUM

From a tax perspective, property is just about the most complicated investment you can make. Which is why I have devoted this short chapter to the subject. The reason it is complicated is that:

- If you make a profit on the rent, you will have to pay income tax.
- If you make a profit when you sell the property, you will have to pay capital gains tax.
- There are all sorts of expenses you can claim against your profits and it is important to make sure you claim all of them.

The benefits of investing in property are huge, especially if you have been a property investor since the early 1980s.

THE TAX ADVANTAGES OF PROPERTY INVESTMENT

There are several generous tax advantages to be had from property investment including:

- In the current climate of low capital gains tax, should you sell the property at a profit you will only have to pay tax at a rate of 20%.
- You can earn up to €10,000 a year in rent tax free from the letting of a room in your own principal private residence.
- All the normal personal allowances are available to you, if you haven't already used them against other income.
- The Revenue Commissioners will allow you to set a surprisingly wide range of expenses against your rental income, thus helping to keep your income tax bill to a minimum.

A WORD OF WARNING

It is worth bearing in mind that rental income is treated in the same way as self-employed income. As a result, it may have the effect of pushing you into the higher tax bracket (in other words, 41% tax plus 5% PRSI and levy). Many people wrongly believe that they will reduce their tax liability by holding property through a limited company. This is not the case, because:

- The rate of **corporation tax** on rental income is 25%.
- Undistributed investment and rental income in a **close company** is liable to a further tax charge of 20%. (A 'close' company is one that is controlled by five or fewer shareholders or is controlled by any number of shareholders who are directors.)
- The effective corporation tax rate can be as high as 40%.

TAX INCENTIVES

Over the last few years, there have been two property tax incentives you could have availed of:

1   Capital allowances in relation to **industrial buildings.** The term 'industrial buildings' includes not just factories but nursing homes, crèche facilities, and even – in certain cases – holiday cottages.

2   Tax incentives to **designated areas.** These designated areas are to be found in run-down parts of Cork, Dublin, Galway, Limerick and Waterford. The idea is to encourage urban renewal. The best known of these tax incentives was the 'Section 23' relief in respect of expenditure on the construction, conversion or refurbishment of residential property in certain inner-city areas.

'GENEROUS' EXPENSES

Below is a list of the expenses that can normally be deducted from your rental income for tax purposes:

- any rates you have to pay on the property
- any rent (such as ground rent) that you have to pay on the property
- interest paid on money borrowed to acquire or improve the premises. Note that there is no upper limit on this interest relief, and in this it differs from the mortgage interest relief you receive on your main residence
- the cost of anything you supply to your tenant that isn't covered by their rent. For instance, if you pay for the electric light in the hallways, or for the lawns to be mown, it is an allowable expense
- the cost of any maintenance, repairs, insurance or management fees
- a capital allowance of 12.5% a year on the value of any fixtures, fittings or furniture you have purchased specifically for the property. In plain English, this means that if you buy furniture for the flat you can write it off over an eight-year period.

Do note that where your costs exceed the income from your rental property, the loss you incur may only be offset against future rental income. In other words, you can't use a loss from property investment to reduce – say – the tax you pay on your monthly salary.

27

TAX AND THE COMPANY CAR

There was a time, in the distant past, when being provided with a company car was a genuine perk. Not only were there major tax advantages but also there was the additional benefit of not having to purchase, maintain or run a vehicle oneself. However, as the table below shows, it may not in fact be to your advantage any more to have a company car.

Civil Service motor kilometric rates from 1 July 2008

Official Motor Travel in a calendar year	Engine capacity		
	Up to 1,200cc (Cent/km)	1,200cc to 1,500cc (Cent/km)	1,501 cc and over (Cent/km)
Up to 6,437 km	52.16 cent	61.676 cent	78.76 cent
6,438 km and over	28.29 cent	31.49 cent	37.94 cent

Nowadays, however, company cars are liable to both PAYE and PRSI. The amount of tax you have to pay is linked to the value of the car and the amount of mileage you do. For instance, if you do less than 15,000 miles a year you will be taxed as if you had received a cash amount equivalent to 30% of the 'original market value' of the car supplied. This calculation does not change even if the car you drive is second hand. Keep in mind, though, that if you do a very high annual business mileage, the amount of tax drops substantially. For instance, if you do more than 30,000 miles a year you only have to pay the cash equivalent of 6% of the 'original market value'. Let's look at a real-life example:

Your company provides you with a car worth €30,000 and your business mileage is less than 15,000 a year. You will be taxed as if you had received 30% of €30,000 – in other words, €9,000 of extra salary a year. Assuming that you're paid monthly, you will be taxed on an extra €750 per month – in other words, one-twelfth of the €9,000 benefit you are considered to have received.

The cost of this can be brought down if you contribute towards the cost of the car and also pay for your own private fuel.

HOW TO SLASH THE COST OF YOUR BENEFIT IN KIND

It is possible to reduce your **benefit in kind** charge to a flat 20% providing the following conditions are met:

- You spend 70% or more of your time away from your place of work.
- Your annual business mileage is between 5,000 miles and 15,000 miles.
- Your average working week is more than 20 hours.

To have any hope of reducing your benefit in kind tax bill, it is very important that you maintain a logbook detailing all your business trips and make it available, if required, to your Inspector of Taxes.

Another clever way to cut your benefit in kind

If, for some reason, the car is not available to you for a period the amount of tax will be reduced. For instance, supposing you gave the car back to your employer for one month a year, you would reduce your tax liability by one-twelfth.

SHOULD YOU HAVE A COMPANY CAR AT ALL?

For many people, the benefit in kind tax is so high that it makes better sense to use their personal car for business and take a mileage allowance instead of a company car. One benefit of this is that if you only receive the civil service kilometric rates (see p. 268), any money paid to you by your employer will be completely free of tax.

If you're entitled to a company car, and forgo it, you may also find yourself better off. As the table below shows, this will be particularly true if you do a relatively low business mileage each year.

Car costing €20,000 and over 1500 cc

Kilometres per year	40,000	30,000	20,000	10,000	5,000
Depreciation	€6,500	€5,500	€4,000	€3,000	€3,000
Petrol	€8,000	€6,000	€4,000	€2,000	€1,000
Insurance	€1,000	€1,000	€1,000	€1,000	€1,000
Road tax	€350	€350	€350	€350	€350
Service/repairs	€2,000	€1,200	€750	€300	€300
Total running costs	€17,850	€14,050	€10,100	€6,650	€5,650
Mileage claims at civil service rates*	€17,803	€14,009	€10,215	€6,421	€3,938
Net running costs	€47	€41	€115	€229	€1,712
BIK **	€1,200	€2,400	€4,800	€6,000	€6,000

* First 6,437 miles at 78.76 cent per mile and balance at 37.94 cent per mile.
** Benefit in kind calculation.

Cost	Mileage	BIK %	BIK
€20,000	5,000	30	€6,000
€20,000	10,000	30	€6,000
€20,000	15,000	30	€6,000
€20,000	20,000	24	€4,800
€20,000	25,000	18	€3,600
€20,000	30,000	12	€2,400
€20,000	40,000	6	€1,200

100% TAX FREE MOTORING!

There is one way in which you can enjoy a company car with absolutely no tax liability whatsoever. Any car included in a **car pool** will be tax free providing all of the following conditions are met:

- The car is available for use (and is actually used) by more than one employee and isn't ordinarily used by any one such employee to the exclusion of the others.
- Private use by any employee is incidental to business use.
- The car is not normally kept overnight at, or in the vicinity of, any of the employees' homes.

Finally, if you work for your own company or are self-employed bear in mind the cost of running a 'business' car will be further reduced by capital allowances. As with other capital expenditure, you're allowed to write off the cost for tax purposes over a period of eight years. So if you purchased the car for €10,000, you can set an allowance of €1,250 per year against your tax bill.

28

CAPITAL GAINS TAX

DON'T PAY A PENNY MORE
CAPITAL GAINS TAX THAN YOU HAVE TO

Just because **capital gains tax** – at a flat rate of 20% – is much cheaper than it used to be (at its peak it was 40%) it doesn't follow that you want to pay any more of it than you have to.

Capital gains tax planning is not easy even though, ironically, the rules relating to it have been much simplified. Nevertheless, there are still some useful allowances and exemptions which do make it possible to reduce, delay, and – in some instances – completely avoid this tax. As you'll discover in this chapter.

HOW THE TAX WORKS

If you buy something for one price and then sell it at a higher price or, for that matter, give it away when it is worth more than you paid for it, then the Revenue Commissioners consider that you have made a 'capital gain' and may, therefore, be liable for tax.

MONEY DOCTOR WEALTH CHECK

Indexation relief

If you owned whatever you have sold prior to 31 December 2002 – good news – before 1 January 2003 something called **indexation relief** was applied to all possible gains and this has the effect of reducing tax liability. Indexation relief was, essentially, an allowance designed to take account of inflation. As such, it meant that only gains over and above the rate of inflation were liable for tax. You can still apply indexation relief to assets held prior to 31 December 2002.

BASIC CAPITAL GAINS TAX PLANNING

Below is a list of the main ways in which capital gains tax can be reduced or avoided:

- It may seem a bit dramatic, but if you **move abroad** prior to making a disposal of your assets (in other words selling them), you will not be liable for any Irish capital gains tax. The only exception to this is if you're selling Irish property or mineral/exploration rights. Obviously, you would want to be selling a fairly major asset to make it worth becoming non-resident. For further information about becoming non-resident see Chapter 31.

- The **first €1,270** made as a capital gain in each tax year is tax free.

- You do not have to pay capital gains tax from the **sale of your principal residence**, including up to 1 acre of land. However, if you sell your home for development, then you will be taxed on the profit attributed to the 'development value'.

- If you've **bought a home for a dependent** relative (this would include a relative who was unable to look after themselves, a widowed mother, and so forth) then any gain you make on the sale of the property would be free of tax.

- If you **give a house site** to a child who then builds his or her private residence on it, providing that site is not worth more than €254,000, no tax will be due.

- There is no capital gains tax on bonuses from **post office** or **state savings schemes**, or from the disposal of **government stocks**.

- You don't have to pay tax if you sell an asset with a 'predictable life' of less than 50 years – for instance, if you sold a car or a horse at a profit.

- If you **hand your business** (including a farm) to a member of your family on retirement, there will be no capital gains tax liability either. This is called 'retirement relief'.

- You can dispose of a 'moveable, tangible asset' worth €2,540 or less without paying capital gains tax.

- Capital gains tax is not applicable to any **winnings** from gambling, the lottery, or competitions.

- Any benefits from **life assurance** policies or **deferred annuities** are tax free.

- If you transfer something to your **spouse** there is no capital gains tax charge.

Incidentally, the retirement relief not only applies when you pass an asset to a member of your family. Providing you're aged over 55, and have owned the farm or business for more than five years, if you sell that farm or business for a sum that is less than €500,000 you won't have to pay capital gains tax. If you sell the asset for more than €500,000 you will pay a reduced level of capital gains tax.

ONE MORE USEFUL WAY TO REDUCE YOUR BILL

If you incur expenses relating to the item you are selling – or if you have improved it in some way – then you may be able to claim them against your tax bill.

For instance, supposing you purchased an investment property and added an extra bedroom to the attic. The cost of doing this could be deducted from the sale price, thus reducing your tax liability.

29

CAPITAL ACQUISITION TAX
DON'T ALLOW YOUR GIFTS AND INHERITANCES TO BE TAXED UNNECESSARILY

The purpose of capital acquisition tax is to tax gifts and inheritances – and the purpose of this chapter is to ensure that your gifts and inheritances aren't taxed unnecessarily!

There are two key ways to lessen the effect of capital acquisition tax (which operates at a flat rate of 20%):

1 Make sure that the value of what you're leaving or giving falls below the tax-free threshold that is available.

2 Make sure that what you're leaving or giving is excluded completely from the tax. As there is a long list of excluded benefits, this is not as hard as it may seem.

TAKE FULL ADVANTAGE OF THE TAX-FREE THRESHOLDS

There are all sorts of gifts and inheritances that the government feel it would be unfair to tax. Or, to be more accurate, they feel it would be unfair to tax them unless the amount involved was fairly substantial. What we are talking about here are gifts and inheritance made to members of your immediate family and other people who are close to you. The tax-free allowances that apply are referred to as tax-free thresholds. I am afraid the tax-free threshold system is not straightforward but I'll do my best to summarise its key features.

Essentially, there are three different groups. The first applies to your closest relatives, the second to your slightly more distant relatives, and the third to everyone else. The thresholds are personal to the recipient, not to the donor (known legally as the disponer). For instance, for the current year the total amount a child can receive as gifts and/or inheritances is €521,208 from a parent. So providing the amount a child inherits from either of his or her parents is beneath this figure, he or she will pay no tax on it. Where it gets complicated is in the case of – say – nieces and nephews, who may receive bequests from a number of uncles and aunts. Anyway, below are the current thresholds:

> **Group 1: Children.** €521,208 where the recipient is a child, or a minor grandchild of the benefactor, if the parent is dead. In some cases, this threshold can also apply to a parent, niece or nephew who has worked in a family business for a period of time. The threshold is also available if a parent receives an inheritance from a child. And foster children may also receive this amount providing they were maintained by and resided with the foster parent for a successive period of five years while under the age of 18.

> **Group 2: Close relatives.** €52,121 where the recipient is a brother, sister, niece, nephew or linear ancestor/descendant of the benefactor or where the gift is made by the child to the parent.

> **Group 3: Everyone else!** €26,060 in all other cases.

> In other words, as an individual you can receive €521,208 from a parent, a total of €52,121 from uncles and aunts, and an additional €26,060 from friends or other more distant relatives without incurring any tax.

The rates indicated apply up to the end of 2008. Current Revenue practice is to revise these rates upwards in line with inflation. Next revision of circa 3% is expected to be available in February 2009. We will publish the new rates on our website when available.

FIVE COMPLETELY TAX-FREE CATEGORIES

Five different categories of gift or inheritance are excluded completely for purposes of capital acquisition tax. They are:

1 Any gift or inheritance made **between spouses**.

2 Any inheritance received from a **deceased child** which was originally given to that child by one or other of their parents.

3 Up to **€3,000 worth of gifts or cash** in any single calendar year.

4 Irish government stock when given to a **non-Irish domiciled beneficiary**. There are conditions attached to this – the main one being that the person receiving it must hold it for at least six years after receiving it. The legal definition of 'non-Irish domiciled' is complicated, but essentially it means someone who wasn't born in Ireland or who hasn't married someone born in Ireland.

5 Your family home. Again, there are certain conditions. It should be your **principal private residence** (or the recipient's principal private residence); the recipient should have been living in the home for the three years prior to the transfer; and the recipient should not have an interest in any other residential property. Furthermore, the recipient mustn't sell the home for at least six years.

As you will see from the list above, with a bit of careful planning it is possible to take the main family home and other assets out of one's estate for inheritance tax purposes.

TWO USEFUL WAYS TO AVOID CAPITAL ACQUISITION TAX

Because the government knows it would be unfair to include **farms** and **business assets** in the capital acquisitions tax net, both can be given away or bequeathed with only minimal tax liability.

The rules are written so that someone who wished to reduce or avoid capital acquisition tax could, in fact, with a little foresight transfer their assets into either a business or a farm and see them escape tax. As you can imagine, the rules governing these two tax loopholes are complex, so I will only summarise them below. It would be unwise (to say the least) to attempt to take advantage of these tax breaks without consulting a professional accountant and/or solicitor.

Farms

With regard to farms, 'agricultural assets are valued at only 10% of their true market value when calculating a liability for capital acquisitions tax'. Farm assets, in this instance, include not just land but buildings, woodland, livestock, bloodstock, and machinery. The recipient of the farm must be a 'farmer', which means that at least 80% of his or her assets are farm assets. You must also hold onto the assets for at least ten years to avoid any claw-back of tax.

A farm may, of course, also be considered a family business, and the Revenue Commissioners very generously allow them to be taxed as such for capital acquisition tax purposes, if it means a lower tax bill in the hands of the recipient.

Businesses

So what are the rules regarding **business** assets? Once again, the primary condition is that the recipient must hold them for at least ten years *after* the transfer. The business itself must be Irish. Most businesses qualify, including property, unquoted shares, buildings, land, and even machinery. However, businesses whose 'sole or main business is dealing in land, shares, or securities' are not covered by this loophole. The transfer of a business by way of gift or inheritance is not entirely tax free under these circumstances, but the assets will be assessed at just 10% of their market value.

Incidentally, keep in mind that the person giving away or bequeathing either farm or business assets need not have owned them for very long. In the case of a gift it should be five years, but in the case of death it need be only two years.

30

LOVE, MARRIAGE AND LOWER TAXES

EXTRA TAX BENEFITS FOR THOSE WHO ARE MARRIED

Billy Connolly, one of my favourite comedians, famously said: 'Marriage is a wonderful invention, but, then again, so is a bicycle repair kit.' However, unlike a bicycle repair kit, marriage has some very tasty tax benefits attaching to it. And in this chapter I will explain how you can take advantage of them.

MARRIAGE BRINGS GREATER FLEXIBILITY

The first big benefit of being married is that you get to choose how you are taxed. The options open to you are:

Joint assessment. This means that you will be taxed as one unit and allowed some tax concessions not used by one spouse to be transferred to the other.

Separate assessment. This is very like joint assessment except that all the available allowances are split evenly between you and your spouse.

Single assessment. This is where you and your spouse decide to be treated as if you were two single people for tax purposes.

Why this flexibility of benefit? Basically, you can choose to be taxed in the way that will produce the greatest possible tax advantage given your personal circumstances.

Under joint assessment and separate assessment, some unused allowances can be passed between husband and wife. This is particularly beneficial in the case of a two-income couple where one spouse earns more than another. Under normal circumstances, the Revenue Commissioners will assume that you wish to be taxed under joint assessment, and will calculate your tax liability accordingly. However, it is worth checking that you are taking full advantage of all the allowances and tax credits open to you, as the Revenue Commissioners may not be fully aware of your financial situation.

> The only circumstances under which most people might wish to be taxed under the single assessment system is where they are separated.

What is interesting is that on a combined salary of, say, €55,000 a couple are likely to save over €1,000 by being taxed under the joint assessment system over and above what they would pay under the separate or single assessment system.

OTHER TAX CONCESSIONS MADE TO MARRIED COUPLES

A number of other generous tax concessions are made to married couples, including:

- Assets may be transferred between husband and wife without being subject to capital gains tax.
- Any capital losses made by one spouse may be used by the other spouse to reduce a capital gains tax bill.
- Any gifts or inheritances given by one spouse to another are completely free of capital acquisition tax.
- Any money received by yourself or your spouse from a life assurance policy (providing you or your spouse were the original beneficial owners) will be completely tax free.
- Married couples do not have to pay stamp duty when they transfer assets from one to another.

EVEN BETTER NEWS IF YOU'RE MARRIED AND SELF-EMPLOYED

If you are self-employed or run your own business, by employing your spouse, you may be able to save up to €5,250 a year in tax. To make this saving, the total amount of income you and your spouse earn each year must be at least €70,800. It doesn't, by the way, all have to come from your own business. Your spouse can earn up to €25,000 and you can still gain a tax benefit.

The reason why the tax saving can be made is the fact that a two-income family can take advantage of a €70,800 standard rate band as opposed to the €44,400 band available to a single-income family.

The best way to illustrate this is with a real example:

One income			Two incomes		
Income	€75,000		Income	€75,000	
€4,400 @ 20%	€8,880		€70,800 @ 20%	€14,160	
€30,600 @ 41%	€12,546		€4,200 @ 41%	€1,722	
Total tax before tax credits	€21,426		Total tax before tax credits	€15,882	
Tax credits			**Tax credits**		
Married person	€3,660		Married person	€3,660	
PAYE	€1,830	€5,490	PAYE	€1,830	€5,490
Tax payable		€15,936	Tax payable		€10,392
Tax saving €15,936 – €10,392 = €5,544					

MONEY DOCTOR WEALTH CHECK

Turn your children to a tax advantage

If you're self-employed, and if you have children, you may be able to avoid tax on up to €18,250 per child a year. This is because your children are entitled – like anybody else – to earn up to this sum every year free of tax. Of course, the child must actually be doing the work for which they are paid – and it may be necessary for you to register as an employer for PAYE and PRSI purposes – but given the tax saving this has to be worth it! Also, depending on the sort of business you run, PRSI may not be applicable.

31

TAX FOR THE EX-PAT

TAX PLANNING TIPS IF YOU'RE LIVING AND WORKING ABROAD

What happens to your tax position if you decide to live abroad? Much depends, of course, on where you go, what you do, and how long you're away. If, for instance, you move to a country with much lower rates of tax than we have here in Ireland you could make a substantial saving. Since there are over 130 different tax jurisdictions in the world, it's obviously beyond the scope of this book to look at all the different possibilities. However, in this chapter I can, at least, explain how your Irish tax situation will be affected by a move overseas.

IT'S ALL ABOUT RESIDENCY AND DOMICILE

Every country in the world has its own rules about whom it taxes and under what circumstances. In some countries it's all about whether you **reside** there for legal purposes. This may have absolutely nothing to do with the amount of time you actually spend in the country. For instance, you can be tax-resident in Malta (thus taking advantage of a very liberal tax regime) but not set foot on the island from one end of the year to the other. Other countries have more complicated rules that are not only linked to your residence but also to your **domicile**, a rather complicated legal concept. Put simply, it is considered to be *the country that you call your natural home*. When you're born you usually have the same domicile as your father. If you marry, or move abroad for a long time, then your domicile may change.

Here in Ireland your tax liability will be determined by *both* your resident status and your domicile. Just to make things more complex, we have *two* types of residence. You may be **ordinarily resident** or simply **resident**.

You will be viewed as being resident here for tax purposes in the current tax year if:

- You spend 183 days or more in the state.
- The combined number of days you spend here in the current tax year and the number of days you spent in the last tax year exceeds 280. In applying this two-year test, a period of less than 30 days spent in Ireland in a tax year will be ignored.

Incidentally, the term 'day' really refers to whether or not you were in the country on the stroke of midnight.

Once you've been in Ireland for three consecutive tax years you are considered to have become ordinarily resident. You stop becoming ordinarily resident in Ireland once you've left the country for three consecutive years.

What happens when you move abroad?

Assuming that you are resident, ordinarily resident, and domiciled in Ireland – what happens when you decide to move abroad on a permanent or, at least, long-term basis?

The year you leave Ireland you will still be considered resident. However, the year after your departure you will not be considered resident. Since this could lead to a very unfair situation – where you're taxed in two countries simultaneously – the law says that:

- As soon as you depart Ireland you may apply to be granted emigrant status, which means that your earnings outside Ireland after that date will be ignored for Irish tax purposes.

If you move to a country that has a double taxation agreement with Ireland, then you won't be expected to pay tax on the same money twice.

A money-back offer: tax rebates

If you leave a job in Ireland and move overseas to work, you may well be entitled to a tax rebate. In fact, you can claim a rebate going back for up to four years. The reason you get this rebate is that under the PAYE system your various tax credits and allowances are spread out over an entire year. Under these circumstances, if you leave your job and move abroad halfway through the year, you'll only ever see the benefit of half your tax allowances and credits. You won't, however, be given this rebate automatically, though you may apply for it before you've even left the country.

What is your tax status?

So, what is your tax status? There are four different possibilities:

1   If you are resident and domiciled in Ireland then you pay Irish tax including income tax on your Irish income and on your worldwide income.

2   If you are resident in Ireland but not domiciled here, and if you haven't lived here for at least three years (in other words you are not ordinarily resident in Ireland), then you pay Irish income tax on your Irish and UK income, and on any foreign income paid to you in Ireland. In other words, foreign income (unless it comes from the UK) that you don't deposit in an Irish bank or spend in Ireland escapes Irish tax.

3   If you are ordinarily resident in Ireland, but not resident here for a particular tax year, then your tax status changes dramatically. In theory you're liable to Irish income tax on your whole worldwide income. However, employment or income which you earn wholly abroad (plus an extra €3,810) will be ignored for tax purposes. Furthermore, you may be able to take advantage of double taxation agreements to further reduce your tax bill.

4   If you are not resident, or ordinarily resident – in other words, if you haven't lived in Ireland for at least three years – then your only liability to Irish tax is on Irish income.

Put in plain English, you have to live abroad for **one full tax year** in order to benefit from any income tax saving which may arise from living in a country with a lower income tax level. And you must stay out of

Ireland for at least three years to make sure that all your world-wide income (with the exception of your Irish income) is tax free in Ireland.

Your personal tax credits and reliefs

What happens to all your personal tax credits and allowances if you cease to be resident in Ireland? The answer will be determined by the source of your income, and your resident status.

Get professional help!

In the excitement of moving abroad, many people omit to take professional advice on their tax position, and end up with an unexpected tax bill or – just as bad – missing an opportunity to claim back tax they've already paid. The Money Doctor's advice to anybody moving abroad is get professional tax help sooner rather than later.

32

SPECIAL TAX ADVICE FOR FARMERS

We city folk have an idyllic view of farming life – sun-drenched fields, wholesome food, healthy lifestyle, happy people. There is all that, but there is also the everyday issue the farming community face that we all face – tax. Tax is and always has been a thorny issue from both sides of the fence. Some city folk may think that farmers don't pay enough and farmers might say that they should be given special status because of the importance of their role in Irish heritage – not to mention the produce they yield from Irish soil. Being married to a farmer's daughter, I tend to agree with the latter!

If you are a farmer, you need to consider a number of areas:

- income tax
- capital acquisitions tax

- capitals gains tax
- VAT
- stock relief
- compulsory disposal of livestock
- capital allowances
- milk quotas
- stamp duty
- farm consolidation relief
- leasing of farm land.

Let's look at them all in more detail now.

INCOME TAX

The Finance Act allows for a deferral of tax on FEOGA income. This is the European Agricultural Guidance and Guarantee Fund, support through funding from the Common Agricultural Policy. (FEOGA are the French initials!) However, you must meet certain conditions:

- You must be a farmer in receipt of payments under the EU single payments scheme for farmers and certain terminated FEOGA scheme payments in 2005.
- You must not be availing of farm averaging.

The provision allows payments received under terminated FEOGA schemes to be disregarded for tax purposes in 2005, and instead to be deemed to arise in three equal instalments in 2005, 2006, and 2007. If you cease to farm during this period, any untaxed payments will fall to be taxed in the year the farming stopped. Once agreed to go this route, it cannot be changed.

CAPITAL ACQUISITIONS TAX

A gift/inheritance of land, buildings and other agricultural property (e.g. machinery and livestock) may be reduced by 90% of its market value for gift/inheritance tax when received by a qualifying farmer as long as:

- the farmer is domiciled in Ireland
- 80% of the market value of the property after taking the gift/ inheritance consists of agricultural property.

However, do keep in mind that this relief is lost if the assets are disposed of within a six-year timeframe, without being replaced within one year of sale, or within a period of six years in the case of a sale or compulsory acquisition made on or after 25 March 2002. Make any claims for agricultural relief on **Form I.T.41**.

Gifts or inheritances of agricultural property qualify for **business relief** (where the relevant criteria are met) in circumstances where it fails to qualify for agricultural relief. This reduces the market value of the gift/inheritance by 90%. Again, business relief will be clawed back if the assets are disposed of within six years, without being replaced.

Before you receive a gift of farm assets, make sure that 80% of your personal assets are agricultural assets after you have received the gift.

CAPITAL GAINS TAX

Retirement relief means that a **disponer** (the person who is giving the legacy, generally the mother or father), can hand over land to a child without capital gains tax liability for that child. However, the conditions are:

- The disponer must be over 55 years of age.
- She or he must have used the business assets for at least ten years prior to handing over to the disponer's child.

You should also note these other key points:

- Periods of ownership of a deceased spouse may also be included.
- 'Child' includes anyone who has worked substantially on a full-time basis for five years before the handover.

- Where proceeds do not exceed €500,000, relief on the disposal can be given to an unconnected person. There is marginal relief exceeding this amount.

In addition, land that has been let for up to five years prior to a compulsory purchase order being made will qualify for retirement relief if it was used for farming for ten years prior to the letting.

Note that a farmer who participates in the EU 'Early retirement from farming scheme' by leasing the land qualifies for the relief. Therefore, while it is called 'retirement relief', you don't actually have to retire to qualify for this relief!

VAT

- A flat rate of 5.2% applies to supplies of agricultural goods or services.
- If you engage in any other services and your turnover exceeds €35,000 in a calendar year, normal VAT rates will apply – this includes the farming itself.
- Keep in mind that if you are a flat rate (5.2%) farmer, you can also reclaim this VAT on any expenditure incurred in the construction or improvement of farm buildings, farm structures, fencing, drainage and land reclaimation.
- VAT on farm vehicles (vans, pick-up trucks but not passenger vehicles) can also be reclaimed.
- VAT on diesel is also reclaimable.

STOCK RELIEF

Stock relief is a basic relief for first-time farmers (who meet certain required criteria) whereby they can reduce their taxable trading profit by 100% of the increase in their farming stock at the end of their trading year over their farming stock at the beginning of that year. The Finance Act 2006 extended this relief to 31 December 2008. The existing 25% general stock relief for farmers was also extended to this date.

COMPULSORY DISPOSAL OF LIVESTOCK

There is a special relief for farmers (individuals and companies) in respect of profits resulting from the **disposal of livestock** due to statutory disease-eradication measures.

You can have tax on profits spread over four consecutive annual instalments *after* the year in which the profits arise or spread equally over the four years including the year in which the profits arise.

This relief extends to all animals and poultry.

CAPITAL ALLOWANCES

Relief is available for farmers who have:

- incurred expenditure on necessary pollution-control measures
- who have a **Farm Nutrient Management** plan in place.

The maximum allowed is €63,500. This scheme has been extended to 31 December 2008 with the Finance Act 2005 shortening the write-off period to three years in respect of expenditure incurred after 1 January 2005.

MILK QUOTAS

Capital allowances are available to farmers incurred in purchasing a milk quota. The period for write-off is seven years – 15% for the first six years and 10% for the seventh year. Do note that capital allowances may be claimed by a farmer who leases a milk quota from a relative and who later purchases that quota.

STAMP DUTY

Essentially a tax on buying or transferring property or land, this duty payable is restricted to half for related bequests (e.g. giving your son your farm) but to young trained farmers this duty is nil. There are clawbacks whereby within five years of receiving a stamp duty relief, the proceeds of that disposal of the property are not reinvested within one year in other land.

FARM CONSOLIDATION RELIEF

This is another type of stamp duty relief for exchanging farm land between two farmers to consolidate each other's holding. There are a number of conditions attached to this relief and you should consult your accountant for more advice on this.

LEASING OF FARM LAND

If you are over 40 and you lease your farm land, you are eligible for income tax exemption subject to certain thresholds – bear in mind the lease income of the husband and wife are treated separately for the purpose of the relief, whether jointly assessed or not.

In January 2007, a new exemption of €20,000 per annum was introduced for leases of 10 years or more duration. This measure was subjected to clearance with the European Commission under state-aid rules.

PART 9

This section of the book offers advice and information relating to four highly sensitive subjects:

- *redundancy*
- *separation*
- *divorce*
- *the death of a loved one.*

In each of these situations, of course, the last thing you'll want to think about is money. And yet, unfortunately, each of these difficult experiences has important financial implications.

33

REDUNDANCY

TOP TIPS, INCLUDING ADVICE ON YOUR RIGHTS
SHOULD YOU EXPERIENCE REDUNDANCY

Whether you have opted for redundancy because of the financial benefits it offers you, or whether it was thrust upon you, it is vital that you know your rights and that you can make sure that you come out of it in as strong a financial position as possible. In this chapter I will explain your rights and offer general advice on making the most – from a money perspective – of the situation.

BACKGROUND BRIEFING ON 'REDUNDANCY'

The term 'redundancy' applies to a very specific situation, so the first thing you must do is find out whether or not you are covered by the relevant legislation. Essentially, in order to be eligible for a redundancy payment, you must:

- be aged between 16 and 66
- have been working for at least eight hours a week for your employer
- have at least 104 weeks (in other words, two years) of continuous service for the same employer.

Redundancy can only exist when an employee is dismissed because:

- The employer is no longer undertaking the business activity which necessitated employing you.
- The employer is moving the location of the business.
- The employer has decided to carry on business with fewer employees, or to carry out work in some different manner.

Voluntary redundancy – also known as 'voluntary parting' – is where an employer wants to lose members of staff and asks for volunteers for redundancy. If you do volunteer, you will automatically become entitled to a **statutory lump sum payment**. Note that employers must give you at least *two weeks' notice* before making you redundant, and notice must be given using the specific form – **Form RP1** – at that time.

HOW MUCH ARE YOU ENTITLED TO?

The law is very precise about the amount of money an employer must pay you if you are to be made redundant. It is calculated as follows:

- You should receive two weeks' pay for each year of employment continuous and reckonable between the ages of 16 and 66.
- You should also receive an equivalent of one week's normal pay.

However, there *is* an upper limit. No matter what your salary, one week's pay will never be more than €600.

WHAT HAPPENS IF THE EMPLOYER DOESN'T PAY UP?

There are many situations where employers either don't – or can't – make the lump sum redundancy payment. For instance, the employer may be inefficient, insolvent, or even dead. Under these circumstances, it may be possible to receive a payment from the government. To pursue this, contact the:

> Department of Enterprise,
> Trade and Employment
> Davitt House, Adelaide Road
> Dublin 2

or contact your local FÁS office.

WHAT'S THE TAX SITUATION?

Depending on your circumstances, and the amount of money being paid, your redundancy lump sum may or may not be liable to tax. It will be totally exempt from tax if the payment was made:

- under the Redundancy Payments Acts of 1987–1991
- as a result of injury or disability
- from an approved pension scheme.

Even if your lump sum isn't entirely tax free, you may be able to claim an extra tax-free amount. How much you can claim will be the highest of the three different exemptions outlined below. Where you are receiving a larger sum, it is likely to become taxable. Under these circumstances, you can either treat it as income in the year in which you receive it, and have it taxed as such, or else you can take advantage of something called top slicing relief, which works by calculating your average rate of tax for the five years prior to the tax year in which you received a lump sum.

Do note that it is often possible to reduce your tax bill on a redundancy lump sum by using it to make an additional voluntary contribution to a pension scheme (see Chapter 20).

CLAIMING TAX RELIEF ON A REDUNDANCY PAYMENT

You can claim tax relief under one of these three exemptions:

Basic exemption. You can receive up to €10,160 as a lump sum together with an additional €765 for each complete year of service without paying a cent of tax.

Increased exemption. The tax-free sum you are entitled to receive may be increased by €10,000 to a maximum of €20,160 (plus the additional €765 for each complete year of service) if you haven't made a claim for an increased exemption amount in the previous ten years, nor received a tax-free lump sum under an approved pension scheme.

Standard capital superannuation benefit (SCSB). This is a way for those with a long service record to receive a higher tax-free sum. The SCSB formula involves taking your average salary over the past three years, multiplying it by the number of years of service, dividing it by 15, and deducting any tax-free lump sum paid, or due, from a pension scheme.

Let me give you an example:

> Peter, aged 65, has given 44 years service to his company. His average salary over the last three years was €47,500. If you multiply this by 44 (the number of years service), you would get a total of €2,090,000. Then divide it by 15, giving you a total of €139,333.33 tax free.

THE MONEY DOCTOR SAYS...

- If you have been working for an employer for a sufficiently long period of time to entitle you to a redundancy payment, then there is no doubt in my mind that it's worth seeking professional help to ensure that you not only optimise that payment but that you pay the least possible amount of tax on the benefit.

34

SEPARATION

THE FINANCIAL CONSEQUENCES OF SEPARATION

Sadly, no book dealing with personal finances is complete without chapters covering separation and divorce. First of all, it's worth pointing out that from a legal perspective the breakdown of a marriage actually has three separate stages:

1 When a couple make the decision to live apart.

2 When a couple seek a legal separation.

3 When a couple seek a judicial separation.

In this chapter I will explain the consequences and issues surrounding a separation, and in the next chapter I will explain what happens as a result of a divorce.

The implications of living apart

Living separately from your husband or wife does not in any way alter the legal status of your marriage. For example, you don't automatically lose your Succession Act entitlements (see p. 302 for further details) if you are separated from your spouse. However, do note that if a spouse is found guilty of desertion or bad conduct, they might well be deemed by a court to have forfeited these rights.

What happens when you 'live apart'?

The financial effects of living apart can be summarised as follows:

- In the case of a temporary or short-term separation, there will be no alteration in the income tax situation and you can still elect for joint, separate or single assessment.

- If the separation is considered to be permanent, then the husband and wife will be assessed for income tax under the single assessment system. The only situation where this really alters is if there are legally enforceable maintenance payments being made. In some circumstances, these will be tax deductible to the payer, and taxable in the hands of the recipient; in other circumstances, they will be ignored for income tax purposes.

- With regard to capital gains tax, a temporary separation will make no change in either spouse's tax status. In the event of a permanent separation, any transfer of assets that are connected with the separation itself will remain capital gains tax free. However, other transfers will become taxable and unused capital gains tax losses will no longer be permitted.

- Couples who live apart continue to be exempt from capital acquisitions tax on the transfer of assets between each other.

- Life assurance proceeds continue to be tax free – providing the beneficiary was originally named in the policy as such.

Couples who are separated continue to enjoy exemption from stamp duty when transferring property between each other.

What happens when you get a 'legal separation'?

A **legal separation** (often referred to as a 'Deed of Separation') is a voluntary agreement made between a husband and wife who have decided to live apart on a permanent basis. Interestingly, it does not change the *legal* status of a marriage. Its purpose is really to resolve the key financial and, where relevant, child-custody arrangements. Under normal circumstances, a legal separation makes provision regarding two key financial matters:

- any maintenance payments to be made by one spouse for the benefit of the other spouse and/or their children
- any desired change regarding rights under the Succession Act 1965.

With regard to **Succession Act rights**, these only change if altered legally by the Deed of Separation. However, on becoming legally separated, many people alter their wills to account for the new circumstances.

From an **income tax** perspective, a legal separation is no different from a married couple simply deciding to live apart. Thus, if the separation is likely to be permanent and legally enforceable maintenance payments have been agreed, most couples decide to opt for separate assessment. If this happens, then **maintenance payments** are ignored for income tax purposes.

While the income tax situation may be relatively straightforward in the first year of separation, in subsequent years it may become slightly trickier. This is because a number of different factors come into play, including:

- voluntary maintenance payments, whether made to a spouse or for the benefit of a child
- legally enforceable maintenance payments, whether made to a spouse and/or child
- interest relief on mortgage repayments
- single-parent credits.

PRSI and **health levies** may be payable on maintenance payments, depending on whether the separated couple have opted for single or separate assessment.

Keep in mind that – in most circumstances – there is a **tax benefit** to legally enforceable maintenance payments. This is because they are tax deductible for the spouse paying them but will not, necessarily, be large enough for the recipient to have to pay tax on them.

The situation regarding capital gains tax, capital acquisition tax, and stamp duty do not alter if you become legally separated as opposed to simply living apart.

WHAT IS A JUDICIAL SEPARATION?

If a couple cannot agree to a legal separation, one of them may apply to the courts for a **judicial separation**. In this case, instead of a voluntary arrangement regarding the marital assets, maintenance and so on, the court will make a number of **Ancillary Orders**, which are legally enforceable.

From a financial perspective, there is little difference between a legal separation and a judicial separation. There is one area, however, where a judicial separation is more like a divorce, and this is with regard to **pension benefits**. Under the Family Law Act of 1995, if a judicial separation takes place, a spouse's pension benefits will be treated in one of three different ways:

1   **Earmarking** may occur. This means that when a pension becomes payable, a share of it is earmarked for the other spouse.

2   **Pension-splitting** results in the pension benefits being split on a pre-set formula between the two spouses.

3   **Off-setting** whereby the spouse with pension rights may be entitled to keep them in exchange for something else. For instance, the spouse with pension rights might give up all entitlement to a family home.

Keep in mind that a decree of judicial separation does *not* affect the legal status of a marriage – it merely means that a husband and wife no longer have to live together. The key difference between a judicial separation and a divorce is that a judicial separation will not allow either party to re-marry.

THE MONEY DOCTOR SAYS...

- Sadly, many separating couples take legal but not financial advice. I strongly recommend a thorough review of your finances both before and after separation.

- You should consider every aspect of your finances – life cover, income protection, critical illness cover, borrowings, savings, investments and (especially) pension plans.

- Given that after a separation both parties are likely to be managing on a lower income, it is also important to work out a new monthly budget.

35

DIVORCE

Although a great deal has been written about the legal, emotional, religious, moral and logistical aspects of divorce, there are very few sources of reference relating to the *financial* consequences of ending a marriage.

The financial consequences will, of course, vary considerably depending on a variety of factors including:

- each partner's age

- the income of each partner
- whether or not there are any children
- whether or not there is a family home
- other joint and individually held assets
- the pension entitlements for each partner
- the health of each partner
- whether or not any life assurance is in place for one or other partner
- whether or not they both live in Ireland.

Decisions over whether or not the family home should be be sold, or concerning maintenance payments are legal rather than financial and, therefore, outside the scope of this book.

If you are divorced, whatever settlement was reached – whether voluntary or decided by the courts – you need to now re-consider and review your financial planning.

In this chapter then I look at the key issues facing a newly divorced person, and I make a number of specific suggestions relating to your personal finances.

THE IMPORTANCE OF BUDGETING

There is no doubt that divorce is expensive. Leaving aside the legal costs, both husband and wife are likely to find themselves now having to fund two homes where, previously, they only had to pay for one. By the same token, other assets are likely to be depleted:

- Extra life cover may become necessary.
- All sorts of living expenses will increase.
- You may be required to start or increase retirement savings.

In addition, the emotional strain of divorce is often such that people become somewhat reckless about their spending and borrowing habits. If you do find yourself in this unfortunate position, my advice is that – at the earliest possible moment – you sit down and work out a **new budget**.

If you would like assistance with this, I would refer you to my website (www.moneydoctor.ie) where you will find a free, online monthly budget planner.

HOW YOUR SITUATION WILL HAVE CHANGED

Once you are legally divorced, your financial position in relation to succession, tax, pensions, insurance and social welfare will all have changed:

- Your **succession rights** will automatically be lost. However, if you have made any specific bequests in your will to your former spouse, they will stand unless you change your will or make a new one.

- In terms of **income tax** your position is broadly the same as if you were simply legally separated (see Chapter 34). The main thing to remember is that if there are legally enforceable maintenance payments then you can usually opt to be taxed either under the single assessment or separate assessment systems. Under the single assessment system, maintenance payments are tax deductible for the person paying them, and taxable for the person receiving them. If you decide to be taxed under the separate assessment system, then maintenance payments will be ignored for income tax purposes.

- Any transfer in assets that is made because of the divorce will be **capital gains tax** free. Do note however that after that point transfers will no longer be exempt from capital gains tax.

- Any transfer of assets or gifts that take place as a result of the divorce settlement are exempt from **capital acquisition tax**. As with capital gains tax, once you are divorced, the spouse exemption for capital acquisitions tax no longer applies.

MAKING PROPER PENSION PROVISION

Pension rights can be a very important part of the financial arrangements resulting from a divorce. Indeed, for many married couples, their pension rights can be as valuable, if not more valuable, than the family home. For this reason, I advise you strongly to take expert advice when you separate.

In fact, the law recognises the vital importance and value of pension rights – as a result, spouses are *not allowed* to arrange a **pension adjustment order** between themselves. Only a court of law has the right to decide what happens to pension rights after a couple separate or divorce.

Deciding on the value of the pension is not easy. It will depend on the beneficiary's salary, type of pension scheme, level of contributions, prescribed benefits, years of service, and scheme performance.

A court will not necessarily make any decision regarding pensions if it believes that the rest of the agreed settlement is fair to both parties. However, there are three things concerning pension benefits that divorcing couples should be aware of:

1   A court can make orders about the pension benefits of either spouse.

2   Normally any decisions about pensions will be made at the time of the divorce, but if this doesn't happen either spouse can go back to court for a **pension adjustment order** at any time during the lifetime of the pension scheme member.

3   A court can order that part of a pension is paid to either a spouse or to a dependent child.

THE MONEY DOCTOR SAYS...

If you are getting divorced, do not rely solely on the services of a solicitor – call in one or more financial professionals to help with financial planning, tax planning and pension planning. I cannot stress how important it is to do this at the earliest possible opportunity.

36

COPING WITH BEREAVEMENT

WHAT TO DO ABOUT THE MONEY SIDE OF THINGS WHEN SOMEONE CLOSE DIES

When somebody close to you dies, tax and other financial matters are obviously the last thing on your mind. If there are dependants involved, however, it may be necessary to tackle such matters with a degree of urgency. Even if dependants aren't involved, there is a legal obligation for the personal representative to carry out certain responsibilities within a reasonable period of time.

Making and executing a will, especially after purchasing a property, is probably the most important legal task a person should perform. Despite that fact, very few people during their lifetime actually execute a will. Many of us have a psychological or emotional difficulty addressing thoughts of a will, or with meeting a solicitor or other persons to instruct the drafting of a will and then executing it. These aversions are very understandable as nothing can be as stressful or as morbid as planning for one's own death. However, as anybody who has been touched by bereavement knows, creating a will during one's lifetime will in fact minimise the grief and distress felt by surviving relatives.

A will also guarantees that the affairs of a deceased person will be dispensed with and distributed far more urgently than someone who dies either without having made a will (intestate) or with an invalid will, thereby minimising stress for surviving loved ones.

A SHORT LIST OF DEFINITIONS

Below you'll find a plain English definition of the different legal terms and expressions that are used to sort out the affairs of someone who has died.

The administrator. Where the deceased hasn't appointed a personal representative (in his or her will), the person looking after the financial situation is known as an administrator.

The beneficiary. A beneficiary is someone who inherits either part or the whole of the deceased's estate.

The deceased. The 'deceased' refers to the person who has died.

The estate. The 'estate', or the 'deceased's estate' is made up of all the assets that the deceased person owned. This includes bank accounts, property, jewellery, stocks and shares, furniture, and so on.

The executor. If the deceased has written a will, he or she will have appointed an executor to ensure that his or her wishes are carried out. Many people appoint several executors, and it is normal for the personal representative to be one of them.

Intestate. If the deceased did not write a will, they are said to have died 'intestate'. The word 'intestacy' refers to the situation where no will exists. What happens to the assets where there is no will is set out in the 1965 Succession Act.

The personal representative. The personal representative is the person ultimately responsible for sorting out and finalising the deceased's affairs.

The Succession Act. This piece of legislation sets down the requirements for a valid will. Under Irish law, a spouse and children are legally entitled to a certain share in the property of a deceased parent or spouse – whether a will has been made or not. As it currently stands, if there are children then the spouse's share, by legal right, is at least one-third of the estate. Where there are no children, the spouse is entitled to at least one-half of the estate.

The trustee. If there is some reason why some or all of the deceased's assets cannot be distributed immediately to the beneficiaries, then the will may provide for certain assets or property to be held 'in trust'. This situation might arise, for example, if the deceased was leaving something to someone who was under the age of 18. The person whose responsibility it is to look after such property or assets is called the trustee. Many people appoint more than one trustee in their will.

The will. This is the legal document in which the deceased set out his or her wishes regarding his or her assets.

WHEN THERE IS A WILL

If there is a valid will, the following rules apply:

- On the death of a married person with no children, their surviving spouse is entitled to one-half of the deceased's estate.
- On the death of a married person with children, their surviving spouse is entitled to a one-third of the deceased's estate.
- The spouse is legally entitled to the appropriate share, regardless of the actual terms of the will. The fact that the parties may have lived apart for many years does not of itself affect their entitlements under the Act.

WHEN THERE IS NO WILL OR NO VALID WILL

In these circumstances, under the Succession Act 1965, the following rules apply:

- On the death of a married person with no children, the surviving spouse is entitled to the entire of the deceased's estate.
- On the death of a married person with children, their surviving spouse is entitled to two-thirds of the deceased's estate and their children are entitled to the remaining one-third.
- If a single person or widowed person passes away without having made a valid will, their next of kin will be entitled to inherit their estate as outlined in the Succession Act 1965.

THE RIGHT OF THE SPOUSE TO INHERIT

A spouse, i.e. somebody who is legally married to another person, is entitled to share in the estate of that person on death regardless of the will made by that person prior to their death.

If a person has made a will and passes away, regardless of what is mentioned in that will (e.g. entire estate left to a third party), the spouse is entitled to one-half of the deceased's estate if there are no children.

If a person has died having made a will with a spouse and children, the spouse is entitled to one-third of the deceased's estate.

The spouse is also entitled to a portion for their own benefit of the family home, namely the place where the husband and wife normally resided prior to the death of a spouse.

However, note that the right to apportion the family home should not exceed the legal right share (i.e., one-half if there are no children; one-third if there are children of the spouse to share in the estate of the deceased).

In order to explain this element of the law more clearly, it may be useful to give an example:

> Mr and Mrs Murphy are legally married. Mr Murphy makes a will. They have no children and live in a house which is registered in Mr Murphy's sole name.
>
> Mr Murphy dies and when his will is read it appears that under his will he has left everything to charity.
>
> The value of Mr Murphy's estate is €2m. Regardless of the will of Mr Murphy, his spouse is entitled to:

- The family home *and*
- One-half of the share of Mr Murphy's estate to include the family home.

If in this example, Mr and Mrs Murphy had children but the facts were exactly the same, Mrs Murphy would be entitled to only one-third of the value of the estate (to include the family home).

Status of children under a will

If a party dies leaving children and no surviving spouse, these children will be deemed to be the next of kin of the deceased and entitled to share in the estate of the deceased.

However, they are only entitled to share in the estate of the deceased because they are the next of kin of the deceased for legal purposes.

It is a common misconception that an individual has an obligation to their children to leave a portion of their estate to them. Unlike a wife or husband (spouse), children over the age of eighteen have no right to share in the estate of their parents and rank as a beneficiary to the estate of a parent purely in their position as next of kin.

A child (again over the age of 18) of a deceased person who has been disinherited in a will may challenge this will in the courts on very strict legal grounds to the extent that the parent **failed during their lifetime to make proper provision for the child**.

Just because a child has a right to challenge the will of a parent, this does not mean that the parent has an obligation under law to leave anything to that child in their will. Irish children beware!

Confusion often arises because spouses have certain rights in the estate of a deceased person by virtue of the fact that they were married to the deceased, plus the fact that children often share in the estates of deceased persons not because they are children, but because they are legally the next of kin of the deceased. In other words, a party may make a will during their lifetime wherein they endeavour to disinherit their spouse and children. Once he or she has passed away, the spouse has an automatic right to share in the estate despite what is in the will but the children do not have such automatic right. However, if a party dies without making a will, the children may share in the estate of the deceased person by virtue of the fact that they *are* the next of kin.

Non-marital children

The status of children born to an individual outside marriage is exactly the same as children born inside marriage.

For example, a couple may have never married but have three children. If this individual does not make a will and passes away, the partner will not be entitled to any share in the estate of the deceased but rather the children as next of kin will be entitled to a share. In this example, if the deceased had made a will leaving everything to the surviving partner and the children over the age of eighteen, the children have no right to share in the estate of the parent who has passed away.

The matter becomes even more complicated in the following example:

A married couple have three children. One party to the marriage has a fourth child *outside of the marriage* with another party. This parent passes away without making a will: all four children as next of kin are entitled to a proportionate share in the estate of the deceased parent.

Non-marital relationships

Non-marital partners have no right to share in the estate of a deceased partner. For example, a man and woman may have lived together all their lives as husband and wife (often referred to as a common law wife or husband) and the male partner passes away without having made a will. The surviving partner has no right to share in the estate of the deceased and the estate will be inherited by the next of kin of the deceased person, e.g. parents, brother or perhaps even children.

Accordingly, one can envisage the situation whereby a man and woman live together as husband and wife for thirty years and have three children but never marry. One party to the relationship passes away without having made a will and the surviving party is entitled to no benefit in the estate of the deceased. Instead, the estate passes to the children of the couple as the next of kin, legally speaking, of the deceased person.

THE ROLE OF THE PERSONAL REPRESENTATIVE

When someone dies, it usually becomes clear fairly quickly whether he or she has left a will. If they have, then this will list one or more executors, one of whom will be appointed as the **personal representative** of the deceased.

If a personal representative has not been appointed in the will, or no valid will is in existence, then the courts will appoint an administrator to act as a personal representative (usually the next of kin).

It is the personal representative's or administrator's responsibility to finalise the deceased's affairs. The administrator or executor is usually referred to as the personal representative. The personal representative should within a reasonable period of time collect the deceased's assets, pay any debts and distribute the remaining assets to the beneficiaries.

Obtaining the Grant of Representation

The primary obligation of the personal representative is to obtain a **Grant of Representation**. If somebody has died with a will, they will be entitled to a **Grant of Probate** and if somebody has died intestate (without a will) they will be granted a **Grant of Representation**.

The grant is made by the Probate Office which is an office of the High Court. If the application is made for the grant in Dublin, one applies to the Probate Office in the Four Courts. Outside of Dublin, every County Hall or Registrar will have a Probate Office. Only somebody with a valid will may apply for probate. If somebody has died with an invalid will or no will, the personal representative applies for administration rights called **Letters of Administration.**

Commonly, regardless of the status of the will and the estate of the deceased person, somebody is said *to apply for Probate* even if they are applying for a **Grant of Administration.**

The Grant of Representation (i.e., Grant of Probate or Letters of Administration) is an Order from the High Court which allows the party to whom the grant is issued to deal with the affairs of the deceased person. It is effectively a Court Order or an authority from the Court for this person to step into the shoes of the deceased person and carry out the wishes of the deceased person if there is a will or alternatively, deal with the estate as per the law of the land if there is no will.

A Grant of Representation allows the personal representative to execute documents for the sale of property, the lease of property and the remortgage of same, for the transfer of property to other members of the family who may inherit under the will or the law, to close bank accounts, transfer money and discharge debts.

In order to obtain the grant, clearance must be sought from the Revenue Commissioners.

The importance of notifying the tax office

Prior to obtaining the Grant of Representation from the Probate Office, the Personal Representative must settle the deceased's **tax affairs**. Furthermore, before financial institutions can release money, the personal representative must apply to the Capital Taxes Office of the Revenue Commissioners for something called a **Letter of Clearance** – effectively stating that all taxes have been paid to date or are in the process of being paid. Without this Letter of Clearance from the Revenue Commissioners, banks, building societies, credit unions, insurance companies and other financial institutions are prohibited by law from releasing any monies other than those:

- held in a current account lodged or
- deposited in the joint names of the deceased and another person or persons.

The only exception to this is money that is being held in the joint names of the deceased and his or her surviving spouse.

Furthermore, the application to the Revenue Commissioners will also contain details of the beneficiaries to the estate of the deceased person.

A Personal Representative must obtain a Grant from the Probate Office to deal with the affairs of the deceased person. The Probate Office will not release such a Grant until such time as the **Tax Clearance Certificate** or **Letter of Clearance** from the Revenue Commissioners has been delivered which does not just address the tax affairs of the deceased but also the tax affairs of the beneficiaries to the estate.

What the personal representative could be liable for

If the personal representative makes payments or passes assets to the beneficiaries of the estate without paying any outstanding tax liabilities, he or she will be liable to pay the tax out of his or her own pocket. By the same token if, as personal representative, you fail to claim a tax rebate due to the deceased then the beneficiaries will be entitled to come after you for this money.

If the deceased was an employee, there may be a PAYE tax rebate due. This can be arranged by asking the deceased's employer to send a **Form P45** to the tax office. If, on the other hand, the deceased was self-employed, you will need to file an outstanding income tax return and business accounts to the deceased's tax office. Don't forget that you may also need to deal with outstanding VAT and PRSI matters.

Before the Probate Office can process the application for the Grant of Representation, they will require a certified **Revenue Affidavit** from the Capital Taxes Office. It is the responsibility of the personal representative to provide the Revenue Commissioners with a Revenue Affidavit. The Revenue Affidavit requires the personal representative to supply:

- full details of the deceased's assets and liabilities
- information about assets passing outside of the will
- details of the beneficiaries and the value of the benefits taken.

How the assets are passed on

The deceased's assets will be passed on to the beneficiaries in one of three different ways:

1 Assets left by will pass to the beneficiaries in accordance with the terms of the will.

2   If there is no will, assets that would otherwise have passed by will
    instead pass by special laws laid down by law.

3   Assets may also pass outside of the will or intestacy.

The benefits of Joint Ownership

Regardless of the law in relationship to intestacy or the will drafted by an
individual, the **Rule of Joint Ownership** is extremely important. Joint
Ownership effectively takes precedence over either the law or the will.

Under law, two parties or more can own property in two ways. They can
own it as **Tenants in Common** or by **Joint Tenancy**. I do not propose to
set out in depth details of the differences between Joint Tenancy and
Tenants in Common as this is a very particular legal issue, but it is
important that the concept be understood – particularly in relation to
any post-death planning.

When two parties or more are said to own property as Tenants in
Common, they are said to own shares in that property. For example:

> Mr Murphy and Mr Smith buy a house as Tenants in Common.
> They own a half share each. On the death of either person, their
> share is passed on to that person's *devisees* or heirs, either by will or by
> *intestate succession.*

If in our example given above, Mr Murphy and Mr Smith buy a
property and own the same as **joint tenants**, they do not own shares in
the property but rather they own the property jointly.

If Mr Smith was to die, Mr Murphy would be the surviving/remaining
owner of the property and would be deemed to automatically inherit the
property. If, for example, Mr Murphy, Mr Smith and Mr Jones were to
purchase a property as **joint owners** and Mr Smith was to pass away, Mr
Murphy and Mr Jones would be the surviving joint owners. If Mr Jones
was then to pass away Mr Murphy would be the remaining owner of the
property.

The relevance of Joint Ownership is extremely pertinent, particularly in
relation to family financial planning. If a husband and wife have bank

accounts in joint names they do not own shares in this bank account but rather they own the bank account jointly. If the husband or wife pass away, the surviving spouse is said to be the surviving or remaining owner of the property i.e. the bank account.

The same concept applies to all property, including the family home. If a family home is held in joint names, neither the husband nor wife own a share of the property but rather own the property jointly. If one party passes away the other is deemed to be the surviving owner of the property.

Regardless of the law or any will made, if property is held jointly it cannot be severed.

How is it that assets can pass outside of the will or intestacy?

This is best explained by an example. The deceased may have taken out a life insurance policy or pension scheme where the beneficiaries have been named. Under these circumstances, the insurance or pension company would pay the beneficiaries direct without any reference to the will or estate.

THE MONEY DOCTOR SAYS...

- Sorting out the financial dealings of someone who has passed on is an emotional business. Help whoever will be looking after your affairs by making a proper will and keeping a file somewhere containing all your financial documents.

- Many parties believe that there is no necessity to make a will as they are happy to allow their spouse or their next of kin inherit as per the Succession Act Rules. However, a will should *always* be made – this means that the estate is distributed more quickly and also distributed in accordance with your wishes – there may be relatives, next of kin or bequests you may want to acknowledge. Remember it is also a simple process – you will need two independent witnesses (who cannot gain from the will) and a nominated person to execute your wishes (executor/executrix), then date the will and sign it.

- It is extremely important if you are involved in a non-marital relationship to ensure that you have proper wills drafted to ensure inheritance for your surviving partner and your or their children.

- It is also important to take professional and perhaps legal advice in relation to the drafting and execution of a will especially where there are complications. Many homemade wills can be ineffective and can often lead to further confusion after death. Remember the bulk of wealth in Ireland is in property – to convey the transfer of ownership, a solicitor will be required to effect same.

- One other reason for making a will is you can direct who is your Personal Representative and who is charged with the responsibility of dealing with your affairs after your death. This way, you will avoid any application to the Courts to appoint somebody who is inappropriate for that purpose.

- Many people apply to the Revenue Commissioners and the Probate Office to be appointed as the Personal Representative of the deceased themselves. Both the Revenue Commissioners and the Probate Office are extremely co-operative when dealing with members of the public. Again, depending on the complexity of the estate, legal accounting and financial advice should be sought prior to contact with these offices.

- Ensure that all family and marital property is held jointly, including the family home – it is better for all concerned.

- If involved in a non-marital relationship, both partners should ensure that all property is held *jointly* as the death of one partner will ensure the other partner inherits, which is denied under law or via the will.

Appendix 1

LEARN TO SPEAK
THE LANGUAGE

A QUICK GUIDE TO THE MOST IMPORTANT 'PERSONAL FINANCE' TERMINOLOGY

One of the first things about finance that puts people off is the *language*. The moment an expert starts to bandy around terms like 'dividend', 'yield', 'compound interest' and 'net present value' it can all start to sound very intimidating.

Like every other area of life, finance has a specialised language. It has its own jargon. Jargon is actually very useful – we need precise terms that are clearly defined so that there is no confusion about what is being said. On the other hand, if you don't understand what the jargon means you are automatically at a disadvantage. This is something which I believe many financial institutions use to confuse their customers. After all, customers who don't understand something are hardly in a position to ask awkward questions – or to compare value for money.

In this appendix then we will look at four important terms used in personal finance. Never again will you be dependent on someone else to explain any of the following to you:

1 Percentages.

2 The difference between capital and income.

3 Compound interest.

4 Gearing.

Please note that other terminology you may find useful is explained in the 'Jargon Buster' section in Appendix 2.

PERCENTAGES MADE EASY

You are not alone

If you aren't entirely comfortable with percentages you are not alone. In a survey designed to test graduates on their knowledge of percentages, only 8% could calculate a percentage accurately, and only 19% actually understood what a percentage was. In other words, more than eight out of ten people with a third-level education were completely at sea when it came to one of the key mathematical concepts used in personal finance. Under the circumstances, is it any wonder that the majority of people struggle to sort out their money matters?

What is a percentage?

The word 'percentage' literally means 'parts per 100' – 'cent' being the Latin word for 100. Because percentages always deal with parts per hundred, they allow you to compare things that would be very difficult to compare otherwise. They are particularly useful when it comes to choosing a loan or deciding on the relative worth of different investment opportunities.

How to work out percentages

You calculate the percentage by turning your numbers into a fraction, divide it out and then multiply by 100.

Imagine that you have three apple trees and you want to know which one of the trees produces the highest number of good – as opposed to rotten – apples. When you harvest the apples from each tree you keep a note of the total number of apples picked and the number of apples that have to be thrown away. Your note looks like this:

Tree	Apples on tree	Apples spoiled
A	750	150
B	550	88
C	670	101

Clearly, from the above figures, it isn't easy to gauge which is your best tree. However, if you express the figures in percentage terms it will immediately become obvious.

On Tree A, 150 out of the 750 were rotten. So your calculation would look like this:

$$\frac{150}{750} \times 100 = 20 \text{ percent}$$

If you were using a calculator you would key it in like this:

150 ÷ 750 = 2 x 100 = (**answer 20**)

For Tree B, 88 apples out of the 550 were rotten so the calculation would be like this:

$$\frac{88}{550} \times 100 = 16 \text{ percent}$$

For Tree C, 101 apples out of the 670 were rotten so the calculation would be like this:

$$\frac{101}{670} \times 100 = 15 \text{ percent}$$

Converting the numbers to percentages allows us to make a fair comparison between the 'performance' of the apple trees. So, 20% of the apples on Tree A were rotten; 16% of the apples on Tree B were rotten; but just 15% of the apples on Tree C were rotten – making it the best performing apple tree in the orchard!

It is hard enough comparing apple trees with apple trees – but even harder to compare apple trees with – say – orange trees. This is where percentages come in so useful. By giving everything a base of 100, we can compare things which aren't alike in other ways.

Now let's put percentages into context – you are told the yield in a property you wish to buy is 6% while the internal rate of return (IRR) is 11%. The first element, the yield, is the return or rental income in proportion to the cost of the property excluding stamp duty and costs.

For example, an investment property costing €300,000 with a rental income of €18,000 per annum will give you an initial rental yield of 6% per annum. Capital growth on the property is expected over the next few years and just taking the first five years of ownership together with the yield, the combination is called the Internal Rate of Return (IRR) and is generally in excess of the initial yield.

For example, an investment property costing €300,000 with a rental income of €18,000 per annum will give you an initial rental yield of 6% per annum. Capital growth on the property is expected over the next few years and just taking the first five years of ownership together with the yield, the combination is called the Internal Rate of Return (IRR) and is generally in excess of the initial yield. If in five years' time the property is worth €450,000 the returns would be:

- Growth = 50% (five years)
- Annual rental yield = 6%
- IRR = 16% per annum (on an un-geared investment and before tax).

MONEY DOCTOR WEALTH WARNING

Don't trust your calculator!

Don't always believe the answer the calculator gives you. Why not? Because the tiniest slip of your finger could give you a completely wrong answer without you being aware of it. Here are five things you can do to avoid calculator error:

1 Estimate your answer before you begin a calculation.

2 Do every calculation twice.

3 Know your calculator.

4 Don't be overawed by your calculator.

5 Hang on to common sense and what you know.

The vital difference between capital and income

All money is not equal

One of the most important financial concepts to understand is the difference between capital and income. **Capital** is something – it could be money, a property, shares or some other investment – that generates an **income** for whoever owns it. A good way to remember the difference is to think of a fruit tree. The tree itself is the 'capital'. The fruit it produces is the 'income'. You continue to own the tree (capital) and it continues to bear fruit (income) every year. Your wage or salary is the income which comes from the capital of your labour – hence, the expression 'human capital'. Money is not just money – it is either capital or income.

And then there is 'interest'

When you own capital and it produces an income you have a number of choices:

- You can hold on to the capital and spend the income.
- You can hold on to the capital, add the income to it, and generate even more income.
- You can dispose of some or all of the capital and thus reduce the income you receive.

Let's use the example of chickens and eggs! You have some hens (capital) which lay eggs (income). You can do one of three things:

1 You can hold on to the chickens (capital) and eat the eggs (income).

2 You can hold on to the chickens (capital) and leave the eggs to hatch into more chickens (more capital) that in turn will produce even more eggs (income) for you.

3 You can eat your chickens (thus eating into your capital) and thus reduce the total amount of eggs (income) you receive.

There are lots of different names for the income produced by capital. In the case of property, for instance, it is called 'rental income'. In the case of a cash deposit in a bank it is called 'interest'.

THE MIRACLE OF COMPOUND INTEREST

A financial concept that can make – or break – you

When you are earning it, it has the power to make you very rich. When you are paying it, it has the power to make you very poor. Albert Einstein described it as 'the greatest mathematical discovery of all time'. It is the reason why banks, building societies, credit card companies and other financial institutions make so much profit from lending money. And it is the reason why ordinary investors can make themselves rich simply by doing nothing. It is the fiendishly simple concept of 'compound interest'.

Compound interest in one easy lesson

Perhaps the easiest way to understand compound interest is to look at a hypothetical example. Imagine that you have €1,000 and that you invest it in a savings account which pays interest at a rate of 10% per year. At the end of one year you will be entitled to €100 interest. If you withdraw this interest but leave your capital, at the end of the second year you will be entitled to another €100 interest. Supposing, however, that you don't withdraw the interest but leave it to 'compound'. At the end of your first year your €1,000 is worth €1,100. At the end of your second year you will have earned €110 interest, meaning that your original €1,000 is worth €1,210. Put another way **your interest is earning you more interest.**

> You will sometimes see the initials **CAR** in relation to interest. This is the **compound annual rate** … in other words it is the amount of interest you will receive if you keep adding your interest to your capital in the way I have just described.

Now let's look at a real example:

According to research, the Irish stock market has produced an annual average return of 14% since 1989. At this rate, if you invested €1,000 today it would be worth €3,700 in less than ten years.

Still not impressed? How much do you think your money would grow by if, at the age of 25, you had started saving €100 a month (that's €25 a week) for just 10 years at the same return? €15,000? €18,000? You are not close. At the age of 35 your money would be worth €25,000. Better still, at the age 65 your money would be worth €1.5 million!

No wonder lenders love you

When you **borrow** money, compound interest is working against you. Supposing, for instance, you borrow €5,000 on a credit card at an interest rate of 15% – which isn't high by today's standards. The credit card company allow you to make a minimum payment of 1.5% each month. Aften two years, you will still owe approx. €4,700, having made repayments of €1,750, of which €1,450 has been swallowed up in interest. Work out for yourself how long it will take you to pay off the full debt!

Compound interest is your greatest enemy and your greatest ally. When you are in debt, it works against you. But when you have money to invest you can make compound interest really work for you.

GEARING

Allowing other people to make you rich

Using borrowed money to buy an asset is called gearing. If you can make it work in your favour, gearing can dramatically boost your profits. For instance:

> Supposing you buy a €200,000 apartment using a €40,000 deposit and a €160,000 mortgage. After one year the apartment is worth €240,000. It isn't just that you have made a €40,000 profit – you've actually doubled the €40,000 you originally invested. In other words, you've achieved a 100% gain in just 12 months.

Even if you deduct the mortgage interest you've had to pay for the year you've owned your apartment – you have still done very well. However, what goes up can also come down. In the UK between 1987 and 1989 house prices fell by around one-third. If this happened to someone selling an apartment they bought for €100,000 using an €80,000 mortgage they would not only have seen their €20,000 deposit wiped out they would owe an additional €13,333 (the difference between the mortgage of €80,000 and the €66,666 you would get for the apartment). When this happens it is called being in 'negative equity'.

> Gearing is the easiest and most effective way of increasing the potential profit from any investment. It is also the most effective way of increasing the potential loss, something every investor contemplating gearing would be well advised to remember.

There is a commonly held view that owning property is a one-way bet. But in the recent history of many European countries there have been periods when residential property prices fell. In fact, over the long term the Irish stock market has outperformed Irish property. Furthermore, it is vitally important to diversify your investments – thus spreading your risk.

> Many people re-mortgage their homes in order to have a deposit with which to buy a second investment property. This can be very sensible. However, if you have an existing mortgage on your home it might make more sense to pay that off first and then to invest in another area – such as the stock market. It very much depends on your circumstances.

Without gearing, most of us would never be able to own our own homes. It also allows us to make other, highly lucrative investments. Nevertheless, you should think carefully before you embark on any investment that requires you to borrow money. You want to make sure that the investment is going to earn you more than the loan is going to cost you.

THE MONEY DOCTOR SAYS...

- It is well worth your while to practise calculating percentages as these are the most common way of comparing both investment and lending products.

- If you are trying to remember the difference between capital and income think of an apple tree. The tree is your capital and its annual crop of fruit is your income.

- Compound interest can make you rich and it can make you poor, too. In the case of an investment it is the process whereby the interest you earn from something is added to the capital to produce even more interest. In the case of a loan it is the process whereby the interest you owe is added to the capital making it harder to get out of debt.

- Gearing allows you to buy an asset with borrowed money. There is no better way to achieve dramatic investment returns but, remember, it can work the other way, too.

- You'll find a full explanation of all the most commonly used financial expressions and terms in the 'Jargon Buster' section next.

Appendix 2
THE MONEY DOCTOR'S JARGON BUSTER

Have you ever noticed that with most contracts the writing becomes smaller as you read through it and the jargon becomes indecipherable? Financial institutions, in particular, have nurtured their reputations through the years for being as obtuse, confusing and ambiguous as possible in their use of the English language. All you have to do is look at a loan offer and you will see what I mean. *Caveat emptor* and all that, but the *caveats* – while I am sure there are valid and necessary reasons for their inclusions – are never fully explained. Therefore, it is hugely important in the first instance, to know what some of these words and phrases mean ... *in plain English*. In this appendix, I explain many of these financial terms.

If you would like to see **your** jargon explained in next year's edition, please write to me at jlowe@moneydoctor.ie.

ACCIDENT INSURANCE

An insurance policy which pays out a lump sum if you suffer an injury. For instance, you might receive €20,000 for the loss of a limb, or €50,000 for the loss of your sight.

ADDITIONAL VOLUNTARY CONTRIBUTIONS (AVCs)

These are extra payments you can make in addition to the normal pension contributions (or premiums) you or your employer make, if you are a member of an employer pension plan. AVCs help boost the value of your pension fund or can be used to contribute to a tax-free lump sum on retirement. You can claim tax relief on AVCs up to certain limits, as long as you earn an income.

ADMINISTRATION FEE

A fee paid to a financial services provider for a service or product.

ALLOCATION RATE

The percentage of your money used to buy units in a pension or investment fund. For example, if you invest €100 and €2 goes towards charges and set-up costs then your allocation rate is 98%.

ANNUAL EQUIVALENT RATE (AER)

This shows what the interest on a savings account would be if the interest were compounded and paid out on an annual basis. This can be used as a basis of comparison for savings plans that may be of less than or greater than 12 months duration. See also **compound annual return**.

ANNUITY

A fixed amount of money paid to you as an income for a particular length of time. The length of time may be the rest of your life (life-time annuity) or for a set period (temporary annuity). You buy an annuity using a lump sum of money. Once you've purchased it you cannot get your original capital back, and you are locked in to the income agreed at the outset.

ANNUITY RATE

Compares the size of an annuity (in other words how much it will pay you each year) with the size of the lump sum required to buy it.

APPROVED MINIMUM RETIREMENT FUND (AMRF)

A type of personal pension fund in which the capital may not be reduced below a fixed limit before age 75.

APPROVED RETIREMENT FUND (ARF)

A personal retirement fund – after you make provision for an AMRF, if necessary – where you keep your pension invested in a lump sum after retirement. Withdrawals from this fund in order to give you an income are taxable.

APR or ANNUAL PERCENTAGE RATE

This is the way in which lenders express the rate of interest and charges they're making. You should always compare annual percentage rates before taking out any loan, and you should bear in mind that there are different ways of calculating the cost of any debt.

ASSETS

These are physical items such as land, or intangible items such as goodwill, that are owned by a company or a person. **Asset Finance** is a loan secured by that asset whether it is a car, boat, helicopter, etc.

AVERAGE CLAUSE

This refers to a condition included in some home insurance policies that limits what you can claim if you are under-insured. For example, if the contents of your home are worth € 50,000 but you insure them for € 25,000, you are under-insured by 50%. If your contents are damaged, destroyed or stolen, the most you will receive from your insurance company is 50% of the claim on your loss.

BALLOON PAYMENT

A reference to one large final payment due at the end of a loan agreement – includes car finance or other short-term loans. It is used to keep monthly payments lower, but must be paid to complete the agreement and so allow you to become the owner of the goods at that point.

BEAR MARKET

The term used to describe a falling stock market.

BENEFIT STATEMENT

A statement giving details of your pension plan that your pension provider must supply you with annually.

BID-OFFER SPREAD

This refers to an investment charge and to the difference between the buying and selling price of a unit in an investment or pension fund on any given day. A typical bid-spread offer would be 5%. This means that if you invest €1000 in a pension or investment fund, its value would be €950 (€1000 less 5%) if you withdrew the funds immediately. Buying and selling price of these units in a fund depend on the value of the assets in the fund, sometimes referred to as the underlying assets.

BOILER ROOMS

In financial circles, this is the name given to unauthorised and unscrupulous investment companies that use high-pressure sales tactics to sell worthless or high-risk shares and foreign currency or other 'investments' to unsuspecting investors. Once bought, these shares are impossible to offload or sell.

BOND

A certificate of debt raised by individuals, companies or governments. In other words, a way for them to borrow money. It can have a fixed date of repayment or a variable one. The dividend (i.e. the payment or return you receive for investing in the bond) is known as the coupon.

BULL MARKET

The opposite of a bear market. This is when a prolonged rise in the stock market occurs.

BUY-OUT BOND

This is a fund into which you can transfer your employer pension fund if you leave or move jobs.

CAPITAL

Capital is, in essence, the total resources you have, or the amount you have available to invest, or the amount you originally invested.

CAPITAL GAINS TAX

A tax on the increase in value of assets during your period of ownership. Once an asset is purchased, if the value increases from day one it is said to have made a capital gain. Governments the world over tax this gain so that they can share in your good fortune.

CFDs

Contracts For Differences – the **Futures & Options** market is a mechanism for buying a small percentage of a commodity or share ownership now, with a maturity date upon which then you must pay the full price. Essentially you are betting that the price will be lower or higher on that date. CFDs do not have a maturity date but if the contract goes below 80% of the original price at the time of purchase, the difference is called in at that point.

CHARGE CARD

A plastic card enabling a purchase to be charged to a current account or store account. It is subject to a credit limit that <u>must</u> be regularly cleared in full – every month if there is an outstanding balance. No interest charges are applied.

COLLATERAL

This is something that a lender will accept as security for a loan – usually an asset such as property or investments which can be easily converted to cash in the event of the loan not being repaid.

COMMISSION

A payment to a sales person or adviser, usually based on the value of the sale from the supplier of the product.

COMPOUND ANNUAL RETURN (CAR)

This is a measure of the rate of return on a deposit or investment enabling you to make a direct comparison between various savings schemes.

COMPOUND GROWTH

The process by which interest-bearing savings mount up. If, for example, you invest €10,000 in a deposit account attracting 5%, at the end of the year you will have a balance of €10,500.

CONVEYANCING

A legal term, carried out by a solicitor, for the process of transferring ownership of a property from seller to buyer.

CORPORATE BOND

A fixed-interest bond raised by a company. See **Bond** above.

COST OF CREDIT

The full cost of borrowing money showing the difference between the amount you borrow and what you will have repaid at the end of the loan period, plus any other 'extras' e.g. valuation fees, etc.

CREDIT CARD

A plastic card from a credit card company that gives you an availability of funds to an agreed limit. The monthly bill – you can receive over 30 days free credit – must be paid within a certain time, or be subject to an interest charge if only the minimum is paid. This amount is less than 5% of the total bill, but because of some credit card company interest rates can take you over 11 years to repay this debt, if you are only repaying the minimum balance each month.

CREDIT HISTORY

Your repayment history on all loans with the front-line credit institutions – 42 members in Ireland – is tracked by the Irish Credit Bureau. Lenders will use this information to assess your credit worthiness. Missed payments stay on record for five years while a **judgment** (when you are successfully sued in court by a creditor who is owed money) is there for life. Guard your good name!

CREDIT INSURANCE

Sometimes called payment protection insurance. This insurance will cover the monthly cost of a debt for a limited period (usually a year) if you can't work because of illness or unemployment. For instance, you might take out credit insurance to cover your mortgage payments.

CREST

CREST is the electronic settlement system used to buy and sell shares on the London and Irish stock market exchanges. CREST also offers investors the opportunity to hold their shares in electronic form in their own name through personal membership.

CRITICAL ILLNESS INSURANCE

This insurance will pay out a lump sum if you're diagnosed with or suffer from any of a list of life-threatening conditions. For instance, if you have a heart attack or cancer you would receive a pre-agreed amount of money. This is also referred to as **serious illness insurance**.

CURRENT ACCOUNT MORTGAGE

Also known as a flexible mortgage. A mortgage – linked to your bank current account – that allows you to vary your monthly payments. By over-paying each month you can save yourself a substantial amount of interest and shorten the length of your mortgage by many years. On a daily basis the balances of your mortgage and current accounts are aggregated and interest is calculated on the net balance.

DEBT CONSOLIDATION

Putting all your short-, medium- and long-term loans into one single loan, or a mix of some into one loan, to reduce your monthly outlay and help cash flow. Consolidating can be a good idea especially if you can then hive some of the saving into a deposit or investment account. You should only ever consolidate once.

DEFAULT

A term used to describe a situation when you fail to pay some of or all of your due installments on a mortgage or loan.

DEFINED BENEFIT PENSION PLAN

A type of pension plan where your income on retirement is related to your final salary and the number of years you have worked for your employer. An example would be an annual pension of 66% of your final salary on retirement after 40 years service.

DEFINED CONTRIBUTION PENSION PLAN

With this type of pension plan, your income on retirement is not related to your final salary but depends on the value of the pension fund accumulated during your working life. If you and your employer's contributions are invested in a pension fund that has not performed, that is your tough luck. Most DB plans were dropped by the bigger employers during the early part of this new century.

DEPOSIT INTEREST RETENTION TAX (DIRT)

This is a tax on interest earned on deposits with the Irish Financial institutions. The current rate is 20% and it is deducted directly from the gross interest and passed on to the Revenue Commissioners.

DEPRECIATION

A loss in value of certain assets such as a car or a machine over time.

DERIVATIVES

These are financial contracts that gamble on the future prices of assets. They are secondary assets, such as options and futures, which derive their value from primary assets such as currency, commodities, stocks and bonds. The current price of an asset is determined by the market demand for and supply of the asset; however, the future price of an asset typically remains unknown. A week or a month in the future, the price may increase, decrease, or remain the same. Buyers and sellers often like to hedge their bets against this uncertainty about future price by making a contract for future trading at a specified price. This contract—a financial instrument – is called a derivative.

DISCOUNT RATE MORTGAGE

A mortgage whose interest rate is kept at a set percentage below the standard variable mortgage rate for an agreed period. You need to make sure that the difference between the normal and discounted rates of interest is not being added to your outstanding loan, which could dramatically increase the overall cost of your mortgage.

DIVIDENDS

The distribution of part of a company's profits to shareholders. It is the money you earn for investing in shares and can be paid in cash or shares.

EMERGENCY FUND

Money you set aside in some reasonably accessible form (such as a bank or building society account) which can be drawn upon in the event of some unforeseen need for funds.

ENDOWMENT MIS-SELLING

In the 1980s and 1990s thousands of endowment mortgages were sold with endowment policies that didn't sufficiently grow in value to repay the lump sum borrowed. In other words, borrowers found themselves unable to pay their entire mortgage off. This crisis continues as borrowers who took out endowment mortgages come to the end of their mortgage term.

ENDOWMENT MORTGAGE

This is a mortgage where your monthly payments consist entirely of the interest on the amount you've borrowed, whilst the loan itself gets paid off using the proceeds of an endowment insurance policy.

ENDOWMENT POLICY

An investment-type insurance policy which pays out a single amount on a fixed date in the future – usually to repay a mortgage or when the policy holder dies – whichever comes first.

EQUITY

This means the net value of your property after allowing for the balance of any remaining mortgage, i.e. the value of the property less the mortgage amount.

EQUITY RELEASE

A scheme whereby you make use of some of the equity (the difference between the value of a property and the loan borrowed against it) in your home by way of remortgage or top-up for refurbishment or other investment purposes.

ESCALATION

An automatic and regular increase in pension over successive years, either at a fixed rate or linked to inflation.

ESTATE

The assets of a person who has died.

EURIBOR

Euro **I**nterbank **O**ffered **R**ate – the interest rate at which eurozone banks will lend to each other. There is a separate rate for each lending period (a lending period can be from one week up to 12 months). Euribor rates may have an effect on the interest rate your bank offers you. These rates change every day depending on quotes from a representative panel of banks. It is not the same as the ECB rate, which is set by the European Central Bank, hence the standard variable mortgage interest rate can be decidedly different to an ECB tracker rate – talk to your financial adviser.

EUROPEAN CENTRAL BANK (ECB)

This is the Central Bank for the eurozone countries. Its main purposes are to maintain the value of the euro by means of keeping prices stable and controlling inflation in the member states. It sets the interest rates for the zone which in turn influence domestic interest rates.

EXCHANGE TRADED FUNDS (ETFs)

An investment fund that tracks the shares of a particular stock market index, such as the top 20 shares quoted in the Irish Stock Exchange. The fund itself is also quoted and traded on the stock market. Entry and exit to ETFs can also be cheaper and better from an administrative point of view (as you don't have to buy 20 separate share holdings, for example).

EXIT PENALTY

This is a penalty applied by financial institutions for cashing in an investment before the specified maturity date. Also referred to as an exit charge or early encashment charge.

EXIT TAX

A tax on the profit made on an investment. On the maturity of that investment or when you have decided to cash it in, you are taxed 23% (the standard rate of tax, currently 20%, plus 3% government levy) on the profit of that investment.

FINANCIAL ADVISER

A person or firm offering advice about investments, insurance, mortgages and other financial products. See the note on the Financial Regulator below.

FINANCIAL REGULATOR

The Financial Regulator (formerly Irish Financial Services Regulatory Authority) is charged with policing the Irish financial services industry – that is, all banks, building societies, credit unions, insurance companies, stockbrokers, financial advisers and intermediaries.

FIXED RATE MORTGAGE

A mortgage whose interest rate is set at a particular level and does not vary during an initial set period. At the end of the period, the rate reverts, usually to the normal variable rate for that lender.

FIXED TERM DEPOSITS

A deposit account into which you put your money for a fixed time and at a fixed interest rate. Any withdrawals before the fixed period expires will usually attract a penalty.

FUTURES AND OPTIONS

A **future** or forward contract is formed when both the buyer and the seller are committed and legally obliged to exchange the underlying asset when the contract matures. An **option**, on the other hand, is a contract that gives its owner the right, but not the obligation, to buy or sell the underlying asset on or before a given date at the agreed-upon price. Both these contracts are time bound.

HOME INCOME PLAN

A scheme usually set up by an insurance company which offers income to the elderly by releasing some of the value tied up in their homes.

HOME REVERSION SCHEME

A scheme to provide extra capital or income once you're retired. You sell part of your home but retain the right to live in it until you die (or both you and your husband or wife have died if it's a joint scheme). The amount raised can either be kept as a lump sum or used to buy an annuity, which would give a monthly income.

HOSPITAL CASH PLAN

This policy will pay out a lump sum in specified circumstances – for instance, if you have to go into hospital, if you become pregnant, and so forth.

INCREASING TERM INSURANCE

Life insurance where the amount of cover – and the cost – automatically increase during the term either by a set percentage each year or in line with inflation. One of the benefits is that the extra you pay assumes that your state of health is still the same as it was when you originally took out the policy even if – in fact – it has deteriorated.

INDEMNITY BOND

A type of insurance policy that in the event of your home being repossessed by your lender as a result of failure to repay the mortgage, it insures the lender against the risk of taking a loss – usually over 80% of the original value of the property – on its subsequent sale. Some lenders will charge you for the costs of this Indemnity Bond.

INDEX LINKING

A method whereby the benefits on your investment, life assurance or house insurance policies are increased annually to keep pace with inflation. Your premiums will also increase proportionately each year.

INFLATION

This is the word used to describe how rising prices cause the purchasing power of your money to decrease. At one point we suffered very high levels of inflation in Ireland – prices increased by as much as one-sixth a year. In recent years, inflation has been pretty much under control but, worryingly, has been on the rise again in the last 2 years. Note that when inflation rises, so do interest rates – hence the steady rate increases of the last 24 months.

INTEREST

Interest is the money charged by a lender to a borrower. It's also the amount of money an investor earns from his or her investments. Here are two short examples: if you borrow €100 and you have to pay an annual interest rate of 20%, that means you have to pay the lender €20 a year. If, on the other hand, you invest €100 and receive interest of 5%, that means that the amount you will receive is €5 a year.

INTEREST-ONLY MORTGAGE

This is similar to an endowment mortgage. Basically, you only pay interest during the term of the loan. Normally, the amount that would go to repaying capital is instead transferred to a savings scheme which should – on maturity – have grown sufficiently to repay the loan. In this case there is no investment planned but the loan reverts to a capital and interest loan (called the repayment or annuity loan) at a future point, or if you have negotiated a 40-year interest-only loan the amount borrowed is repayment, by whatever means, at the end of the term.

INVESTOR COMPENSATION SCHEME

Introduced in 1997, this is a guarantee from the government to protect eligible consumers and investor savings up to €20,000 per person/entity in any Irish bank, deposit taker or authorised investment firm should that credit institution or firm fail or collapse.

This was increased to €100,000 and 100% of this amount during September 2008. Then, on 30 September, the government came in again with a no-limit guarantee on all savings for the Irish-owned banks (AIB, Bank of Ireland, Permanent TSB, Anglo Irish Bank, Irish Nationwide Building Society and Educational Building Society – EBS). And, on 9 October, extended it to five other non-Irish-owned banks (Ulster Bank, First Active, Bank of Scotland Halifax, IIB Bank (now KBC Bank) and Postbank – the An Post/Fortis Bank joint venture.

IRISH CREDIT BUREAU

A credit reference agency that maintains information about individual borrowers' credit history. With 42 credit institution members, one missed payment stays on record for five years, while a **judgment** (a formal decision by a court of law that you owe money) remains forever. Any loan application will always result in an ICB inquiry. You can check your own credit for a fee of €6 by writing to them. Guard your good name!

JOINT LIFE INSURANCE

This is life insurance which covers two people's lives – usually husband and wife – paying out a lump sum when either one or both has died. A 'first death policy' will pay out when one of the people covered has died, whereas a 'last survivor policy' pays out only when both of the people covered have died. This type of life insurance is useful as a way of paying off a mortgage or meeting some other liability. The 'first death' policy is the cheaper while the most expensive is a **dual life policy**, which pays out on both lives irrespective of who dies first.

JUNK BOND

A high yield corporate bond issue with a below-investment rating (BB or lower) that became a growing source of corporate funding in the 1980s. They are the lowest quality bonds and since they are speculative and riskier, they potentially have a greater yield or return, and are generally issued by corporations of questionable financial strength or without proven track records.

LETTER OF OFFER

Usually a letter from your mortgage lender setting out the amount or loan offer they are willing to lend you and listing the requirements and conditions attached to the loan before the funds can be released.

LIFE ASSURANCE

An insurance policy which pays out a lump sum on the death of the insured. The policy holder is not necessarily the insured e.g. a wife could make her children the beneficiaries of an insurance policy on her husband's life.

LIQUIDITY

In simple terms, this refers to the availability of cash – as opposed to assets tied up in long-term investments – to meet any sudden demands.

LOADING

A charge added to an insurance premium because of some specific risk factor, such as the health of an individual looking for life cover insurance.

LOAN TO VALUE (LTV)

Shows the relationship between the value of your home and the amount of your mortgage, expressed as a percentage. Thus, if your home is worth €500,000 and you owe €250,000 the LTV (Loan To Value) is 50%.

MARKET VALUE REDUCTION (MVR)

A reduction in the value of your investment that your Life Insurance Company may apply when you withdraw some or all of your investment except at certain times.

MORTGAGE

This is a loan secured against the value of your home or property – a legal term in French meaning 'dead pledge'. A mortgage is essentially a contract between a lender and a borrower. It obligates the lender to make money available to the borrower, and obligates the borrower to repay the loan over a specified period of time.

MORTGAGE PROTECTION ASSURANCE.

A form of life assurance tailored to provide enough cover to pay off your mortgage in the event of your death. The policy will be set up to run for the same term of years as your mortgage but the level of cover will decrease in line with the reducing balance of your mortgage, so the more you repay on the original amount borrowed, the less you have to 'cover' on the balance. The premiums are fixed for the full term of the policy.

MORTGAGE REPAYMENT PROTECTION INSURANCE

A special policy designed to cover your mortgage payments for a limited period – usually not more than two years – if you can't work due to an accident, illness or unemployment.

NATIONAL TREASURY MANAGEMENT AGENCY (NTMA)

The government agency that manages the national debt and administers the national pension fund. It also administers a fund where unclaimed money from dormant bank accounts is transferred.

NDI

Net Disposable Income – one of the two methods used by lenders to determine how much money can be borrowed by an applicant. Your monthly take home pay amount (that is after tax and deductions) is used to allow up to c. 35% in financial commitments (mortgage, car loan, personal loan, etc.) This leaves the other 65% disposable income to feed, clothe and cover living and luxury expenses. Under certain circumstances, this could be as high as 50%. The other method of calculating your borrowing eligibility is called the Salary Multiplier. Again, as a rule of thumb, your income is multiplied by 4.5 times for a single applicant or twice 4.5 times for joint applicants. If there are no loans outstanding or other financial commitments, the NDI system may give you a greater borrowing eligibility.

NEGATIVE EQUITY

Unfortunately these words are now being used in Ireland since the summer of 2008. When an asset – especially a home – falls below the value of the loan (or loans) taken out to buy it, this is referred to as 'negative equity'. In other words, suppose you have a house worth €200,000 and your mortgage is for €220,000. Your negative equity would be €20,000.

NET WORTH

This is what someone is really worth financially. You calculate it by adding up the value of all your assets and then deducting the total of all your debts. Supposing you have a house, car, and other possessions worth €150,000 and mortgages and loans to the value of €100,000. Your net worth would then be €50,000 (€150,000 less €100,000).

NO CLAIMS BONUS

The reduction you receive on your home or motor insurance, based on the number of years you have been claim-free.

OVERDRAFT

When more money is paid out of your current account than you have paid in, your account is said to be in overdraft or you have overdrawn your account. Your bank must normally approve such overdrafts in advance and when they do, it is generally up to an agreed limit. If you do not have advance permission, your account may still be allowed to overdraw but you will be penalised – a surcharge on top of the already excessive overdraft interest rate, plus referral fees and possibly unpaid charges will apply.

PAY RELATED SOCIAL INSURANCE (PRSI)

A contribution toward the cost of social welfare and pension benefits, payable by employers, employees and the self-employed. It is calculated as a percentage of your earnings and only up to a certain limit.

PRSA

Introduced in 2002, a **P**ersonal **R**etirement **S**avings **A**ccount is a pension plan to give a regular income on retirement plus a lump sum that is tax-free, available through banks and assurance companies. It is regarded as more flexible and cheaper to maintain than the traditional personal pension plan.

RATE OF RETURN

The amount of money you make from an investment, worked out by adding together any capital appreciation and any income you have received. It's expressed as a percentage. When people refer to the 'real' rate of return, they mean the figure after it has been adjusted for inflation.

RENEWABLE TERM INSURANCE

This is life insurance which includes a guarantee that you can take out a second term insurance policy at the end of the original term. Your rights will not be affected by any change in your health.

RE-MORTGAGING

The process of repaying one loan with the proceeds from an existing property by taking out a new consolidated loan with a different lender using the same property as security. Generally, an additional amount of borrowing would be added to the existing debt in a re mortgage situation.

REPAYMENT MORTGAGE

A mortgage that has monthly payments to repay both the capital and the interest on the loan over a stated term.

SECURED LOAN

A loan that is supported by an asset that guarantees repayment of a loan. Mortgages are normally secured by the property being offered as security.

SECURITY

Assets such as title deeds of a property, life policies or share certificates used as support for a loan. The lender has the right to sell the security if the loan is not repaid according to the terms of the mortgage agreement.

SERIOUS or SPECIFIED ILLNESS INSURANCE

This is a form of assurance which pays out if you are diagnosed with one of a number of serious illnesses that are specified in the policy schedule. See **Critical Illness Insurance.**

SHARES

Shares represent, literally, a share in the ownership of a business. Different types of shares will carry different types of benefits. For instance, some may allow you to vote, others may allow you a share of the company's profits in the form of something referred to as 'dividends'.

SHORT SELLING

The selling of a stock (equities or shares in a company; commodities) that a person does not own in the hope of profiting from buying the stock back at a lower price. This is also called shorting. This was banned virtually worldwide in September 2008.

STAMP DUTY

Basically a tax you pay to the government when buying a property. The tax is applied on a sliding scale depending on the property value and there are a number of exemptions, including first time buyers. With shares, the stamp duty is 1%, while there is also stamp duty on credit cards (€30 up to 2008) and cash cards or laser cards (€ 5).

SURRENDER VALUE

The amount of money an endowment policy yields when it's cashed in before reaching maturity.

TAX AVOIDANCE

This is legal tax planning by taking full advantage of the tax laws to minimise your tax liabilities.

TAX EVASION

This is illegal tax planning – where you are breaking the law. If you get paid in cash for doing some work and don't declare it on your tax form – then you are engaging in tax evasion.

TERM ASSURANCE

A life insurance policy which pays out a fixed sum if a person dies within a fixed number of years – the term of the policy.

TIED AGENT

Sales people selling products and services on behalf of one company. Their financial advice is neither impartial nor independent.

TRACKER MORTGAGE

A mortgage where the interest rate is set at a fixed percentage above the ECB rate for the duration of the loan.

TRUST

A trust is a legal entity – like a company, or a person for that matter. It allows assets by one set of people – beneficiaries – to be managed and run by other people – known as trustees. Trusts are a useful way of protecting your loved ones and also saving tax at the same time.

UNIT TRUST

This is where investors pool their money into a fund which in turn invests in a number of different companies. It's a good way to spread your risk because it allows you to diversify without having to buy lots and lots of shares.

UNSECURED LOAN

A loan that is not supported by any asset to guarantee repayment of the loan. Personal unsecured loan examples are car loans, overdrafts, holiday and short-term personal loans.

VALUATION

This can be either a report by a registered valuer on the value of a property and will be required when applying for a mortgage, or an estimate from a fund manager of the value of the assets in your investment or pension fund.

VARIABLE RATE MORTGAGE

A mortgage that permits the lender to adjust its interest rates periodically, but generally on the back of interest rate rises around the globe and, in particular and pertinent to Ireland, from the European Central Bank.

WHOLE OF LIFE POLICY

A type of life policy that, as its name implies, provides cover for your whole life and pays out on your death providing the policy is still on force. Premiums are not fixed and will be reviewed – upwards – at regular intervals. Policies would also have an encashment value.

WITH PROFITS POLICY

An insurance policy that offers a policy holder a share of any surplus in the insurance company's life insurance and pension business.

Appendix 3
100 TOP TAX TIPS

Tax avoidance is perfectly legal, and while I am a great believer in the responsible citizen approach and also in John F. Kennedy's immortal words: *'Ask not what your country can do for you – ask what you can do for your country'*, I also believe in the adage: *'Don't look a gift horse in the mouth.'* Therefore, I attach hereunder 100 top tax tips for your benefit.

Special thanks to Frances Brennan of Kieran Ryan & Company Chartered Accountants, Lower Mount Street, Dublin 2, who has revised and updated this section, incorporating the Budget 2009 changes.

INCOME TAX

1. Due dates for payment of income tax

    The 'Pay and File' deadline is 31 October each year. By this date the taxpayer must:

    *   Submit an Income Tax return for the year ended the previous 31 December.

    *   Pay any balance of Income Tax and Capital Gains Tax (CGT) due for the year covered by the return.

    *   Pay the Preliminary Income Tax for the current year.

    *   Pay CGT in respect of chargeable gains arising in the period 1 January to 30 September of 2008.

    For 2009, the payment date for CGT for disposals in the period January to November will be mid-December in the year of disposal. CGT for December disposals will be due for payment on 31 October of the following year.

2. Pay tax on time to avoid interest, penalties and surcharges

    Interest on overdue tax is 0.0273% per day from 1 April 2005. Surcharge is calculated at the rate of 5% of the amount of tax subject to a maximum of €12,695 if the tax return is submitted within two months after the due date or 10% of the amount of tax subject to a maximum of €63,458 if the return is submitted more than two months after the due date.

3.   Utilise your pension contribution limits

Remember you can now borrow to fund your self-administered pension fund.

The maximum amount on which tax relief may be claimed in respect of qualifying premiums is as follows:

Age	% of NET Relevant Earnings
Up to 30 years	15
30 but less than 40	20
40 but less than 50	25
50 but less than 55	30
55 but less than 60	35
60 years and over	40

A 30% limit also applies to individuals who are engaged in specified occupations and professions – primarily sports professionals – irrespective of age.

There is an earnings cap of €262,382 for 2007, €275,239 for 2008 and €150,000 for 2009 on net relevant earnings. Contributions may be made until an individual reaches 75 years of age.

'Net relevant earnings' are earnings from trades, professions and are non-pensionable employments, less certain payments and deductions. Earnings of a husband and wife are treated separately for purposes of determining relevant earnings and the relief is available in respect of each spouse with non-pensionable earnings. Where a qualifying premium is paid after the end of the tax year but before 31 October in the following year, it may be treated as paid in the previous year, for example: pay the premium in 2008, the tax relief can be obtained for 2007. Any surplus premium that is paid can also be rolled over to be used the following year.

4. Consider investing in BES (Business Expansion Scheme)

You can invest in a Revenue-approved BES scheme and set the amount invested off against income in the year of investment.

After a minimum of five years any repayment of your investment will be free of tax with the exception of any capital gain made.

The capital gain, if any, will be taxable at 20% after taking into account any reliefs, such as indexation relief and expenses incurred.

Such a scheme cannot be guaranteed and there is a risk of losing all or part of your investment – research and choose the scheme carefully.

The relief applies to shares issued on or after 6 April 1984 and on or before 31 December 2013. The relief is only available to individuals who subscribe for new ordinary shares. The relief is calculated separately for each spouse.

Relief is given as a deduction from total income and the maximum amount which qualifies for relief in any one tax year is €150,000 for the tax years 2007 et seq. Any unrelieved amount may be carried forward and claimed as a deduction in future years.

5. Consider investing in Section 23 properties or properties with similar designation

Section 23 – Relief for investment on rented accommodation. This relief applies to new, refurbished or converted property, let by its owner to a tenant on an arms-length basis.

A clawback of relief will arise where the property ceases to be a qualifying premises or the lettor's interest passes to another party (including on death) within ten years of the first letting of the premises under a qualifying lease.

6.   If you are self-employed and your spouse helps with the business, pay him/her a salary

For the tax year 2009 the following tax bands apply at 20% with the balance of income taxed at 41%:

Single person	€36,400
Married Couple – One Income	€45,400
Married Couple – Two Income	€72,800
One-parent families	€39,400

The €72,800 band for the two-income couple is transferable from one earning spouse to the other, subject to a maximum individual band of €45,400 for either spouse.

7.   Employing family members

For the tax year 2009 family members who work part time in your business and have no other income can be paid up to €335 per week without incurring PAYE or PRSI.

8.   Pay all business expenses by cheque/credit card thereby ensuring a record is kept

9.   Have a petrol/diesel account with a local garage to keep track of business expenditure

10.   Direct debit mandate to pay Revenue Commissioners

Set up a direct debit mandate to pay your tax liability to Revenue Commissioners over a 12-month period. This leaves it easier to manage cash flow.

11.   Pension mortgage

Consider a pension mortgage e.g. pension mortgage on Section 23 property and get double relief.

12. Tax-based investments

Tax-based investments are more advantageous to people on the higher rate of tax (41%).

13. Claim an element of household expenses

If you work from home, claim an element of household expenses e.g. light, heat and phone.

14. Subsistence

If you work away from your business, you are entitled to subsistence rates per civil service rates.

Domestic Subsistence rates from 1 July 2007–30 June 2008

Class of Allowances Rate	Overnight Rates		Day Rates		
	Normal Rate	Reduced Rate	Detention Rate	10 hours or more	5 hours but less than 10 hours
A Class	€144.45	€133.17	€72.21	€43.13	€17.60
B Class	€141.60	€121.11	€70.83	€43.13	€17.60

Domestic Subsistence rates from 1 July 2008

Class of Allowances Rate	Overnight Rates		Day Rates		
	Normal Rate	Reduced Rate	Detention Rate	10 hours or more	5 hours but less than 10 hours
A Class	€145.32	€133.97	€72.64	€44.81	€18.28
B Class	€143.58	€122.81	€71.82	€44.81	€18.28

15. Entertainment expenses

Client entertainment is not tax deductible and should be categorised separately from other expenses such as advertising, promotion, etc. Staff entertainment is fully tax deductible.

16. Tax-free Lump Sums on Retirement

The tax-free element of payments made on or after 1 December 1998 is based on the following:

(i) Basic exemption

The basic exemption is €10,160 together with €765 for each complete year of service in the employment in respect of which the payment is made.

(ii) Increased exemption

If you are not a member of an occupational pension (superannuation) scheme or if you irrevocably give up your right to receive a lump sum from the pension scheme the basic exemption as outlined in (i) above can be increased by €10,000 provided you have not made any claims in respect of a lump sum received in the previous 10 tax years.

(iii) SCSB (Standard Capital Superannuation Benefit)

This relief generally benefits those with high earnings and long service. It is a relief given for each year of service equal to 1/15th of the average annual pay for the last three years of service to date of leaving less any tax-free lump sum.

SCSB is calculated by the formula:

$$\frac{A \times B}{15} - C \quad \text{Where:}$$

A = The average annual remuneration (including BIK, pension contributions less Revenue agreed flat rate expenses) for the last 36 months service to date of termination.

B = The number of complete years of service.

C = The value of any tax-free lump sum received or receivable under an approved pension scheme.

17. Medical Expenses

Ask your family doctor/chemist to issue an annual statement. For 2007 et seq there is no requirement for a relationship between the taxpayer and the person on whose behalf the relief is being claimed. For example, an individual can pay for medical expenses for his/her friend and claim the tax relief. Also, tax relief can be claimed on the full amount of the health expenses.

Medical expenses include the cost of maintaining a person in an approved nursing home.

Tax relief is also available to an individual who employs someone to take care of a family member who is totally incapacitated by old age or infirmity.
For 2009 et seq tax relief on health expenses will be reduced from the marginal rate to the standard rate of 20%. Tax relief for nursing home expenses will be standard rated from 1 January 2010.

18. Leasing/Hire-Purchase

When deciding whether to lease or hire-purchase try and anticipate profits over the lifetimes of the lease or hire-purchases so to maximise the write-off of the costs of the asset.

19. Exemptions

Exemptions exist in relation to income of artists and income from patent royalties, stallion services, forests and personal injury compensation. Artists whom Revenue determine have produced works recognised as having cultural or artistic merit are entitled to exemption to income tax on this income. The artist exemption can be obtained in the following categories: for writing a book, a play, a musical composition; a painting or picture, a sculpture.

Other exemptions exist in relation to greyhound stud fees, payments made by Haemophilia HIV Trust, Hepatitis C Compensation and trusts for permanently incapacitated individuals.

20. Limitation of Certain Reliefs used by High Income Individuals

An individual who is a high income individual is restricted to the extent that specified reliefs can be used to lower their tax liability for 2007 et seq. The specified reliefs are limited to 50% of the individual's adjusted income.

The specified reliefs include: capital allowance incentive schemes, film relief, BES relief, artist's exemption, patent royalty income, interest deductions on funds borrowed to purchase shares in companies or partnerships, donations to certain sports and approved bodies, exempt distributions and profits or gains from income from stallion fees, stud greyhounds, the occupation of woodlands and certain mining profits.

21. Rental Income

All rental income from properties in Ireland and abroad must be reported on your annual tax return. Deductions can be made from the rental income for expenses relating to the rental income. If a property is rented for residential use, apart from holiday rentals, it must be registered with the Private Residential Tenancies Board, otherwise a deduction cannot be claimed for the mortgage interest on the property.

A €200 charge will be applied by local authorities to all private rented accommodation and holiday homes in their area.

22. Rent a Room relief

Renting a room in your principal private residence is tax free up to a limit of €10,000 per year – no expenses may be deducted. This is not available between connected parties. One-bedroom apartments do not comply.

23. Tax relief on private rented accommodation

If you live in private rented accommodation you are entitled to tax relief. Tax relief at the standard rate of 20% is available from 1 January-31 December 2008 as follows:

Age	Single tax credit @ 20%	Married/widowed tax credit @ 20 %
Aged under 55 years (max. relief)	€2,000	€4,000
Aged over 55 years (max. relief)	€4,000	€8,000

24. Donations to charities

Donations to charities qualify for tax relief under certain conditions.
Minimum donation in any year is €250.

The legislation differentiates between donations made by PAYE taxpayers, self-employed tax payers and companies as follows:

(i)   PAYE Taxpayers
        Relief granted on a 'grossed up' basis to the approved body.
        Donor must supply an 'appropriate certificate' to enable the approved body to reclaim the tax.

(ii)   Self-employed Taxpayers
        Relief is granted to the taxpayer when filing the tax return.

(iii)   Companies
        Can be made as trading expenses or expense of management and to be included in the companies tax return.
        The charities must be an approved body under **Section 26 TCA97**.

25. Permanent health schemes are deductible

Premiums paid to permanent health insurance schemes are tax deductible. The amount on which relief is granted cannot exceed 10% of the individual's total income for the year of the assessment.

26. Trade Union subscriptions

Trade Union subscriptions are tax deductible up to €70.

27. Third-level tuition fees

Tax relief at the standard rate is available for tuition fees paid for approved courses in approved third level colleges. For 2007 et seq there is no requirement for the fees to be paid in respect of a relative. The maximum limit for qualifying fees is €5,000.

28. Relief for retirement of certain sports persons

Main features of the relief are as follows:
(i)   Resident in the state in the year of retirement.
(ii)   Allows a deduction of 40% against gross earnings (before deducting expenses) for up to any 10 tax years back.
(iii)   Earnings derived are directly from actual participation in the sport concerned (not sponsorship).
(iv)   Given by way of repayment of tax and is claimed in the year in which the sportsperson ceases permanently to be engaged in that sport.
(v)   Clawed back if the sportsperson recommences in that sport but relief still allowed in future.
(vi)   Relief cannot create or augment a loss and cannot affect the calculation of 'Net Relevant Earnings' for the purpose of ascertaining maximum pension contributions.

29. Exemption from Income tax for Low Earners

For the tax year 2008 total exemption from income tax is available to individuals over 65 years of age whose total income does not exceed €20,000 (€40,000 in the case of a married couple jointly assessed).

30. Interest on loans applied in acquiring shares/lending money/ acquiring an interest in a partnership

Interest on loans applied in acquiring shares and lending money to a qualifying company and acquiring an interest in a partnership is tax deductible. Relief can only be claimed for loan on bona fide commercial purposes and not allowable where BES/Film relief is applicable.

31. Interest on mortgages on personal residence granted at source (TRS)

With effect from 1 January 2002 there was a change in the way mortgage interest relief in Ireland is granted. Your mortgage lender now gives you the benefit of tax relief on mortgage interest paid. In the past, this tax relief was granted to you by the Revenue Commissioners.

Mortgage interest relief is given at the standard rate of 20%. The relief is subject to upper limits, depending on your personal situation. The following are the maximum amounts allowable for 2008. (To calculate what this is worth to you each year after tax, you multiply the tax credit amounts below by 20%.) The higher limits for first-time buyers apply for the tax year in which the mortgage is taken out plus six subsequent tax years.

From 1 January 2009 mortgage interest relief is being increased for first time buyers from 20% to 25% in year 1 and 2, and 22.5% in years 3, 4, and 5. This relief will be backdated to those who made a purchase in the last 4 years.

Mortgage interest relief for non-first time buyers will be reduced from 20% to 15%.

Single	Widowed/ Married	First Time Mortgage	Others
€10,000	€20,000	€6,000	€3,000

32.   Benefit–in-Kind exemptions

Bus passes.
Childcare services.
Canteen meals if generally provided for all staff.
Laptop/mobile phones/home high speed internet if the personal use is incidental.
Examination Awards.
From 1 January 2009 the provision of bicycles and associated safety equipment to employees who agree to use the bicycles to cycle to work to a limit of €1,000 per employee.

33.   Covenants

Tax relief is available for covenants made to the following:
*   Persons over 18 years of age who are permanently incapacitated.
*   Permanently incapacitated minor child if paid by person other than the parent.
*   Persons who are aged 65 years or over.

- A university or college for the purposes of research or the teaching of the natural sciences.
- Certain bodies established for the promotion of human rights.

All the above covenants will be restricted to 5% of the covenantor's total income except for permanently incapacitated persons where unrestricted relief is available.

34. Farming profits

Farmers can average their profits for tax purposes over the last three years.

35. Farming stock relief

Stock relief is available to farmers. They can reduce any increase in their stock value by 25%.

36. Joint Assessment

Joint Assessment is invariably the most efficient manner for married couples living together to maximise tax credits and rate bands.

37. State pension

Keep tabs on your PRSI contributions to ensure that you will qualify for a contributory state pension, and pay at least the lowest PRSI contributions so as not to let your pension lapse.

38. Terminal loss relief, etc.

On cessation of trade, check if terminal loss relief can be claimed or how unused losses and capital allowances can be utilised.

39. Incorporation

It is more advantageous to incorporate your business if a major consideration for you is to build up a pension fund.

40. Casual labour

Remember, there is no such thing as casual labour. Revenue need to see to whom all sums were paid and that PAYE/PRSI was properly operated. It is the employer's responsibility to ensure that PAYE/PRSI is deducted and paid and there are strict rules laid down by Revenue to determine if an individual is self-employed or employed.

41. Motor vehicles

Investing in an expensive motor vehicle is not efficient as motor expenses allowances are restricted by the Revenue. The Finance Bill 2009 will contain provisions to link the basis for assessing the BIK charge on cars to CO_2 emmissions.

42. Leasing & Capital Allowances on Motor Vehicles

Since 1 July 2008 there are new rules introduced for leasing and capital allowances on motor vehicles. These rules limit the availability of allowances for leasing charges and capital allowances in relation to the car's carbon emissions. The level of emissions the vehicle produces will determine the restriction imposed.

43. Kilometre/mileage expenses

It may be more beneficial to own your own car and charge your company a kilometre/mileage rate as opposed to having a company car and paying benefit in kind (BIK).
BIK is liable to PRSI since 1 January 2004 and is collected through the payroll.

VAT

44. Turnover thresholds for VAT registration

Persons supplying services from 01/05/08	€37,500
Persons supplying goods from 01/05/08	€75,000

45. Dealing with VAT-registered customers

Monitor your turnover to establish whether you should be registered for VAT. Remember, if you are dealing with exclusively VAT-registered people you will be better off by an amount equal to your VAT on business purchases.

46. Turnover for cash receipts basis

Ensure you are on the correct output VAT scheme i.e. Sales or Cash Receipts basis. To qualify for the cash receipts basis, not less than 90% of your turnover must be from sales to unregistered persons or your total turnover must be less than €1m in any continuous 12-month period.

47. Trading from outside the state

If you are from another jurisdiction and are trading in Ireland, you are obliged to register for VAT regardless of your turnover.

48. VAT on disallowable expenses

Carry out regular checks to ensure input VAT is not being claimed on expenses that are disallowable e.g. petrol, car leases, accommodation, food and drink.

49. VAT on property

VAT on property is a minefield and there are major new rules in effect since 1 July 2008.
Take professional advice on all property transactions other than those relating to your principle private residence.

50. Bad debts

Reclaim VAT on bad debts – you (will) have paid VAT you did not receive.

51. Flat rate farmers

A flat rate farmer is a farmer who is not an accountable person for VAT. Where they supply produce or goods to an accountable person, the accountable person is entitled to input credit of 5.2% of the tax exclusive consideration for the supply.

52.   Farmers

Farmers may reclaim VAT on capital expenditure without registering for VAT.

53.   Make sure you are charging VAT at the correct rates

The standard rate of VAT in Ireland has increased to 21.5%. There are various other rates, for example 13.5% and 0%, certain goods and services are charged at these rates. Consult professional advice for further information.

54.   VAT on Property leases, etc.

VAT implications of various transactions such as leases, etc. must be understood. There are major changes in this area since 1 July 2008 and professional advice should be sought.

55.   Monthly statements

Ask your suppliers to issue you with monthly statements to facilitate the tracking of all input invoices.

56.   VAT numbers of supplier

For large purchases from new suppliers check the VAT number with the Revenue to ensure it is valid before paying the bill.

CAPITAL ACQUISITIONS TAX

57.   Thresholds for CAT liability

Tax free thresholds applicable to gifts or inheritances arising after 1 January 2006 (cumulative in the lifetime of the recipient) are:

Group 1 –   €521,208 (e.g. Child of the person giving or bequeathing)

Group 2 –   €52,121 (e.g. Lineal ancestor, brother, sister, etc. of the person giving or bequeathing)

Group 3 –   €26,060 (e.g. All others)

CAT is payable at a rate of 20% above these limits.

58.   Gifts

In addition to the above thresholds a beneficiary is entitled to receive a gift from any one person of up to €3,000 annually tax free. This can facilitate tax-efficient payments to children/grandchildren without utilising the CAT thresholds applicable to a recipient's lifetime. The allowance only applies to gifts. This exemption is not transferable between spouses.

59.   Dwelling House Exemption

A donee or successor who receives a dwelling house plus up to one acre as a gift or inheritance, and who has used this house as their only or main residence for three years prior to the date of the gift or inheritance and retains the property for six years thereafter as their main or only residence, can receive this house free of CAT. There are some restrictions if the disponer is the parent of the donee and professional advice should be sought in this respect.

60.   Business Property Relief

This applies to business property acquired through a gift or inheritance and applies to chargeable business assets i.e. land, buildings, machinery, plant and certain shares. The relief available is 90% of taxable value of the gift or inheritance. The business property must be owned by the disponer for at least 5 years prior to transfer or at least 2 years for inheritance.

61.   Agricultural relief

Agricultural relief is applicable where 'agricultural property' is passed to a qualifying individual. Relief is given by reducing the market value on which CAT is calculated by 90%.
If you have received a gift of or inherited agricultural land seek professional advice to ascertain if the necessary criteria are met

and relief is applicable. An individual must qualify as a 'farmer' to obtain the relief.

62.   Agricultural Relief – farmer definition

A 'farmer' for the purposes of 'agricultural relief' means that 80% of your total assets for one day is agricultural property. A 90% relief on the market value of the agricultural property will be allowed for CAT purposes.
Clawback will arise if assets or farm is sold within 6 years of ownership.

63.   Will

Make a Will. It will avoid tax complications when you die.

64.   Section 60 policy

If you anticipate a large CAT liability on your death you may take out a Section 60 policy. This qualifying insurance policy will be used to pay tax arising on CAT except inter vivos discretionary trust.

65.   Capital Acquisitions Tax paid against a Capital Gains Tax liability

This is available for same event disposal where the net tax payable on the earlier event will be allowable as a credit against tax on the later event. The property must be held by the beneficiary for two years post acquisition.
Seek professional advice.

66.   Family business

Consult your business adviser regarding family business partition and transfer to the next generation.

67.   Consider purchasing properties in adult children's (over 18 years) names using security, not cash

68. Favourite nephew/niece relief

If you have no children, study conditions necessary for 'favourite nephew/niece relief'. A nephew/niece who has worked substantially on full-time basis for a period of five years up to date of gift/inheritance in business will receive a Group I threshold similar to a child of disponer.

69. Double taxation treaties

Double taxation treaties exist between Ireland and various countries including the UK and US. An inheritance from a person resident outside the state may have incurred tax which can give rise to a credit against any CAT liability attaching to the inheritance.
Seek professional advice.

70. Valuing property for probate

When valuing property for probate, do not be tempted to value it at an artificially low value. Remember this is the base cost for future disposals.

71. Disposal of assets by a widow or widower

When planning, do not forget that a disposal of assets by a widow or widower has a base cost value when their spouse dies, which is the market value at the date of death.

CAPITAL GAINS TAX

72. Self assessment

Since the tax year 2003 payment of Capital Gains Tax must be made in two installments:

On or before 31 October in respect of chargeable gains arising in the period 1 January to 30 September.

On or before 31 January in respect of chargeable gains arising in the period 1 October to 31 December of the prior year.

For 2009, the payment date for Capital Gains Tax for disposals in the period January to November has been changed to mid-December of the year of disposal. CGT on December disposals will be due for payment on the following 31 October. Budget 2009 has increased the CGT rate to 22% with immediate effect.

73. Capital losses

If you have incurred losses on the sale of assets you can carry forward the losses indefinitely and set them off against future gains, except gains on development land.

74. Selling farm land

If you own farm land and are considering selling it, consult your professional adviser first. You may be able to avail of lower tax rates or defer the date when tax becomes payable if you are considering developing it or entering into some kind of agreement with a developer.

75. Gifting an asset

The gifting of an asset despite the fact that no consideration has been received can give rise to a CGT liability.

76. Transfer of a site to a child

A parent can transfer a site to their child to the value of €500,000 subject to certain conditions without incurring Capital Gains Tax or Stamp Duty if the child builds a house on the land and occupies the house as their principal private residence. The child must occupy the house for a period of three years otherwise the child will suffer a clawback of the relief granted to the parent.

77. Business Retirement Relief (where over 55) on disposal of a family business

Where the consideration does not exceed €750,000, an individual aged 55 years or over can claim relief from Capital Gains Tax on gains accruing on the disposal of:

- the whole or part of his/her business assets/farm.

- shares in his/her family company (to the extent to which their value is derived from chargeable business assets).

In the case of business assets, they must have been owned and used by the individual in the business throughout the ten-year period ending with the disposal. In the case of shares in a family company the shares must be owned for 10 years ending with the disposal and the individual must have been a working director for at least 10 years, five of which he/she must have been a full-time working director.

Examples of such disposals are:

- disposal of business assets or shares in a family company up to value of €750,000.

- farmers transferring land into early retirement scheme provided that the farmer used the land for the purposes of farming for a period of at least 10 years ending date of transfer.

- compulsory purchase of farmer's land by local authority for the purposes of road widening.

Consult your professional adviser to ensure full advantage is taken of possible relief in these circumstances.

78. Business Retirement Relief (where over 55) on disposal of a family business within the family

Irrespective of the amount of the consideration for the disposal, total relief may be claimed by an individual aged 55 years or over on the disposal to his/her child of the whole or part of his/her business assets or farm, or shares in his/her family company (to the extent to which their value is derived from chargeable business assets). The ownership, use and working director requirements are similar to relief outside of the family as in 76 above. A disposal to a niece or nephew who has worked full time on the farm or in the business for the previous five years will also qualify for relief.

Consult your professional adviser to ensure full advantage is taken of possible relief in these circumstances.

79. Transfer of a business to a company

Where an individual transfers a business to a company, together with the whole of the assets of the business, or the whole of the assets other than cash and the business is transferred in exchange for shares issued by the company to the individual, the chargeable gains arising is deferred until such time as the shares are disposed of.

80. Compulsory purchase

When assets are disposed of under a compulsory purchase order and proceeds are reinvested within the same class as the original assets, Capital Gains Tax is not payable, the whole gain being deferred to be assessed on the disposal of the replacement asset.

81. Exempt chargeable gains

The first €1,270 of chargeable gains of an individual is exempt. This exemption is not transferable between spouses.

82. Maximising Capital Gains Tax allowances

You can transfer assets to your spouse without any CGT or Stamp Duty. This will effectively double the annual exemption of €1,270 or allow losses carried forward to be applied against gains from both spouses.

83. Disposal of life assurance policies and deferred annuities

The disposal of life assurance policies and deferred annuities by the original beneficial owner in respect of policies issued by an Irish life assurance company is exempt from Capital Gains Tax.

84. Irish Government Securities

Irish Government Securities are exempt from Capital Gains Tax.

85.   Principal private residence

Gains on the sale of your principal private residence and up to one acre can be exempt from Capital Gains Tax. However, if part of the property was used for business purposes, that part will not be exempt. Also, if the house was not occupied throughout it's entirety as the principal private residence – subject to some exceptions – then the full gain would not be exempt.

86.   Properties owned by companies

Remember properties owned by companies are subject to double tax on disposal if you want to access the proceeds. Firstly, the company will be liable to CGT on the disposal of the property. Secondly, the individual will be liable to either Income Tax or CGT depending on how the funds are extracted from the company. If the company is liquidated, then the individual will pay CGT on the disposal of their shares. If the individual extracts the funds through salary or bonus then they will be liable to Income Tax and PRSI on the monies.

CORPORATION TAX

87.   Liability to Corporation Tax

Corporation tax is due by all companies incorporated in the state and all non resident companies which carry on a trade in the state through a branch or agency.

88.   Close companies

Be aware of special rules regarding 'close companies' (i.e. most private companies). Breaking them can be expensive and in contravention of the CA 1963-2003.

89.   Salary level

Only take what remuneration you need from your family company as you may become entitled to Business Retirement Relief (see 77 above – no Capital Gains Tax payable up to

€750,000) when you dispose of your shares or assets at age 55 or over. Because the rate of Corporation Tax is significantly lower than PAYE/PRSI you will be maximising the amount retained in the company on which to claim this relief.

STAMP DUTY

90. Young trained farmers

Farmland transferred to young trained farmers (young being under 35 years of age) does not attract any stamp duty. This relief was due to terminate on 31 December 2008 and Budget 2009 has extended it for four years. The relief will apply in respect of instruments executed no later than 31 December 2012.

91. Transactions between relatives

Property other than shares transferred to certain relations attracts a rate of Stamp Duty which is half the normal applicable rate.

RESIDENTIAL PROPERTY TAX

92. Residential Property tax clearance certificate

From 5 April 2004 the new threshold for clearance certificates is €1,389,000 for disposals between 5 April 2006 and 31 January 2007. This means that where the sale price of a residential property exceeds this amount the seller must provide the purchaser with a clearance certificate from Revenue confirming that all RPT has been paid. In the absence of such a certificate the purchaser is obliged to withhold a specified amount from the sale proceeds and remit it to Revenue.

GENERAL

93. Planning

Plan in advance, you cannot plan retrospectively.

94.   Expert advice

If in any doubt on a tax matter always consult a qualified independent adviser. The cost will probably be less than the tax you will save.

95.   Non-disclosure

If you are worried in relation to non-disclosure of liabilities consult your professional adviser with a view to correcting the situation. It is much cheaper than having the Revenue come to you.

96.   Revenue Officials

Be courteous to the Revenue Official; remember he/she is fulfilling a very important function.

97.   Revenue Audit

Familiarise yourself with Revenue Audit procedures. Note the opportunity and benefits of making a voluntary disclosure. You should also have your accountant sit in with the Inspector of Taxes when the disclosure is being made.

98.   Expression of doubt

If you are unsure of a matter included in your tax return, include an expression of doubt. You can avoid penalties this way.

99.   The internet

Visit the Revenue site http://www.revenue.ie/. Many helpful and informative publications can be read and/or downloaded.

100.   Do not make unwise commercial decisions simply for the tax incentives

Appendix 4

DECISION TREES

What to do about your pension arrangements if you are self-employed

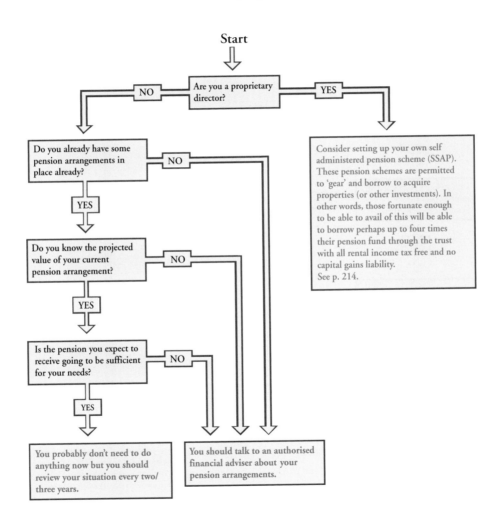

Start

Are you a proprietary director?

NO → Do you already have some pension arrangements in place already?

YES → Consider setting up your own self administered pension scheme (SSAP). These pension schemes are permitted to 'gear' and borrow to acquire properties (or other investments). In other words, those fortunate enough to be able to avail of this will be able to borrow perhaps up to four times their pension fund through the trust with all rental income tax free and no capital gains liability.
See p. 214.

Do you already have some pension arrangements in place already?

NO →

YES → Do you know the projected value of your current pension arrangement?

NO →

YES → Is the pension you expect to receive going to be sufficient for your needs?

NO →

YES → You probably don't need to do anything now but you should review your situation every two/three years.

You should talk to an authorised financial adviser about your pension arrangements.

What to do about your pension arrangements if you are an employee

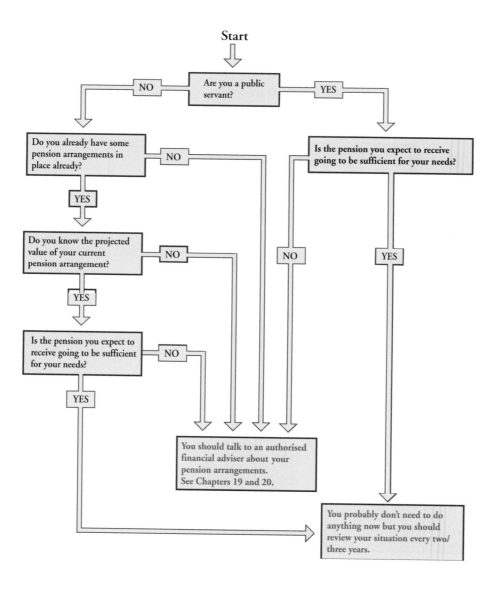

How to generate a regular income from a lump sum?

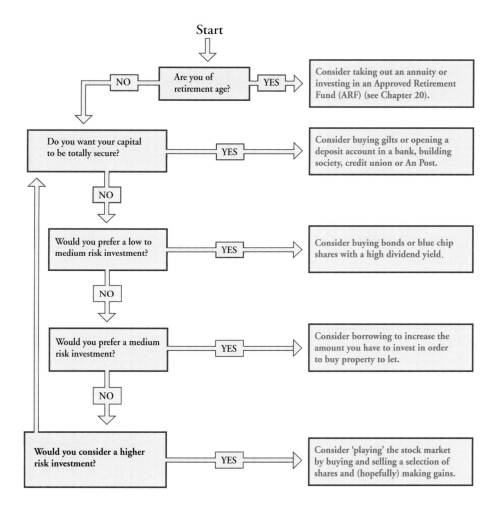

How to create a financial plan

Start

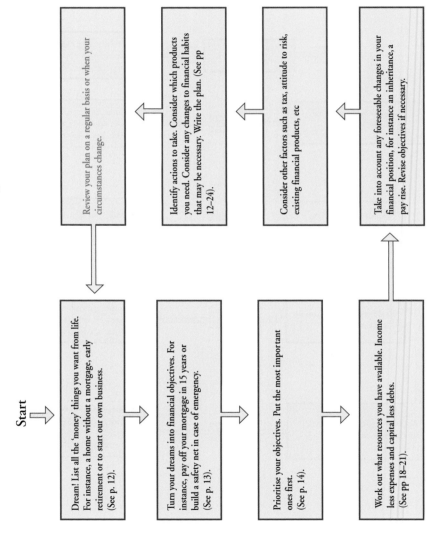

Dream! List all the 'money' things you want from life. For instance, a home without a mortgage, early retirement or to start our own business. (See p. 12).

Turn your dreams into financial objectives. For instance, pay off your mortgage in 15 years or build a safety net in case of emergency. (See p. 13).

Prioritise your objectives. Put the most important ones first. (See p. 14).

Work out what resources you have available. Income less expenses and capital less debts. (See pp 18–21).

Take into account any foreseeable changes in your financial position, for instance an inheritance, a pay rise. Revise objectives if necessary.

Consider other factors such as tax, attitude to risk, existing financial products, etc

Identify actions to take. Consider which products you need. Consider any changes to financial habits that may be necessary. Write the plan. (See pp 12–24).

Review your plan on a regular basis or when your circumstances change.

Do you need life cover?

Start

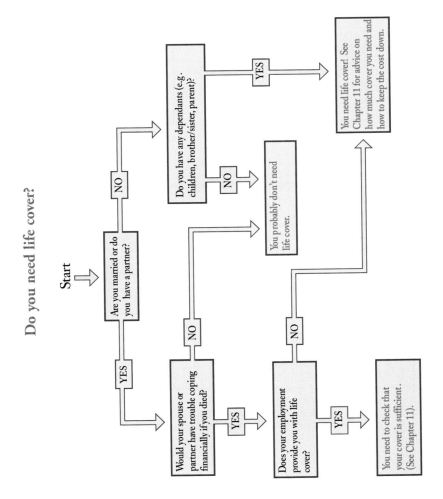

Are you married or do you have a partner?

YES

Would your spouse or partner have trouble coping financially if you died?

NO

Does your employment provide you with life cover?

NO

You need to check that your cover is sufficient. (See Chapter 11).

YES

You probably don't need life cover.

NO

Do you have any dependants (e.g. children, brother/sister, parent)?

YES

You need life cover! See Chapter 11 for advice on how much cover you need and how to keep the cost down.

Do you need income protection insurance?

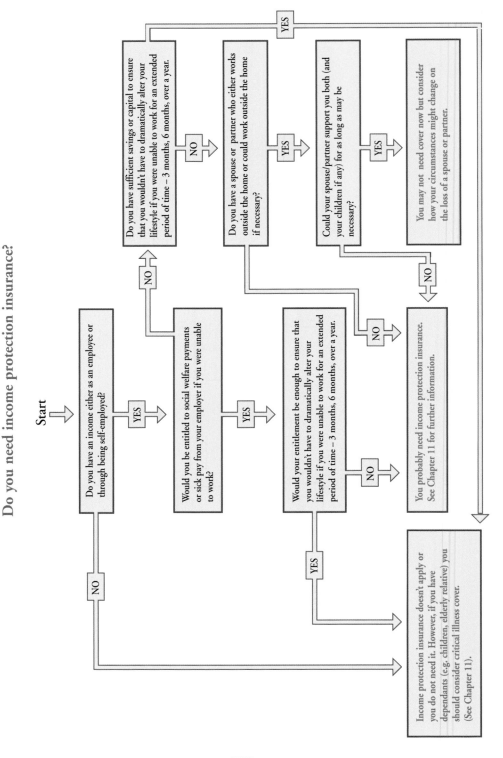

Start

Do you have an income either as an employee or through being self-employed?

NO

YES

Would you be entitled to social welfare payments or sick pay from your employer if you were unable to work?

YES

NO

Do you have sufficient savings or capital to ensure that you wouldn't have to dramatically alter your lifestyle if you were unable to work for an extended period of time – 3 months, 6 months, over a year.

NO

Would your entitlement be enough to ensure that you wouldn't have to dramatically alter your lifestyle if you were unable to work for an extended period of time – 3 months, 6 months, over a year.

YES

NO

Do you have a spouse or partner who either works outside the home or could work outside the home if necessary?

YES

Could your spouse/partner support you both (and your children if any) for as long as may be necessary?

YES

NO

You may not need cover now but consider how your circumstances might change on the loss of a spouse or partner.

YES

You probably need income protection insurance. See Chapter 11 for further information.

Income protection insurance doesn't apply or you do not need it. However, if you have dependants (e.g. children, elderly relative) you should consider critical illness cover. (See Chapter 11).

Do you need private medical insurance?

Start

If you needed medical treatment would you opt to be treated privately?

YES →

Can you comfortably afford to pay from savings/investments for an operation which might vary in cost from €4,000 to €20,000?

NO →

Are you self-employed?

YES →

Does your business depend on your input on a day-to-day basis to the extent that delay in your getting treatment would damage the business?

NO →

YES

Do (or might) you or members of your family suffer from illness which might require urgent and expensive treatment.

YES →

You should definitely consider taking out private medical insurance (see Chapter 11 for more information).

NO

NO

YES

Private medical insurance is not applicable or you probably don't need to take it out.

How to maximise the value of regular saving

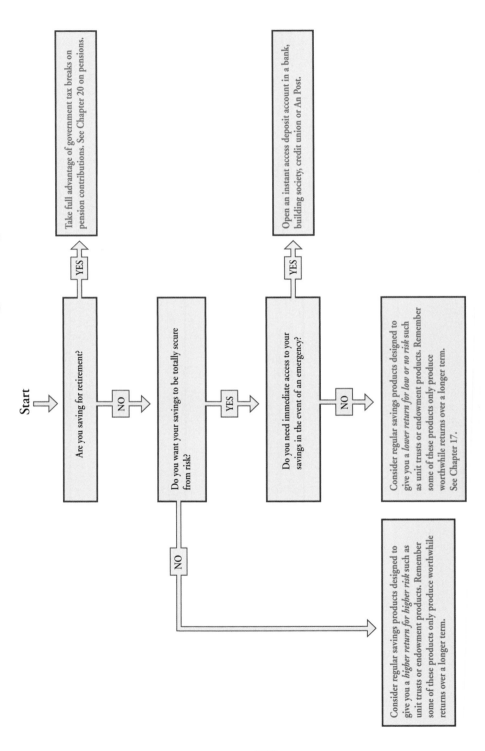

Start

Are you saving for retirement?

YES → Take full advantage of government tax breaks on pension contributions. See Chapter 20 on pensions.

NO →

Do you want your savings to be totally secure from risk?

YES → Do you need immediate access to your savings in the event of an emergency?

YES → Open an instant access deposit account in a bank, building society, credit union or An Post.

NO → Consider regular savings products designed to give you a *lower return for low or no risk* such as unit trusts or endowment products. Remember some of these products only produce worthwhile returns over a longer term. See Chapter 17.

NO → Consider regular savings products designed to give you a *higher return for higher risk* such as unit trusts or endowment products. Remember some of these products only produce worthwhile returns over a longer term.

Note: If you are not averse to risk and would like to invest in say, the stock market, the best way is to build up a lump sum via regular savings and invest the lump sum or part of it. Stock market investment is not feasible for regular savers.

Inheritance on intestacy (no will in existence)

The diagram below outlines how your assets will be distributed under the Terms of the 1965 Succession Act, should you die without a valid will.

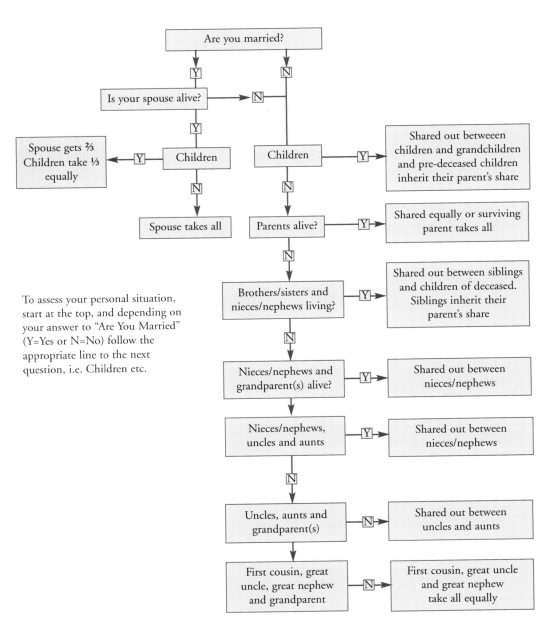

To assess your personal situation, start at the top, and depending on your answer to "Are You Married" (Y=Yes or N=No) follow the appropriate line to the next question, i.e. Children etc.

Appendix 5

TAX RATES

Tax Credits @ 20%	BUDGET 2009	2008
Personal Tax Credits	€	€
Single Person	1,830	1,830
Married (assessed jointly)	3,660	3,660
Widowed Person in year of bereavement	3,660	3,660
Widowed Person – no children	2,430	2,430
Additional allowances for widowed persons in the years after bereavement		
Year 1	4,000	4,000
Year 2	3,500	3,500
Year 3	3,000	3,000
Year 4	2,500	2,500
Year 5	2,000	2,000
One-Parent Family	1,830	1,830
Home Carer's Credit (max.)	900	900
PAYE Tax Credit	1,830	1,830
Age Tax Credit		
(a) Single/Widowed	325	325
(b) Married	650	650
Incapacitated Child Tax Credit	3,660	3,660
Blind Person's Tax Credit (one spouse blind)	1,830	1,830
(both spouses blind)	3,660	3,660

Bin charges – if eligible, the maximum allowance claimable is still €400 per annum on a prior year basis.

Tax allowances @ marginal rate		
Additional Allowance for Guide Dog	825	825
Incapacitated Person –		
Allowance for Employing a Carer (max.)	50,000	50,000

Exemption Limits	2009	2008
	€	€
Single/widowed under 65	5,210	5,210
65 years of age or over	20,000	20,000
Married under 65	10,420	10,420
65 years of age or over	40,000	40,000

Additional for Dependent Children

1st and 2nd child (each)	575	575
Each subsequent child	830	830
Marginal Relief Tax Rate	40%	40%

Tax Rates and Tax Bands	2009	2008
Personal Circumstances	€	€
Single/Widowed without dependent children	€36,400 @ 20% Balance @ 41%	€35,400 @ 20% Balance @ 41%
Single/Widowed qualifying for One-Parent Family tax credit	€40,400 @ 20% Balance @ 41%	€39,400 @ 20% Balance @ 41%
Married couple (one spouse with income)	€45,400 @ 20% Balance @ 41%	€44,400 @ 20% Balance @ 41%
Married couple (both spouses with income)	€45,400 @ 20% (with an increase of €26,400 max.) Balance @ 41%	€44,400 @ 20% (with an increase of €26,400 max.) Balance @ 41%

Note: The increase in the standard rate tax band is restricted to the lower of €27,400 in 2009/€26,400 in 2008 or the amount of the income of the spouse with the lower income. The increase is not transferable between spouses.

INCOME LEVY

Under €100,000 per annum	1%
All income in excess of €100,000 per annum	2%

Appendix 6

TAX COMPUTATION TEMPLATE

	Example	Enter your figures
Gross income	40,000	
Benefit in Kind	1,000	+
	41,000	
Pension contributions	2,000	–
	39,000	
Tax allowances at marginal rate	1,000	–
Taxable	38,000	
Tax		
36,400 (46,400 married) @ 20%	7,280	
38,000–36,400=1,600 @ 41%	656	
Tax before tax credits	7,936	
Income Levy		
1% of Gross Income	400	
Personal	1,830	
PAYE	1,830	
	3,660	–
Tax payable	4,676	

Appendix 7
THE MONEY DOCTOR'S ANNUAL BUDGET ACCOUNT

Description	Monthly/quarterly	Total
Electricity		€
Home heating (oil/gas)		€
Telecoms (land/mobile/broadband)		€
TV licence/cable TV		€
Household insurance (contents)		€
Car insurance/tax/service/fuel		€
Food/drink/eating out/cinema/concerts		€
School fees/uniform and sportswear; extracurricular school costs		€
Alarm/security		€
Repairs/cleaning/waste/garden		€
Health insurance/medical expenses (incl. dentistry)		€
Christmas and birthday expenses		€
Mini breaks/holidays		€
Clothes/footwear		€
Club subscriptions/donations		€
Other		€
Totals		€

When you have totalled your expenditure, divide by 12 and that is the amount you have to provide monthly. All other costs (e.g. capital expenditure, new washing machine, TV, etc.) must be found outside of this budget.

THE MONEY DOCTOR'S
STUDENT MONTHLY BUDGET

Category	Totals	
	Weekly	Monthly
Rent		€
Home heating (oil/gas)		€
Mobile		€
Books		€
Course materials		€
Printing/Photocopying		€
Commuter expenses (Bus/Train/DART/Luas)		€
Food		€
Household items/toiletries		€
Medical expenses/dentistry		€
Clothes		€
Gym/club subscriptions		€
Movies/theatre/concerts		€
Other (pubs, clubs & incidentals)		€
		€
Total		€

When you have totalled your expenditure, multiply by 12 and that is the money you have to provide annually. All other costs (e.g. holidays, buying iPods, etc.) must be found outside of this budget.

Appendix 8

MONEY DOCTOR ADVISERS

Providence Finance Services Limited, now trading as **The Money Doctor**, was founded on 1 December 1999 with an intention to *tell* and not *sell*. The company, an **Authorised Advisor** and a **Mortgage Intermediary** fully regulated by the **Financial Regulator**, has built up an enviable reputation of executing solid, independent and transparent advice, with no bias to any one supplier, delivered through a first-class service and administrative back up. This is our company mission statement:

*As an independent financial advisory company for mortgages, insurance and investments, **Money Doctor** (the trading name of Providence Finance Services Limited) aspires to give to clients the best financial advice, service and aftercare in the most transparent, honest and professional manner. We are always at your service.*

Now you can experience not just meeting with one of our advisers but can choose an experienced professional who has been selected, vetted and promoted to carry out the duties of a first-class, authorised, independent financial adviser – a **Money Doctor adviser**. One of the key tasks of a Money Doctor adviser is to carry out a **Money Doctor Personal Financial Review**. This is a full wealth check on every aspect of your finances. We do for your wealth what a good doctor would do for your health. There is no point in a piecemeal approach to your finances, you will only find the symptom and not the cause. We analyse the A to Z of your finances from top to toe and then recommend and implement any corrections required.

The **Wheel of Services** includes:

All aspects of your personal finances are covered as you can see, and you WILL save money. Here is what will be reviewed:

Debt advice

All lending is dependent on repayment capacity – can you afford it? We tell you *precisely* how much you can afford, whether it is for your home, commercial property or unsecured personal loan.

* Financial planning – we show you how to budget your annual household spending and create your own 5-year plan, 10-year plan, even life plan.

- Are you attracting the best interest rates? With 20 + credit institutions and hundreds of lending products, have you been 'sold' the right one?

- Can you avail of interest-only options (can save up to half your normal monthly repayment) or do you have an old fashioned endowment mortgage that you don't quite understand?

- Property abroad – perhaps now is the time to take out a loan on that unencumbered (mortgage free) foreign property? What are the risks, the costs and the advantages?

- Are your financial commitments greater than the income being generated? Are you at a stage where you JUST WANT TO KNOW WHAT TO DO? We will give you options to immediately reduce that debt and create an action-plan to fully repay all your debts.

- Would a short-term personal loan be better than consolidating within your home mortgage?

- Do you know the difference between asset finance, leasing, hire purchase and an unsecured personal loan?

- Why should you avoid moneylenders?

- Do you want an experienced financial professional to manage your debt and give you options?

Life and health advice

You may have your mortgage protected, but is there a requirement to have stand alone life cover? (Ten times your annual salary is the recommended level.) If you or your business partner are the key persons in your business, have you protected that business interest for you and your family were anything to happen to either of you?

- Is your income protected? Particularly relevant if you are the only breadwinner in your family. Permanent Health Insurance (income protection) is, outside of life cover within a pension, the only insurance plan that is fully allowable against your tax liability at your marginal rate.

- With three health insurers, VHI, Quinn Healthcare and Hibernian Health, are you in the right one?

- Do you need insurance against contracting a serious illness that may leave you incapacitated for up to a couple of years? Serious Illness Cover pays out a lump sum in that event, which tides you over during this period.

- Cost is a major factor – are you paying the most competitive rate for your policies? Have you been oversold - taken out policies that you do not need? We check all costings and policy relevancy as we MUST give *best advice* as an *Authorised Advisor*.

General insurance

Is your home valued correctly? The **Average Clause** catches out many consumers – for example, you place a rebuilding cost of €400,000 on your home but when you have to claim that cost turns out to be only €200,000. So instead of receiving €400,000 from your insurance company, you only receive €100,000 (half of the actual rebuilding cost).

- Have you done a complete inventory on all your contents and valuables, including all risk items (rings, golf clubs, etc.)?

- Have you reviewed your investment property buildings and contents insurance?

- Professional indemnity, public liability, other risk insurance – have you a requirement that you do not know of?

- Car and travel insurance – is it competitive? Does it pay to shop around?

Pension advice

Has anyone ever sat down with you and fully explained how pensions operate? With the range of pension plans and options (personal pension plan, executive pension, PRSA, Additional Voluntary Contributions (AVCs), Self Directed Trusts, personal retirement bonds, Approved Retirement Funds), we demystify the jargon *in plain english*.

- Do you know the difference between defined benefit and defined contribution pensions?

- Are you aware of all the costs associated with a pension – management charges, allocation rates and intermediary fees?

- Are you regularly updated on your pension performance?

- Does the correlation between your pension contribution and income expectancy on retirement match? Are you putting away enough NOW that will give you that income on retirement? Has it ever been worked out for you?

- Are you maximising your tax relief – receive up to 41% on every €1 invested into a pension plan on up to 40% of your annual earnings?

- Do you know when it is practical to move into a Self Directed Trust and what would be the minimum lump sum to start one with? What are the main benefits of a small self-administered pension scheme (SSAPs) or SDT?

- Should you be making AVCs to your employer-sponsored pension?

Investment advice

Savings and deposits – have you all the options? Best rates, best terms and best thresholds?

- Do you have a Rainy Day Fund (RDF) or even a Regular Saver account? Are you aware of why you need an RDF?

- Do you monitor the ever changing deposit rates regularly – monthly at least?

- Are you aware of the Investor Compensation Scheme? (The first €100,000 savings is safe in the event of a deposit-taker collapse. On 30 September 2008 the Irish government introduced a guarantee of all deposits – no limits – for the six Irish-owned deposit takers, namely AIB, Anglo Irish Bank, Bank of Ireland, Educational Building Society (EBS), Irish Life and Permanent (TSB), and Irish Nationwide Building Society. The government then extended this on

9 October to five non-Irish-owned banks, namely Ulster Bank, First Active, Bank of Scotland Halifax, IIB Bank (now KBC Bank) and Postbank – the An Post/Fortis Bank joint venture.)

- Are you aware of how inflation erodes your savings over time?

- Managed funds, tracker bonds, equity funds, alternative investments (CFDs – see Jargon Buster for an explanation - commodities, derivatives and futures) – are you happy with your knowledge of these? No issues on your understanding of this entire sector?

- Property solutions – outside of your home, is there value in creating a diversified property portfolio (French leasebacks, foreign property investment, commercial property syndicates)?

- Have you been 'sold' a property in a foreign destination that could be described as dodgy'? If you did purchase, did you have a second opinion on the investment? And was it from a professional?

- Have you made a will? Do you understand why there is a necessity for making a will? If you own property abroad, have you made a separate will for those foreign countries?

- Have you been briefed on estate planning and the procedures you have to follow? What you can and cannot do with your wealth after you pass on?

- Are you aware of all the tax advantages in estate planning?

Therefore, if you need a **personal one-to-one financial review**, someone to help you navigate through your financial storms and give you solid independent advice, and prescriptive remedies if required, without bias to any one supplier, then consider the advantages of a consultation with a **Money Doctor adviser**. This is not a one-off consultation but a *relationship for life* and with a company you can rely on whatever your financial issues during the coming years. You can either go directly to the website (www.moneydoctor.ie), email me (jlowe@moneydoctor.ie) or contact the **Administration Manager Stephanie Cahill** (scahill@moneydoctor.ie) to organise an appointment with myself or your own preferred Money Doctor adviser.

JOHN LOWE **THE MONEY DOCTOR**

Providence House
Lower Kilmacud Road
Stillorgan
Co. Dublin
Ireland

Tel +353 1 278 5555
Fax +353 1 278 5556
Email info@moneydoctor.ie
Web www.moneydoctor.ie

WEALTH CHECK

We are currently recruiting experienced financial professionals, preferably self-employed. If you have the experience and qualifications, not to mention the desire, enthusiasm and energy, and want to join our Money Doctor adviser team, please call or email recruitment@moneydoctor.ie with your background details.

Appendix 9

USEFUL ADDRESSES

THE REVENUE COMMISSIONERS

Check www.revenue.ie for contact details for your local Revenue office numbers, addresses and email addresses.

You can also avail of the Revenue online service at: www.ros.ie or at:

>Revenue Online Service Helpdesk
>Revenue Online Service
>2nd Floor, Trident House
>Blackrock, Co. Dublin, Ireland.

The opening hours of the ROS Helpdesk (1890 20 11 06) or for callers outside the Republic of Ireland (+ 353 1 2771178) are: Monday to Thursday – 8.30a.m. to 8.30p.m and Friday – 8.30a.m. to 6.00p.m.

COMPANIES REGISTRATION OFFICE

Email info@cro.ie
>Tel. (01) 8045200 LoCall 1890 220 226
>Fax: (01) 8045222
>DX No. 145001.

>Companies Registration Office
>Parnell House
>14 Parnell Square
>Dublin 1.

THE FINANCIAL REGULATOR

C/O Irish Financial Services Regulatory Authority
P.O. Box 9138
College Green
Dublin 2
Tel. (01) 4104000
Fax: (01) 4104900.
Website – www.ifsra.ie

THE INSTITUTE OF CHARTERED ACCOUNTANTS IN IRELAND

http://www.icai.ie/
CA House
83 Pembroke Road
Dublin 4
Tel. (01) 6377200
Fax. (01) 6680842.

THE ASSOCIATION OF CHARTERED CERTIFIED ACCOUNTANTS

http://www.accaglobal.com
ACCA
9 Leeson Park
Dublin 6
Tel. (01) 4988900
Fax: (01) 4963615.

THE INSTITUTE OF CERTIFIED PUBLIC ACCOUNTANTS IN IRELAND

http://www.cpaireland.ie/
9 Ely Place
Dublin 2.
Tel. (01) 6767353

THE IRISH CREDIT BUREAU

www.icb.ie
ICB House
Newstead
Clonskeagh Road
Dublin 14
Tel. (01) 2600388
Fax: (01) 2600390

LAW SOCIETY OF IRELAND

http://www.lawsociety.ie/
The Law Society of Ireland,
Blackhall Place
Dublin 7
Ireland.
Tel. (01) 6724800
Fax: (01) 6724801.

MABS (MONEY ADVICE BUDGETING SERVICES)

http://www.mabs.ie/

Cork MABS
12 Penrose Wharf
Penrose Quay, Cork
Tel. (021) 4552080
Fax: (021) 4552078.
Email: cork@mabs.ie

Dublin MABS
70B Patrick Street
Dun Laoghaire
Co. Dublin
Tel. (01) 2302002
Fax: (01) 2300310.
Email: dun_laoghaire@mabs.ie

Galway MABS
The Halls (3rd Floor)
Quay Street
Galway
Co. Galway
Tel. (091) 569349
Fax: (091) 569478.
Email: galway@mabs.ie

Limerick MABS
87 O'Connell Street
Limerick
Tel. (061) 310620
Freephone: 1800 418088.
Fax: N/A.
Email: limerick@mabs.ie

Waterford MABS
26 Catherine Street
Waterford
Tel. (051) 857929
Fax: (051) 841264.
Email: waterford@mabs.ie

St Vincent de Paul
http://www.svp.ie/

National office
SVP House
91–92 Sean McDermot Street
Dublin 1
Tel. (01) 8550022

The Samaritans
National Helpline 1850 609090
Dublin Branch (01) 872 7700

Appendix 10
IMPORTANT TAX DATES

Form 12 This is the short version for those whose main source of income is from an employment or pension (other than a company director for whom there is a separate Form 12) and is therefore taxed under PAYE.

FORM 11 or Form 11E must be completed each year by self-employed persons or those with income not taxed at source.

To download these forms, go directly to http://www.revenue.ie/forms

The initial instructions for Form 12 are: 'You are hereby required, under Section 879 Taxes Consolidation Act 1997, by the Inspector of Taxes named above to prepare and deliver, on or before 31 October 2009, a tax return on this prescribed form for the year 1 January 2008 to 31 December 2009.'

You must make a return of income on Form 11 if in the year 2007 you:

- opened a foreign bank account
- acquired a material interest in offshore funds in a member state of the EU, EEA, or the OECD with which Ireland has a double taxation agreement and/or
- invested in a Foreign Life Policy issued from a member state of the EU, EEA, or the OECD with which Ireland has a double taxation agreement.

To assist you in completing this return, each section of the form has been colour coded into the different categories of income, tax credits, allowances and reliefs.

All Revenue forms and information leaflets are available from the Revenue Forms and Leaflets Service at LoCall 1890 30 67 06 (ROI only) or from the Revenue's website www.revenue.ie or from any Revenue office.

PENALTIES

The law provides for penalties for failure to make a return, or the making of a false return, or helping to make a false return, or claiming tax credits, allowances or reliefs which are not due. These penalties include fines up to €126,970, up to double the tax in question, and/or imprisonment.

IMPORTANT TAX DATE DEADLINES

October is an important month in the tax calendar as 31 October is the last day by which an individual taxpayer must 'Pay and File' for the tax year ended on the previous 31 October.

The table below uses October as the example because of its importance, and shows what day in October returns and payments become due.

Some returns are required more than once a year (e.g. every month as in the case of PAYE/PRSI) as indicated in Column 2:

Date	Frequency	Category	Description
14	Monthly	Income tax and PAYE/PRSI	Payment of PAYE/PRSI deductions to 30 September.
14	When applicable	Dividend Withholding Tax	Due date for payment and filing of returns of withholding tax on dividends paid by companies in September 2007.
14	Bi-monthly	VAT	Filing of VAT 3 return together with payment of any VAT due.
14	Monthly	VAT	Filing of Intrastat return for September.
21	Annually	Corporation tax	Company year-end 30 November 2007: First instalment due, minimum 72% of total liability for the year.
21	Annually	Corporation tax	Company year-end 30 April 2007:

			Second instalment due, bringing cumulative payment to 90% of total liability for the year.
21	Annually	Corporation tax	Company year-end 31 January 2007: Payment of balance of corporation tax and filing of corporation tax return and Form 46G.
28	Annually	Company Secretarial	Filing of Annual Returns dated 30 September 2007.
31*	Annually	Corporation tax	Company year-end 30 April 2006: Close companies with undistributed profits may have to make a distribution by this date to avoid surcharge.
31st*	Annually	Company Secretarial	Company year-end 31 January 2007: Final date for holding Annual General Meeting and latest possible Annual Return Date for 2007.
31*	Annually	capital gains tax	Filing of return of capital gains tax for 2006. Payment of capital gains tax on disposals from 1 January 2007 to 30 September 2007.
31st*	Annually	Income tax and PAYE/PRSI	Payment of preliminary income tax for 2007. Payment of income tax balance for 2006. Filing of 2006 tax return.
31st*	Annually	Pensions	Payment of retirement annuity premiums, PRSA premiums and personal contributions to occupational pension schemes for tax year 2006 – you must also elect to have these treated as paid in the tax year 2006.
31*	Quarterly	VAT	Filing of VIES return for calendar quarter ending September.

Appendix 11

BUDGET 2009

THE HIGHLIGHTS

- Introduction of income tax levy of 1% on all income up to €100,000 and 2% on the balance.
- Stamp duty on commercial property reduced to 6%.
- Increase in the capital gains tax rate from 20% to 22%.
- Increase in standard VAT rate from 21% to 21.5%.
- Levy of €200 on car-parking facilities provided to employees in main urban centres.
- Increase in employee PRSI ceiling from €50,700 to €52,000.
- Relief for health expenses reduced to the standard (20%) income tax rate, while some pensioners over 70 years of age may lose their Medical Cards.
- New air travel tax of €10 and local authority charge of €200 on non-principal private residences introduced.

Minister for Finance Brian Lenihan delivered his first Budget speech on Tuesday, 14 October 2008, set against a backdrop of massive global financial unrest. He stated: 'Nobody foresaw the speed with which the global and the domestic downturn would gather pace. In the past few months, the world financial system has been turned upside down. Household names in global finance have been rescued by governments and blue chip companies have either failed or been subsumed into other institutions.'

He also went on to say, 'Here at home, we face the most challenging fiscal and economic position in a generation. This Budget sets out a plan to deal with this most unfavourable set of circumstances. The aim is to restore order and stability in the public finances, to increase productivity and competitiveness and to protect those who are most vulnerable in our country.'

Bear in mind that Budget 2009 is debated in the Dáil after its delivery and any amendments will be incorporated in the Finance Bill 2009, which comes into law early 2009.

Essentially the government is borrowing €12 billion to balance the books, so this year the Budget is about raising money, with everyone paying an extra 1%, 2% or 3% tax, depending on income levels and investments. It is one of the toughest Budgets in decades and, in essence, a reality check. This deficit represents about 6.5% of the Gross Domestic Product (GDP – the value of all the goods and services produced by Ireland); the forecast next year is that the deficit will be 4.7%, while unemployment is expected to rise to 7.3% with inflation at 2.5%.

The good news is that members of the government and Ministers for State will surrender 10% of their total pay. The Education budget has gone up 2.7% to €8.7 billion, while class sizes are being increased to reduce teacher numbers, as well as extensive reduced staffing levels right across the public service (see below).

Significant changes that were made in the area of personal taxation.
(See p.233 for an explanation of tax credits and tax allowances.)

- **Income:** A new 1% income tax levy has been introduced for all those earning under €100,000; if you are in the happy position to exceed this income, 2% will be levied on earnings in excess of €100,000. This could raise up to €1.18 billion in the full year. Thirty-four per cent of employees do not pay tax.
  Up to 2008 one could earn up to €18,250 tax free taking into account your tax credits. It now means that this income earner will have to pay €182.50 a year with this new levy.
- **Deposit Interest Retention Tax (DIRT tax):** This has been raised from 20% to 23% with investment funds/life policies raised from 23% to 26%.
- **Tax bands:** Standard rate bands have increased from €35,400 to €36,400 for a single person and from €44,400 to €46,400 for a married couple with one income. The increase for married couples with two incomes is €70,800 to €72,800. For one-parent families it is €38,400 to €40,400.

- **PRSI & medical expenses:** The employee ceiling (the maximum income under which PRSI is payable) increases from €50,700 to €52,000.
  Medical expenses tax relief has been reduced to 20%.
- **Capital Gains Tax:** CGT goes up from 20% to 22% with effect from midnight of Tuesday, 14 October 2008.
  If you made a gain between January 2009 and November 2009, the tax is payable mid-December 2009, while if you made the gain in December 2009, the tax is payable on 31 October 2010.
- Mortgage relief
  For first time buyers, interest relief will rise from 20% to 25% in years 1 and 2, and at 22.5% for years 3, 4 and 5. A single person is allowed €10,000 per annum at 25% for the first two years, which equates to a monthly relief of €208.33 per month (previously it was €166.66 – a saving of €41.67 per month) and for years 3, 4 and 5, the relief will be at 22.5%, or €187.50 per month, a saving of €20.84 per month. Years 6 and 7 remain at 20% relief. This increase for first time buyers is retrospective from 1 January 2005.
  For non-first time buyers, the relief has been cut from 20% down to 15% – effectively a reduction of €12.50 per month from €50 to €37.50.
- Property
  A new levy of €200 per property is being introduced for landlords. This will include all non-principal residences such as rented property and holiday homes.
  Stamp Duty on commercial property has been reduced from 9% to 6%, see table below:

Aggregate Consideration	Rate of Duty
Up to €10,000	Exempt
€10,001 to €20,000	1%
€20,001 to €30,000	2%
€30,001 to €40,000	3%
€40,001 to €70,000	4%
€70,001 to €80,000	5%
Over €80,000	6%

- **Benefit in Kind:** For those fortunate employees who have their own car-parking space, there is a levy of €200 per annum for this privilege.
- **Pensions:** The annual earnings limit for determining maximum tax-relievable contributions for pension contributions is being set at €150,000 for 2009 from the 2008 limit of €275,239 per annum (see table below). This will dramatically affect personal pensions.

Age	Limit	2008	2009
Up to 29	15%	€41,286	€22,500
30 – 39	20%	€55,048	€30,000
40 – 49	25%	€68,810	€37,500
50 – 54	30%	€82,572	€45,000
55 – 59	35%	€96,334	€52,500
60+	40%	€110,095	€60,000

HEALTH & SOCIAL WELFARE

Spending on Health will increase by 2.1% to €15.8 billion for the year and Social Welfare is up 8.4% to €19.6 billion. Measures to reduce staffing levels in the public sector include army barracks, the public service and a voluntary redundancy scheme being introduced in the Health Service Executive (HSE) for some of the 110,000 employees. An extra €454 million is being given to the HSE to support services, including designated cancer centres, therapists for children and the Fair Deal nursing home scheme. Other changes include:

- Charges for attending accident and emergency departments will go up to €100. Private and semi-private bed charges in public hospitals are being increased by 20% to bring them closer to the economic value.
- People will also have to pay up to €100 a month for their medicines before the state begins to reimburse them any additional costs under changes to the Drug Payment Scheme.

Childcare
The Budget 2006 introduced €1000 per annum for all children up to their 6th birthday payable to parents regardless of whether they are in

paid employment or not. This payment will now stop when the child reaches five and a half years of age. There are c. 350,000 children in this age group. This used to be paid quarterly but will now be paid monthly.

- **Family Income Supplement** income thresholds are increased ranging from €197.80 per week depending on family size to €207.80 per week or €10 per week per child.
- **Child Dependent Allowances** are increased to a new maximum rate of €26 per week from January 2009, an increase of €2 per week.
- **Child benefit** payment will cease for 18-year-olds from 1 January 2010 and will be halved for that group to €83 a month.

Pensioners

- The **contributory old age pension** will rise by €7 a week to €230.30 a week while the **non-contributory pension** will rise by €7 to €219.
- **Widow's, Widower's, Invalidity and Occupational Injuries Benefit, and Death pensions** have all been increased by €7.
- **Fuel allowances** have risen by €2 to €20 per week. Many action groups voiced their concerns about this and the soaring food costs over the past 12 months – milk has risen 25%, flour 34% and liquid fuels by 34%.
- The automatic entitlement to a **medical card for those over 70** is being abolished. An annual cash grant of €400 per person will be paid to those over 70 who do not qualify for a medical card or a GP visit card – subject to an income threshold. Health Minister Mary Harney said that of the 140,000 over 70s affected, she expected that around 15,000 people aged over 70 would keep their full medical card, around 35,000 would receive a doctor-only card and 70,000 would get a health support payment. The remaining 19,000 will not benefit. Eight out of ten would be able to visit their doctor free of charge and five out of every 100 would be eligible to a cash payment of €400 for a single person and €800 for a couple. The net weekly income limit to be eligible for a Medical Card will be €240.30 for a single person, the new rate for a single person living with a family will no longer apply while for a married couple the new limit is €480.60. These limits come into effect 1 January 2009.

Carers

The Carer's Allowance is a payment for carers on low incomes who look after certain people who need full-time care and attention. It is a separate scheme from the Carer's Benefit, which is a payment made to insured persons who leave the workforce temporarily in order to care for a person.

The personal rates of all working age payments, including both the Carer's Benefit and the Carer's Allowance, are being increased by €6.50 per week from 1 January 2009.

- **Carer's Benefit** personal rate has been increased from €221.70 to €228.20 per week.
- **Carer's Allowance** has also gone up by €6.50. This will bring the lowest full adult social welfare rate to €204.30 per week.

All carers receiving the carer's allowance also qualify for:

- A Free Travel Pass.
- Electricity/Natural Gas/Bottled Gas Refill Allowance.
- Free Television Licence.
- Telephone Allowance.

Carers receiving the Carer's Allowance are also automatically entitled to a Respite Care Grant of €1,200 per year to pay for respite care when they need a holiday or break from the duties of caring. This is automatically paid in June of each year. People who do not qualify for the Carer's Allowance, because means are too high, may still qualify for the Respite Care Grant.

Indirect taxes include these changes:

- **Air travel:** From 30 March 2009, there will be a new tax of €10 per flight and €2 for short trips.
- **VAT:** The top rate of VAT went from 21% to 21.5%, an increase of 0.5%. There was no change to the 13.5% rate. This change is effective from 1 December 2008.
- **Petrol:** An increase of 8 cent per litre from midnight of 14 October 2008.
- **Motor vehicles:** Increases in motor tax as from 1 January 2009 of 4% on all cars under 2500cc and 5% for all cars over 2500cc. There is also additional Benefit In Kind tax being linked to company cars with greater CO_2 emissions.

- **Cigarettes:** These went up 50 cent per packet of 20. Interestingly, the Minister stated that in a full year this would raise an additional €186 million. This means he expects the 4 million or so Irish residents to continue buying 224 million packets of cigarettes – a pack a week for every man, woman and child in the country – a sobering thought! If ever there was a time to give up...
- **Wine:** An increase in excise duty of 50 cent per bottle of wine. Might not affect those regular imbibers of *Chateau Petrus.*
- **ATM cards:** Government duty charges have been reduced on ATM cards from €5 to €2.50. Combined Debit/ATM cards are also reduced from €10 to €5. On the other hand, duty on cheques has been increased from 30 cent per cheque to 50 cent. This also suits those banks offering current account services as they will claim this service is the most expensive part of their business.
- **Betting tax:** This is being doubled to 2% and allocations for the Horse and Greyhound Racing Fund will be reduced.

Farm taxation was also addressed and a number of changes were made: Next year €3.2 billion will be spent on supporting the farming, food, fisheries and forestry sector. The Minister for Agriculture Brendan Smith estimated spending would be down by 2.6%. Payments in disadvantaged areas and the suckler cow schemes would be reduced, and no new applications would be accepted for the Early Retirement and Young Farmer Installation Schemes.

Mr Smith also confirmed that grants were being cut by between 8% and 9% to Teagasc, Bord Bia, the Marine Institute, Bord Iascaigh Mhara and the Sea Fisheries Protection Authority.

The IFA said there would be a shortfall of €400m in farm schemes next year. IFA leader Padraig Walshe said the budget was particularly damaging to the drystock sector and disadvantaged areas. He said there would be a 26% shortfall in the suckler cow scheme.

While ICMSA president Jackie Cahill said the cuts would have a negative impact on farm incomes and development, Macra na Feirme president Catherine Buckley welcomed the renewal of stamp duty and stock relief which, she said, would benefit young farmers.

- Farmers Stock Relief, Farm Pollution Control Relief and Farm Consolidation Relief is being extended for a further two years.
- Stamp Duty Relief for young trained farmers will be extended for a further four years to 2013.
- No change to the Farmers flat rate VAT for 2009.

BUSINESS INCENTIVES

The Minister extended and improved a number of incentives primarily for the small business community to encourage investment in the SME sector (250,000 small businesses employing over 800,000 people). Included were:

- **Research & Development Tax Credit:** The R&D tax credit available to companies will increase from 20% to 25% putting it to the forefront of R&D regimes globally. This will increase Ireland's attractiveness as a location for R&D activity and it will provide a well-targeted stimulus for such value-added activities. The Minister is going to consider making further enhancements in the forthcoming Finance Bill.
- **Start-up companies:** A welcome measure was introduced in respect of new start-up companies which commence trading in 2009. Such companies will be exempt from corporation tax and capital gains tax in each of the first three years to the extent that their tax liability for the year does not exceed € 40,000.

NO CHANGES TO:

- Corporation Tax (remains at 12.5%).
- Corporation Tax losses.
- Stamp duty on residential property.
- Gift and Inheritance Tax is still 20%.
- Tax planning transactions.
- No additional excise duty on beer, cider, spirits or diesel.

Note: On 20 October 2008, Taoiseach Brian Cowan started the process of a u-turn both on the **medical card** and **income levy**. At the time of going to print, speculation centred on the scrapping altogether of the means test for the over-70s in relation to the medical card; and for the income levy, a threshold of c. €23,000 below which no income levy would be applicable.

Appendix 12
20 CRACKING WAYS TO BEAT THE CREDIT CRUNCH

On a recent golf outing, Kerrie my 12-year-old daughter, and a useful 35 handicapper, posed the question, 'What are green fees, Dad?' It was another prime example of how language can be so ambiguous and misunderstood and funny. Financial and economic terms would probably rank as the number one contender for causing language confusion. While the Financial Regulator is continually at pains to preach the 'plain English' mantra, there are so many words that simply fly over the heads of most people, irrespective of intelligence. One such word is **recession**. The under 25s have never experienced it and only in the last few months has that word raised its ugly head again.

So what is it?

The Wikipedia definition of a recession, in macroeconomics, is generally associated with a decline in a country's real Gross Domestic Product (GDP, also called Gross Domestic Income) or negative real economic growth (measured by a decrease in goods and services produced in that country within a year). **GDP is the total market value of all goods and services produced in a country usually within a year.** According to one widespread definition, a recession occurs when real growth is negative for two or more successive quarters of a year.

However, there are differing definitions. In the United States, the National Bureau of Economic Research's (NBER) Business Cycle Dating Committee ultimately decides whether the economy has fallen into a recession. The NBER defines a recession as 'a significant decline in economic activity spread across the economy, lasting more than a few months, normally visible in real GDP, real income, employment, industrial production and wholesale-retail sales'.

Effectively, there has been a chain reaction since the sub-prime scandal hit the US last year. Not only did the public lose confidence in banks but banks lost confidence in each other. Interest rates have increased as a result – this apart from rising oil prices, rising cost of food and other necessary utilities like electricity.

Everything has been affected and words like **recession** and **credit crunch** are now regularly appearing in print and talk. The GDP decline can last 12 months or longer and is usually marked by job layoffs, high unemployment, reductions in retail sales and a slowing of housing and car markets. Belt and braces stuff. But if the recession continues for any greater period of time and is particularly arduous, it can develop into an **economic depression**. That, hopefully, will not happen here in Ireland.

However, we now have to batten down the hatches and ensure we have enough sustenance to last whatever time it takes to weather the storm, a little like the hoarding of nuts by squirrels at the onset of winter.

What can we do? Address your issues in the first instance – no point in sticking your head in the sand as debt will always eventually consume you if it is not addressed. So, here are **20 cracking ways to beat the credit crunch:**

1. PLAN A YEARLY HOUSEHOLD BUDGET – it makes sense to plan your finances as you would a trip from say Dublin to west Cork so that you know exactly what's ahead of you. It is really very simple – if you haven't got it, you shouldn't spend it. Expenditure should never exceed income unless you are happy to let it eat into your savings – that's of course if you have savings. If expenditure does exceed income, then you have three choices:

- **Earn more money.**

- **Cut costs.**

- **Let the creditors, including the banks, chase you** (though having your name on the Irish Credit Bureau as a defaulter or, worse, with a judgment against you, can scupper any hope of ever receiving a loan again).

You can only discover this surplus or deficit if you know what you are earning and what you are spending, hence the need, the vital need, to plan your annual costs. To start with, you could track all your expenses for a whole month or two just to see where it is all going – a little black book that you keep with you at all times and jot down every cent spent. Then, you simply work out all your *yearly* household liabilities e.g. ESB, heating, gas, car expenses, household insurance, school fees, even the humble TV licence, and then divide by twelve. That figure is the amount you need to put away each month in an account to meet your budget target and is the monthly expenditure you must find to run the home and family.

Any capital or 'luxury' spending must be found outside of this budget e.g. a case of Cristal champagne to tide you over the Christmas celebrations or a new washing machine to replace the broken down old one. You could, if you prefer, adopt a weekly budget. You should also have a 5-year or even a 10-year overall plan – so you can really anticipate all those future costs, goals and dreams (e.g. secondary education for the children, exotic holidays, overseas holiday homes, etc.) Check out the Money Doctor's Annual Household Budget in the Appendix pages of this book or email me for a Budget application form – it's free!

2. CHECK YOUR MORTGAGE AND ALL OTHER LOAN INTEREST RATES – sometimes we go to great lengths, at the initial stages of obtaining a mortgage or personal loan, trying to ensure the most competitive interest rate at the time. Once taken out, there is a tendency to overlook the maintenance of that mortgage or loan. You could very easily find out that your lender's current advertised interest rate bears no resemblance to your own. This is also a time to check and review whether your mortgage or personal loan is currently on a variable standard rate (generally the most expensive), fixed or a tracker rate. It is also worth considering, if your lender is uncompetitive, switching to another lender. Check all your loan rates while doing this exercise as you may be able to save thousands with cheaper options.

The current inter-bank credit issues have virtually brought the loan system to a standstill in comparison with previous years. Not only is it currently very difficult to obtain credit, but should you pass the stringent parameters for these loans, the interest rates are so punitive that borrowers are reluctant to extend their credit requirements. If you are one of the lucky ones who prior to c. April 2008 negotiated tracker mortgages from 0.45% over the ECB rate and even 0.75% for up to 80% loans, then you have nothing to worry about, as those margins (the 0.45% and 0.75%) MUST remain in force for the duration of the loan term. New borrowings attract the new more expensive interest rates. So, whatever you do, do NOT consolidate at this time unless there is no choice. If you are in a position to do so, ask for a separate loan for the new amount sought. Then negotiate that rate. Better still, seek the advice of an **independent financial adviser** (not tied to any one lender and with knowledge of ALL the lenders in the marketplace). **I have included such vetted advisers in Appendix 8 for your information.**

3. SWITCH YOUR MORTGAGE TO AN INTEREST-ONLY FACILITY – for many people, it makes sense to think about switching your mortgage to a lender that offers an interest-only facility or approaching your current lender to swap into an interest-only facility. Primarily, this helps your cash-flow by cutting your monthly repayment dramatically (up to 35% of the normal monthly payment). There are many ways of addressing the capital repayment over or at the end of the term of the loan – you could, for example, pay off the capital by selling the property or selling off other assets/investments to repay the loan on maturity. This interest-only method gives greater flexibility and lets you decide when you want to pay back the capital.

If you are switching, it may also be time to think about consolidating all your short-term loans into one long-term and cheaper loan – interest rates allowing. For those residential investment property owners, it makes sense to maintain your loan on an interest-only basis as the interest is **fully off-settable** against the rental income tax liability. Therefore it pays to maintain the full loan as each year you are availing of the full interest for offset. Currently, with the banks' liquidity issues, it may not be worthwhile switching to another lender if you are looking for an interest-only facility and your existing lender will not comply. However, it is still worth negotiating with your existing lender for a short-term interest-only facility that would help cash flow.

4. CHECK YOUR BANK CHARGES ON A REGULAR BASIS – there are too many cases of overcharging from all the banks to accept that your bank is not one of them! Sometimes, these charges can be waived on the discretion of the manager – if you don't ask, there'll be no waiving. Try and avoid exceeding your overdraft permission if you have an overdraft. The surcharges are simply not worth it. One main bank charges 15.9% for personal overdrafts and if you exceed the limit, three things will happen:

(i) A surcharge is applied – 12% in one bank's case. (This on top of the 15.9% totalling 27.9%!)

(ii) A Referral Fee is also applied – c. € 4.44 every day an item comes in and debits the account. This has to be approved by the bank manager and this is the charge for approval.

(iii) If your bank manager then sends back that item (direct debit/cheque) there is a further charge of €12.70 applied to the account.

Is it any wonder banks are making such huge profits? Overdrafts should be avoided, if at all possible. If you maintain healthy savings with your bank, simply asking them to waive such fees may bring positive results.

5. OPERATE A CHARGE CARD AS OPPOSED TO A CREDIT CARD – you are probably aware that credit card balances are normally charged between 8.5% and 24% depending on the credit card company, and only if you choose to retain a balance. By switching to a charge card (e.g. American Express, Diners, etc.) your monthly balances are debited to your bank current account and even if you decide to leave it on your overdraft – if you have permission, of course – the overdraft interest rate is currently between 12% and 15%. If you can pay off the balance every month, so much the better. You are availing of c. 30 days free credit. If you are one of those people who only pay the minimum balance each month, it is a sobering thought to know that it can take you 11 years to pay off your credit card debt!

If you must have a credit card, you could, first of all, shop around the various credit card companies. Remember, the ideal is to pay the bill in full when due. Tackling debt should always start with repaying the most expensive debt first. While AIB Bank plc's *Click Card* at 8.5% looks good, you would need to check out the 73 conditions to really appreciate what you are getting in to, as well as understand that cash withdrawals will still attract a rate of 22.9%. Bank of Scotland Halifax operate a 0% transfer balance account for the first 6 months (as do Ulster Bank, First Active plc and Tesco), plus if the limit is increased, 0% for the first 6 months on the new limit as well. Permanent TSB's *3V* card is a good idea for those who cannot discipline themselves with their plastic friend – with this card you have to lodge money into the card account before you spend, as you can only spend what is in the account. The same bank offers their credit card at an interest rate of 9.9% on balances. Remember, a credit card is for convenience, not for borrowing.

6. AVOID COMPANY CARS – in about 80% of cases, it does not pay to maintain a company car. Benefit-in-kind on company cars makes it less attractive than simply taking mileage expenses, in particular cars with greater carbon emissions as employers will have to pay more. These expenses also include depreciation, wear and tear, etc. and work out at c. €0.6348 per mile. Of course, you could opt for a classic car – over 25 years old – and the tax payable will be based on the value of the car at the time of purchase!

7. OIL – there are so many ways we can save on this commodity:

(i) **Buy a hybrid car – half petrol/half electric.** On one particular SUV model, apart from the saving on **V**ehicle **R**egistration **T**ax (c. €13,000 on an €88,000 car), there is cheaper annual car tax (€600 *v* €2000), better mileage consumption (c. 30 mpg) and, of course, lower $CO2$ emissions. Roll on the full electric car!

(ii) **Reduce your dependency on car fuel** – pool your car and share it with others, take public transport a couple of days a week. (Tax Saver tickets used at least 4 times a week can save you between 26% and 47% of the normal price of the ticket.) Ensure your car is maintained in tip-top condition – tyres at the right pressures, no unnecessary weights inside the car, driving under the speed limits (speeding causes greater fuel consumption). Better still, buy a bicycle!

(iii) **Home heating** – turn your thermostat down just 1° and you can save as much as 10% of the actual cost. 20° is the normal thermostat setting. Remember to switch off the heating when away - even for weekends, and especially at the onset of summer. If your home heating boiler is more than ten years old, you could consider replacing it with a new condenser boiler – this has much more efficient use of energy and should repay installation costs within two years.

(iv) **Electricity** – there is a direct correlation to the increasing cost of electricity and the increasing cost of oil. Reducing your dependency on electricity is another indirect way of reducing the oil bill. Changing your bulbs to CFLs – this will save you up to 20% of your annual bills, only use washing machines and dishwashers with full loads, turn off lights, use dimmer switches, only boil water needed not the full kettle, use nightlights, reduce peak time electricity usage as much as possible (between 5 p.m. and 7 p.m.), use timers and night timers – do you really hear the washing machine running at 4 a.m. in the morning? Finally, watch the 'stand-by' mode on electrical items such as TVs, computers, etc. – you are using 20% of the normal output on stand by. Switch off.

8. AVAIL OF YOUR ANNUAL CAPITAL GAINS TAX EXEMPTIONS

– the first €1270 of chargeable gains to an individual arising from the disposal of a capital asset (e.g. shares) is exempt. This is allowable for each tax year but is not transferable between spouses. For Capital Acquisition Taxes, remember the thresholds for 2008 from parent to sibling is currently € 521,208 for each sibling. Remember, you do not have to die to pass on your wealth to your children – you can do it now.

9. CHECK YOUR LIFE AND HEALTH COVER

– you could be over insured. Do a review of all your insurances. Are you getting the best value? When was your last review? What happens financially if you or your spouse die or become permanently incapacitated? VHI, Quinn Healthcare (formerly BUPA) or Hibernian Health (formerly VIVAS) – check them all out and do a comparison through your independent and authorised adviser.

10. CHECK YOUR GENERAL INSURANCES – your home buildings and contents – is your cover competitive? If you have commercial or residential investment property insurance, is that competitive? Do you require any special risk insurance that you have 'risked' being without to date – you may not be so lucky next year. Public liability, professional indemnity, multi-trip insurance, PC hacker – virus insurance, not to mention golf insurance.

11. THINK SMART WITH YOUR SURPLUS CASH – do not leave surplus money in your current account. At least transfer it into your bank's deposit account and when you need funds to meet the cheques you have written, transfer amounts over to the current account to meet those cheques as you write them. If that deposit account is sizeable, negotiate with your bank – their rates will generally be far less attractive than their competitors. The inter-bank market is cash-starved and there are some fantastic offers from deposit takers trying to lure your hard-earned savings into their coffers. At the time of going to print, you could avail of lump sum 1-year fixed accounts at 6%, to Regular Saver accounts (save for 12/24 months between €100 to €1000 per month) at a whopping 8% per annum. Even demand accounts are available at 5.5% per annum, so you should avail of the best for your own benefit. **The Investor Compensation Scheme**, set up in 1997, introduced a guarantee of 90% up to a maximum €20,000 of savings with any deposit taker should that credit institution fail. This was increased to €100,000 and 100% of this amount during the second last week of September 2008. Then, on 30 September 2008, the government came in again with a no-limit guarantee on all savings for Irish-owned banks (AIB, Bank of Ireland, Permanent TSB, Anglo Irish Bank, Irish Nationwide Building Society and Educational Building Society – EBS) and, on 9 October, extended it to five other non-Irish-owned banks (Ulster Bank, First Active, Bank of Scotland Halifax, IIB Bank (now KBC Bank) and Postbank – the An Post/Fortis Bank joint venture.

While one should not forget such solid institutions as credit unions and state-backed An Post for savings (the credit unions have the same guarantee – up to €100,000 compensation in the event of deposit-taker collapse – as the main banks and building societies). However, investing in them will not help the banks' liquidity problems. E-mail me for details of the safest and best deposit accounts.

12. TEN WAYS IN WHICH TO KICK-START YOUR SAVINGS –

(i) **Plan it** – there is a difference between saving and investing – saving is generally short term and immediate, while investment is for a minimum period of three to five years. Initially, you have to work out how much disposable income you have – that is, after tax, and after rent/mortgage, household bills, food, petrol and 'spending money'. You might even know how much money you can afford to put away already. The most important decision about savings can be summed up in one word – start. By planning to save you are setting immediate goals – for holidays, that new plasma screen television or funding Christmas presents, etc., and you should have the ultimate goal of having between three and six months annual income in a Rainy Day Fund or emergency account for three very good reasons:

- For emergencies (washing machine breakdowns, weekend breaks).

- As a safety net (in case of loss of income, interest rate increases, etc.).

- For seed capital for unexpected investment opportunities.

(ii) **Budget for a savings account** – find out where all your small change/living expenses go to by writing down everything you spend outside of the usual bills over a period of a couple of weeks. Did you really need that bar of chocolate when you bought your petrol? At a glance, you will be able to see exactly where to make savings and save!

(iii) **Cut down your household utility and travel bills** – when you analyse your household bills you will find you may have left the lights on for too long, or not used the washing machine on the night-time rate or had the central heating blazing while you were away for the weekend. Buy discounted bus passes, a bicycle – over time, not only is it cheaper but better for you physically – or the Last Minute type holidays. You will find many ways to reduce those overheads.

(iv) **Cut down on your banking bills** – overdrafts, and especially those exceeding the limits, should be a no-no. Save on travelling to your bank – open an internet account.

(v) **Cut down your food and toiletry bills** – go generic. Instead of buying the most expensive brand name (after all, you are paying for the marketing and glossy packaging) buy your favourite store's version or at least try it for a few weeks or until you have achieved your savings goal. You could be saving up to 50% of the brand leader's price.

(vi) **eBay it** – a great way to immediately set the ball rolling on your savings is to sell some of your unwanted items from clothing (fashion dresses) to sports and household goods. Your old ipod might be a great way of starting your savings programme. eBay is probably one of the best mediums for this kind of transaction or the *Buy & Sell* magazine.

(vii) **Loose change** – did you ever compile your loose change over the period of a month. You would be amazed at how quickly you can accumulate a few Euro in a short time. A box, basket, jar or anything that collects coins should be left in your hall / bedroom and just wait for the results.

(viii) **Tax yourself** – Joline Godfrey (*Raising Financially Fit Kids*) suggested that when you make non-essential purchases, you should put 10% of the price into an envelope for lodgement into a savings account and continue that habit until your desire to buy non-essential items wanes. She also suggests that you should cultivate your children to save by encouraging them to save one third of their pocket money into a savings account and as parents, match it.

(ix) **Monthly checks** – while you will be saving from your income, remember you will also be saving from some of the other ideas. Be sure to record these and ensure that those savings are being lodged into your account. Keep a colour coded graph or something pictorial to remind you of your savings progress. Even after you have reached that saving goal, continue the habit – it'll be in your best interest!

(x) **Find the right savings/deposit account** – there is no point in saving in a current account. Albert Einstein was accredited as saying: 'Compounding is mankind's greatest invention as it allows the reliable systematic accumulation of wealth.' Many of the top deposit accounts have some minimum and maximum thresholds so you need to do a little research to find out where is the best account for you (for starters, check best rates at http://www.moneydoctor.ie). You may even decide to start in your local Credit Union and after you have built up a certain sum, transfer it to a higher yielding savings account.

13. ENSURE OF ANY EXEMPTIONS ON INCOME TAX LIABILITY – you may be unwittingly exempt from paying income tax (e.g. an Irish resident artist producing originals that have cultural and artistic merit, income from woodlands, etc.), while you should also ensure, if self-employed, and your partner is working in the business, that the full entitlement of income tax exemptions is taken up by the partner. In other words, pay her/him her/his dues tax free! Your accountant will advise.

You should also ensure that you are receiving all the tax allowances irrespective of your status. Check out my chapter on Why pay more tax than you have to (see Part 8) and find out all about your entitlements and credit allowances. Young earners – under 30 – especially rarely claim all their allowances e.g. rent allowance, Single Person's tax credit, etc.

14. THINK PENSIONS – if you are self-employed, a 5% equity holding director or even in an occupational pension scheme (where pension holders can make further payments through an Additional Voluntary Contribution), you should review your pension requirements.

For every Euro you will save tax at your marginal rate, depending on the type of pension, plus all profits are tax free and on maturity, you can cash up to 25% of the fund tax free. You also do not pay PRSI contributions on pension payments. Just remember if you were retiring now, ask yourself could you live off the €223.30 per week from the state pension if you qualified through your stamps? You should talk to an adviser and specifically those regulated by the Central Bank – Authorised Advisors, or your preferred pension adviser.

15. ARFs (Approved Retirement Funds) & AMRFs – for self-employed, owners and directors of companies, recent changes in the pension laws now allow you to decide what you want to do with your retirement fund when you have reached the age of retirement. Up to a couple of years ago, the only choice you had was to take out an **annuity** (a kind of deposit account where you received a monthly interest cheque until you died – the interest rate is fixed for life) with a Life Insurance Company. When you died, the capital stayed with that Life Insurance Company and your estate lost out – winning meant outliving the insurance company's life expectations until more was paid out to you than was originally invested. That system has all changed now anyway and an ARF fund can now eventually be left to your estate, if you wish; while you also have choice as to how and where your pension fund is invested. The annuity system is still available and has its merits too. Contact your Authorised Advisor or your preferred pension adviser for further details.

16. THINK ABOUT OTHER FORMS OF INVESTMENT – for instance, if your preference is to stay in property, you could try French leasebacks – guaranteed rental income for up to 11 years plus the French government give you a VAT rebate of up to 19.6% on the cost of the property, also guaranteed is Spanish off-plan property buying, gold or even rock memorabilia!

Diversify – it is imperative that you do not place all your eggs in the one basket. At a time when there can be few guarantees on any investment or asset, diversifying your portfolio should be a priority. Property, bonds, equities and cash are the main four asset classes. But add alternative investments to this list to reduce that risk even further.

You could do worse than buy *The Money Doctor – 50 Ways to Wealth*, a compilation of 50 *Sunday Independent LIFE* magazine articles on making money from art and wine investment, rock memorabilia, investment clubs to classic cars, philately and numismatics. (Published in April 2008 by Gill & Macmillan.)

17. GO GREEN – forestry investment. Ireland is the least afforestated country in the EU with forest cover of 9% as compared with the EU average of 31%. The Irish climate is the most ideal in the Northern Hemisphere for tree growing due to our mild wet climate and trees grow three times faster here than elsewhere in Europe. Timber products are also the second largest import into the EU after oil.

The EU and the Irish government promote forestry through grants and premia payments. They are keen to reduce agricultural output of which there is a surplus in the EU and substitute it with timber producing forests for which there is a growing internal EU shortage. The government through the Department of the Marine and Natural Resources offer **capital grants** and **tax free income grants** under certain conditions as an encouragement to investors buying appropriate and approved lands for the planting of trees.

18. TELECOMS – if you have not heard of the word SKYPE, then you are missing out on incredible savings for both national and international calls. Broadband would be a prerequisite to register on www.skype.com – with over 310 million subscribers and usually at least 12 million online at the same time, the savings are significant. Free Skype to Skype calls, 0.017c per minute for landline calls, 0.16c per minute for mobile calls, and that's all over the world! Parents, unfortunately your children all operate pay-as-you-go mobiles but when they are at home they are using your landline. If you block all outgoing mobile calls, the saving could again be significant. Check your bill next time, and see the top ten most called and most expensive – you might just be surprised!

Check with ComReg's website (www.callcosts.ie), it gives you all the broadband operators and various costs associated. One to be watched is

Network 3's mobile broadband box at €19.99 per month – you simply plug it in to your laptop and off you go. Also, check out all the main telecom players to obtain the best deal for you and your family.

Finally with the new eurotarriff legislation on roaming charges in Europe, it may be cheaper to phone home for a couple of minutes than send a text message (which is not covered under the new legislation).

19. FOOD – the cost of food has soared over the last 12 months and it has shaken the Irish nation from their lethargy. Thirty per cent of us, according to the National Consumer Agency, have already started to change the way we shop with generic brands the big winners to date. Here are a few other tips we should adopt:

Clubcards – apart from helping the supermarkets to know their customers better, they can considerably reduce the cost of your food purchases over time with the discounts on offer.

Online shopping – this can be cheaper because impulse buys no longer apply. Delivery charges are negated by the cost of petrol to travel there and parking.

Cut out 'nibbles' – when you next fill your petrol tank, just pay for the petrol and give the two chocolate bars a miss. Stick to your three meals a day – good for your health and good for your pocket.

Collect cut-out coupons and discount offers – there is no shame in giving a voucher that gives you two for the price of one. Even the back of your receipt may have a discount offer that will save you money.

Check the dates on all your foods – be careful that the sell-by date has not passed and you might be better advised to shop in the evening – the supermarkets have special offers on pre-cooked foods and perishables.

Buy in bulk if you can – economies of scale will give you better value if you can buy for a month or two as opposed to the week.

Make your own lunch – you would really be surprised at the savings you would make if you made your own lunch rather than pay the local deli for your BLT and latte. That's of course if you are working outside of the home!

Grow your own – if you have your own garden, try putting down a few carrots, potatoes or onions. Our Irish soil cries out for them.

20. FINANCIAL MAKE-OVER – if ever there was a time to take a holistic view of your finances, this is the year. Better still, seek out a professional adviser who can help you make those difficult financial decisions to improve your lot. In the world of golf, Tiger Woods regularly consorts with his coach, relying on feedback and observation to improve his game, and let's face it, he's the best! Similarly, with our finances, we should follow suit. In life, you get what you pay for, so be prepared to spend if you want the best. The best things in life may be free, but independent financial advice is definitely worth paying for!

The Money Doctor advisers – these experienced financial professionals will review the A to Z of your personal finances. They have come through a process of careful selection and can be relied upon to give solid, independent and trustworthy advice. Money Doctor advisers are here to 'tell' and not 'sell', and are fully authorised. See Appendix 8 for details.

INDEX

abroad
    banking, 85–6
    capital gains tax, 273
    health insurance, 58
    property investment, 418
    social welfare benefits, 56–7
    tax, 282–5
    travel insurance, 130
accident insurance, 116, 117, 328
    decision tree, 376
    tax relief, 237
accommodation expenses, 249
accounting dates, 257–8, 396–8
administration fee, 328
adoptive benefit, 51
advisers, financial, 10, 35–40
    choosing, 36–40
    complaints against, 67–8
    Money Doctor advisers, 385–91
    regulation of, 39
    tied agents, 345
    trust and, 2, 10
AER (annual equivalent rate), 329
affordable housing, 167
Agricultural Relief, 362–3
aims, financial, 12–17
air travel tax, 404
allocation rate, 329
AMRFs (approved minimum retirement
    funds), 218, 329
Ancillary Orders, 301
annual budget, 383, 408–9
annual leave entitlement, 61
annual rest system, 137
annuity, 188–9, 329
annuity mortgages, 136–7
annuity rate, 329
antiques, investing in, 187
approved profit share scheme, 254

APR (annual percentage rate), 103–4,
    162–3, 329
ARFs (approved retirement funds), 218,
    329
arguments about money, 25–30
art investment, 187
artists' tax exemption, 353
assessing your finances, 17–22
asset finance and leasing, 108, 330
assets, 19–20, 330
Association of Chartered Certified
    Accountants, 393
assumptions, 21–2
asylum seekers, 51–2
ATM cards, 76, 79
    abroad, 85
    charges, 405
attitudes to money, 2–3, 26
    compatibility with partner, 26–7
attorney, power of, 15
audits, 260–1, 370
AVCs (additional voluntary
    contributions), 206, 210–11,
    217–19, 328
average clause, 330, 388

back-to-work allowance, 53–4
back-to-work enterprise allowance, 53–4
balloon payment, 330
banking, 74–86
    abroad, 85–6
    bank charges, 79–81, 411
    complaints, 67
    current accounts, 74–5, 76–7,
        80–1
    deposit accounts, 82, 176, 414
    Investor Compensation Scheme,
        70, 339–40, 389–90,
        414–15

joint accounts, 81–2
online and telephone, 77, 81
overdrafts, 79, 80, 96, 108, 343, 411
Regular Saver Accounts, 176–7, 178, 414
'baskets' (stock investment), 187
bear market, 330
belief patterns and money, 2–3, 26
compatibility with partner, 26–7
beneficiary, 308
benefit in kind, 247, 269–71, 357, 402
benefit statement, 330
bereavement, 307–18, 364, 379
grant, 54
BES (Business Expansion Scheme), 196, 348–9
BES (relief for investment in corporate trades), 242
bid-offer spread, 330
blind person's pension, 56
blind person's tax credit, 237
blind welfare allowance, 56
'boiler rooms', 330–1
bonds, 193–4, 331
corporate, 332, 340
government, 193, 194
guaranteed, 189
junk, 340
tracker bonds, 185
bonuses, and tax, 251
borrowing see loans
broadband, 419–20
Budget 2009, 399–406
budget account, annual, 383, 408–9
budget account, students, 384
budgeting services see MABS
building societies, 83–4
complaints against, 67
buildings insurance, 127–8
bull market, 331
Business Expansion Scheme (BES), 196
business premises, 263–4

capital acquisition tax, 277–8, 287–8, 362
Business Property Relief, 362
Business Retirement Relief, 288–9, 365–6, 368–9
buy-out bond, 331

calculators, 322
capital, 323, 331
for future income needs, 22
capital acquisition tax, 224, 275–8, 361–4
business assets, 277–8, 287–8, 362
divorce and separation, 299, 305
dwelling house exemption, 362
farms, 277–8, 287–8, 362–3
life assurance policy and, 123–4
thresholds, 275–6, 361
capital allowances, 196
farms, 290
industrial buildings, 267
capital expenditure, 264
capital gains tax, 224, 272–4, 364–8
exempt chargeable gains, 367, 413
divorce and separation, 299, 305
farms, 273, 274, 288–9, 365–6
home working, 261–2, 368
rates, 401
shares, 192
start-up companies, 406
CAR (compound annual rate), 324–5
car expenses and tax, 247–8, 350, 359
carbon emissions, 359
car pools, 271
company cars, 268–71, 412
mileage rates, 247–8
motor tax, 404
parking, 252
self-employed, 271
car fuel savings, 412–13
car insurance, 128–9
car parking levy, 399
carer, employing a carer, 353

carer's allowance, 56, 404
carer's benefit, 54, 404
carer's tax credit, 235–6
cash card, pre-paid, 86
casual labour, 359
CFDs (contracts for differences), 187, 331
charge cards, 332, 411–12
charitable donations, 239, 355
cheque books, 76
cheque guarantee card, 77
cheques, bouncing, 81
child benefit, 52, 403
childcare, tax relief, 236, 252, 402–3
child dependent allowances, 403
children
    involving in family finance, 31–4
    savings, 416
civil service mileage rate, 247–8
civil service subsistence rates, 249
'close' company, 266, 368
clubcards, 420
collateral, 332
collectibles, investing in, 188
college fees, and tax relief, 239
commission, 332
commodities, 182, 334
common law spouse, 312
Companies Registration Office, 392
company cars, 268–71, 412
company directors, and pensions, 212, 217
compartmentalised approach to money, 7
compatibility with partner, 26–7
competitive analysis, 38
complaints, financial consumers, 67
compound annual rate (CAR), 324–5
compound interest, 90–1, 324–5
compulsory purchase, 367
consolidation loans, 99–100, 334
constant attendant's allowance, 54
consumer rights (financial), 66–71
contents of house insurance, 128

contract work, 60
contractors, and self-employment, 262
contracts for differences (CFDs), 187, 331
contributory pension, 46, 403
contributory social welfare benefits, 43–4
conveyancing, 332
corporate bond, 332, 340
corporation tax, 266, 368–9
    important dates, 397–8
    start-up companies, 406
coupon, 193, 331
covenants, 241, 357–8
credit, 87–94
    cost of credit, 332
    credit rating, 68–9, 105, 149–50, 333, 340
    see also credit cards
credit cards, 109, 332–3, 411–12
    abroad, 85
    gold, 109
    insuring, 130
    interest rates, 83, 103, 325, 412
    minimum payment trap, 91–2
credit crunch, 407–8
credit insurance, 333
credit unions, 84
    complaints against, 67
    loans, 108
    saving with, 177, 415
CREST, 333
critical illness insurance, 116, 118, 333
current accounts, 74–5, 76–7
    reducing bank charges, 80–1
current account mortgages, 140–1, 333

daily tax allowances, 249
Data Protection Commissioner, 69
death and bereavement, 307–18, 364, 379
    bereavement grant, 54
death-in-service benefit, 217
death-in-retirement benefit, 217

debentures, investing in, 187
debit cards (Laser), 78–9, 344
debt, 87–102
    assessing liabilities, 96–7
    borrowing sensibly, 103–11
    getting out of, 95–102
    increase in consumer debt, 88
    loan consolidation, 99–100, 334
    minimum payment trap, 91–2
    secret debts, 28
    sub-prime lending, 144–51
    transferring debt, 94
decision trees, 371–9
deed of covenant, 241, 357–8
default, 334
defined benefits pension schemes,
    209–10, 217, 334
defined contributions pension schemes,
    210, 214, 217, 334
definitions of terms, 328–46
dental treatment benefits, 51
dental treatment, tax relief, 238
Department of Enterprise, Trade and
    Employment, 64
Department of Social & Family Affairs,
    43
dependent relative tax credit, 236
deposit accounts, 82, 176, 414
    fixed term, 337
    Investor Compensation Scheme,
        70, 339–40, 389–90,
        414–15
depreciation, 334
depression, economic, 408
derivatives, 187, 334–5
deserted wife's benefit, 49
designated areas, tax incentives, 267
diamonds, investment in, 188
diary, money diary, 96
direct debits, 78
director's executive pensions, 212, 217
DIRT (Deposit Interest Retention Tax),
    177–8, 334

rate, 400
disability allowance, 56
disability benefit, 54
disability payments, and tax credits, 250
disabled people, social welfare benefits,
    42–3, 50, 54, 56
disabled persons grant (housing), 168
discount rate mortgage, 335
dismissal from work, 62–3
disponer, 275, 288
disposable income, 342
diversification strategy, 182–3, 187, 419
dividend, 191–2, 335
Dividend Withholding Tax, 397
divorce, 303–6
doctor visit card, 51
domicile, 282–5
domiciliary care allowance, 56
donations, 239, 355
double taxation treaties, 283, 364
drugs payment scheme, 55, 402
dual life policy, 340

early childcare supplement, 52–3
early retirement pension, 54
earmarking, 301
e-Bay, 416
ECB (European Central Bank), 336
economic recession, 407–8
education fees, and tax relief, 239, 250
elderly
    annuity, 188–9
    loans for, 152–9
    tax credit, 235
electricity savings, 413
emergency fund, 173–7
emergency tax, 245
emergency time off work, 63
emigrant status, 283
employment rights, 60–5
endowment mortgages, 138, 335
    mis-selling, 335
endowment policy, 335

enduring power of attorney, 15
energy savings, 412–13
entertainment expenses, 249, 263
equity, 336
equity release, 336
escalation, 336
ESOTs (employee share ownership
     trusts), 254
estate, 308
ETFs (exchange traded funds), 336–7
EURIBOR, 336
euro, 85
European Central Bank (ECB), 336
European Health Insurance Card, 58
European Union (EU)
     farmers, 287
     health insurance, 58
     interest rates, 336
     Ombudsman, 70
     social welfare benefits, 56–7
exam payments, and tax relief, 253
exchange traded funds, 336–7
executor of a will, 308
exemptions (tax), 229–31, 353–4, 356,
     417
exit penalty, 337
exit tax, 337
expectant mothers, time off work, 64
expenses, and tax
     PAYE, 247–53, 351
     self-employed, 263–4, 350–1
Experian Ireland, 69
extended warranties, 129–30
eye treatment benefits, 51

family finance, 25–34
     compatibility, 26–7
     involving/educating children, 31–4
     joint bank accounts, 81–2
     money arguments, 25–30
family income supplement, 55, 403
farm consolidation relief, 291
farms, 286–91

agricultural relief, 362–3
Budget changes, 405–6
capital acquisition tax, 277–8,
     287–8, 362–3
capital allowances, 290
capital gains tax, 273, 274, 288–9,
     365–6
farmer definition, 363
income tax, 287, 358
leasing, 291
profit averaging, 358
stamp duty, 290–1, 369
stock relief, 289, 358
VAT, 289, 360–1
FEOGA (European Agricultural
     Guidance and Guarantee Fund), 287
film industry, investment and tax relief,
     242
financial advisers, 10, 35–40
     choosing, 36–40
     complaints against, 67–8
     Money Doctor advisers, 385–91
     regulation of, 39
     tied agents, 345
     trust and, 2, 10
financial institutions, consumer rights,
     66–71
financial objectives, 12–17
financial pages, 191
financial planning, 5–40, 374
     advice see financial advisers
     annual budget, 383, 408–9
     assessing resources, 17–22
     benefits of, 5–11
     family and partners, 25–34
     objectives, 12–17
     writing a plan, 12–24, 374
Financial Regulator, 39, 67–8, 79
     address, 393
Financial Services Ombudsman, 67, 69
financial year, 257–8
fixed rate mortgages, 139, 337
fixed term deposits, 337

flexible (current account) mortgages, 140–1, 333
foreign banking, 85–6
foreign property investment, 418
forestry investment, 419
Form 11, 257, 259, 396
Form 12, 396
free travel, 56
fuel allowance, 403
fuel savings, 412–13
fund managers, 184–5
futures & options, 331, 338

gambling, 274
GDP (Gross Domestic Product), 400, 407
GE Money, 147, 149
gearing, 325–6
general insurance, 125–30, 388
gifts
    tax see capital acquisition tax
    tax-free, 250, 253, 255
gilts (gilt-edged securities), 193, 194
Godfrey, Joline, 416
gold, investing in, 187
government bonds, 193, 194
Grant of Administration, 313
Grant of Probate, 313–14
Grant of Representation, 313–14
grants (forestry), 419
grants (housing), 167–8
greyhound stud fees, 353–4
gross tax payable, 244
guaranteed bonds, 189
guardian's payment, 49–50

Habitual Resident's Test, 52
Hall, Alvin, 96
health insurance, 114–18, 120–1, 338
    abroad, 58
    decision trees, 376–7
    tax relief, 237, 251
health screening, and tax relief, 253

health, State spending, 402
hearing treatment benefits, 51
heating, savings, 413
hedge funds, 187
hire purchase, 110
    business equipment, 353
holiday pay and entitlement, 61
home carer's tax credit, 235–6
home improvement grants, 167–8
home income plan, 338
home insurance, 127–8
    home working, 261–2
    under-insurance, 126, 330, 388
home reversion schemes, 155–9, 338
home working, 261–2, 351, 368
hospital cash plan, 338
Household Benefits Package Scheme, 47–8
household budget account, 383, 408–9
house purchase, 131–51, 160–9
    costs involved, 163–5
    deposit, 162
    house prices and, 131, 194, 195
    mortgages see mortgages
    negative equity, 326, 342
    shared ownership schemes, 167–8
    see also property investment
housing, affordable, 167
housing grants, 167–8

ICB (Irish Credit Bureau), 69, 105, 149–50, 340
    address, 150
IFSRA (Financial Regulator), 39, 67–8, 79
    address, 393
illness and insurance, 114–18, 120–1, 333, 344
    decision trees, 376–7
improvement grants, 167
incapacitated child tax credit, 236
incapacitated person's tax allowance, 236
income, 323
    as an asset, 14

income, *continued*
  assessing your income, 18
  different to capital, 323
income equalisation, 201
income exemption limit, 222
income protection cover, 116, 117, 328
  decision tree, 376
  tax relief, 237
income tax, 223, 227–64, 347–59
  computation template, 382
  credits and allowances, 233–42,
    246, 380
  emergency tax, 245
  exemptions, 229–31, 353–4, 356,
    417
  expenses allowable (PAYE),
    247–53, 351
  expenses allowable (self-
    employed), 263–4, 350–1
  farmers, 287
  gross/net tax payable, 244
  levy, 400
  marginal relief, 230–1
  PAYE, 243–55, 351
  rates, 228–9, 380
  refunds, 245–6
  schedules, 227–8
  self-employed, 256–64, 280–1,
    350–1
  standard rate cut-off point, 243–4
incorporation of business, 358
increasing term insurance, 338
indemnity bond, 148, 165, 338
Independent Mortgage Advisers'
  Federation (IMAF), 68
indexation relief, 272
indexed funds, 186
index linking, 339
industrial buildings, 267
inflation, 21–2, 339
inheritance, 23, 307–18
  divorce and separation, 300
  intestacy, 308, 379

tax *see* capital acquisition tax
injury benefit, 54
injury payments, and tax, 250
Instalment Savings scheme, 176–7
Institute of Certified Public Accountants
  in Ireland, 393
Institute of Chartered Accountants in
  Ireland, 393
insurance, 113–30
  accident, 116, 117, 328
  advisers, 118, 121, 388
  brokers, 126
  complaints, 67
  decision trees, 375–7
  disclosure and invalidation, 123
  endowment policy, 335
  excess, 128
  general insurance, 125–30
  life cover and illness, 114–24, 251,
    338, 375
  mortgage repayment, 169, 333,
    338, 342
  regulations, 122
  tax and, 123–4, 237, 251
  under-insurance, 126, 330, 388
interest, 323–5, 339
  compound, 90–1, 324–5
interest rates, 22
  AER, 329
  APR, 103–4, 162–3, 329
  CAR, 324–5
  changes in, 105–6
  comparing rates for loans, 103–4
comparing rates for mortgages, 83
credit cards, 83, 103, 325, 412
  EURIBOR, 336
  mortgage repayments, 135
  sub-prime lending, 147–8
internal rate of return (IRR), 321–2
intestacy, 308, 379
invalidity pension, 42–3, 50, 403
investment, 22, 171, 179–97, 418–19
  basic planning and strategy, 180–4

decision tree, 373
diversification, 182–3, 187, 419
fund managers, 184–5
gearing, 325–6
growth comparison graph, 181
pooled investments, 184–7
risk and, 182, 189
stocks and shares, 187
tax relief, 242
see also property investment
investment club, 193
investment funds, 184–7, 336–7
investment mortgages, 137
Investor Compensation Scheme, 70,
   339–40, 389–90, 414–15
Irish Brokers' Association (IBA), 68
Irish Credit Bureau (ICB), 69, 105,
   149–50, 340
   address, 150
Irish Financial Services Regulatory
   Authority (IFSRA), 39, 67–8, 79
   address, 393
Irish Stock Exchange, 193
IRR (internal rate of return), 321–2

jargon, 319, 328
jewellery, investing in, 188
jobseekers allowance, 53
jobseekers benefit, 53
joint assessment, 279–80
joint bank accounts, 81–2
joint life insurance, 121, 340
joint ownership, 316–17
joint tenancy, 316
judgment, 333, 340
judicial separation, 301
junk bond, 340

Labour Relations Commission, 64
land registry fees, 164
Laser cards, 78–9, 344
Law Society of Ireland, 394
leasing, 108, 353

farms, 291
legal fees (house purchase), 164
Letter of Clearance, 314
Letter of Offer, 341
Letters of Administration, 313
levy on income tax, 400
liabilities, assessing, 20–1, 96–7
life assurance, 114–24, 341
   advisors, 118, 121
   annuities, 188–9
   cooling-off period, 122
   decision tree, 375
   joint, 121, 340
   pensions and, 217
   regulations, 122
   tax and, 123–4, 251
   term insurance, 119–20, 345
   term insurance, increasing, 338
   term insurance, renewable, 344
   types of life cover, 118–20
   whole of life assurance, 120, 346
Life Insurance Association (LIA), 68
LifeLoan, 158–9
lifetime mortgage, 153–4, 157–9
limited company, 262
liquidity, 181, 341
livestock, compulsory disposal, 290
loading, 341
loans, 87–111, 409–10
   borrowing sensibly, 103–11
   changing rates, 106–7
   comparing rates, 103–4
   consolidation, 99–100, 334
   credit rating, 68–9, 105, 149–50,
      333, 340
   debt, 87–102
   minimum payment trap, 91–2
   over-60s, 152–9
   secured, 105–6, 344
   security against, 344
   sub-prime lending, 144–51
   tax relief, 239–40
   unsecured, 105–6, 346

local authority mortgages, 166–7
lottery winnings, 274
LTV (loan to value), 341
lump sum payments, and tax, 217, 250, 351–2

MABS (Money Advice Budgeting Services), 169
   addresses, 394–5
maintenance payments, 300–1, 305
managed funds, 186
marginal tax relief, 230–1
market value reduction (MVR), 341
marriage and tax, 279–80
   tax credit, 235
maternity benefit, 51
maternity leave, 63
maturity date, 193–4
meals expenses, 250
means testing, 44–6, 56
medical cards, 50–1
   over-70s, 403
   threshold, 403
medical expenses, tax relief, 238, 352–3, 402
   ceiling, 401
medical insurance, 114–18, 120–1, 338
   abroad, 58
   decision trees, 376–7
   tax relief, 237, 251
membership fees, and tax relief, 253
mileage rates, 247–8
milk quotas, 290
minimum payment trap, 91–2
minimum wage, 60–1
mobile phones
   insurance, 130
   savings, 419
   tax relief, 252
money arguments, 25–30
money diary, 96
Money Doctor advisers, 385–91
Money Doctor – 50 Ways to Wealth

(book), 419
money lenders, 110
mortgage protection assurance, 341
mortgage repayment protection scheme, 341
mortgages, 132–51, 160–9, 341
   adding purchases to, 107–8
   advisers, 68, 142
   current account mortgages, 140–1, 333
   difficulty in repaying, 169
   discount rate mortgage, 335
   endowment, 138, 335
   fixed/variable rate, 139, 337, 346
   interest and repayment figures, 135
   interest-only/repayment mortgages, 136–9, 339, 344
   interest rates comparison, 83
   lifetime mortgage, 153–4, 157–9
   local authority, 166–7
   mortgage allowance scheme, 167
   paying off early, 141, 168
   pension-linked mortgages, 138–9
   protection insurance, 169, 333, 338, 342
   re-mortgaging, 326, 344
   reviewing, 409–10
   self-employed and, 147, 163
   size of, 162
   sub-prime mortgages, 144–51
   switching your mortgage, 163, 410–11
   tax relief, 165, 239–40, 356–7, 401
   tracker mortgages, 140, 345
motor expenses *see* car expenses and tax
motor insurance, 128–9
motor tax, 404
motorised transport grant, 56
multi-agency intermediaries, 39
MVR (market value reduction), 341
mystification of money, 2

national minimum wage, 60–1

National Treasury Management Agency (NTMA), 342

NDI, 342

needs, universal, 15–16

negative equity, 326, 342

negotiation services, 38

nephews, favourite nephew/niece relief, 364

net disposable income (NDI), 342

net relevant earnings, 348–9

net tax payable, 244

net worth, 343

no claims bonus, 343

non-contributory pension, 46–7, 403

non-contributory social welfare benefits, 43–4

non-residents, and tax, 85–6

NTMA, 342

nursing home subvention, 55–6

objectives, financial, 12–17

occupational injuries benefit, 403

occupational pension schemes, 209, 214

offshore entity, 260

oil and fuel savings, 412–13

Ombudsman

European, 70

Financial Services, 67, 69

Pensions, 68, 203

on-call workers, 62

on-line banking, 77, 81

on-line shopping, 420

on-line tax see ROS

one-parent family payment, 48–9

one-parent family tax credit, 235

options, 338

Organisation of Working Time Act, 61–2

outgoings, assessing, 18–21

overdrafts, 79, 80, 96, 108, 343, 411

overnight tax allowances, 249, 351

P45, 245

P50, 245

P60, 246

parental leave, 64

parking

levy, 399

tax relief and, 252

partnerships, 356

Pay and File, 257, 347

PAYE, 243–55

refunds, 245–6

tax credit, 57–8, 237

tax-free expenses, 247–53, 351

tax returns and, 226

payment protection insurance, 333

payroll deduction schemes, 174

P/E (price-earnings ratio), 191

pension adjustment order, 306

pensioner trustee, 212

pensions, 199–218

advisers, 215, 388–9

ARFs/AMRFs, 218, 329

AVCs, 206, 210–11, 217–19, 328

complaints, 68, 203

costs, 215–16

decision trees, 371–2

divorce and separation, 301, 305–6

early retirement pension, 54

employees, 209–11, 372

pension-linked mortgages, 138–9

property investment and, 213

PRSAs, 206, 211–14, 217–18, 241, 343

self-employed, 211, 371, 417–18

social welfare pensions, 46–7, 54, 403

tax on lump sums, 217, 351–2

tax relief, 213–14, 241, 348, 402

Pensions Board, 203

Pensions Ombudsman, 68, 203

percentages, 320–2

permanent health insurance, 116, 117, 328

permanent health insurance, *continued*
    decision tree, 376
    tax relief, 237
pet insurance, 130
planning *see* financial planning
pooled investments, 184–7
Post, An, 84
    saving with, 176–7, 415
power of attorney, 15
precious metals, investment in, 187–8
preliminary tax, 257, 347
premises, business, 263–4
pre-paid cash card, 86
presents, tax-free, 250, 253, 255
price-earnings ratio, 191
prime lending, 144
prioritising, 14–15
probate, 313–14, 364
Professional Insurance Brokers'
    Association (PIBA), 68
profit share scheme, 254
property, charge on non-principal
    residences, 401
property insurance, 127–8
    home working, 261–2
    under-insurance, 126, 330, 388
property investment, 194–6
    abroad, 418
    house prices and, 131, 194–5
    house purchase, 131–51, 160–9
    local authority charge, 401
    mortgages see mortgages
    negative equity, 326, 342
    pensions and, 213
    renting out property, 166, 195–6,
        265–7, 354
    tax, capital gains, 272–4
    tax on rental income, 195–6,
        265–7, 349
PRSAs (personal retirement savings
    accounts), 206, 211–14, 217–18,
    343
    tax relief, 241

PRSI (pay related social insurance), 225,
    231–2, 343
    ceiling, 401
    pensions and, 213–14
    self-employed, 261
    social welfare payments and, 42–4,
        46
public liability insurance, 127

R&D tax credit, 406
RAIPIs, 39
rate of return, 343
    internal rate of return (IRR),
        321–2
recession, economic, 404–5
recreational facilities, and tax relief, 252
redundancy, 65, 294–7
refugees, 51–2
Regular Saver Accounts, 176–7, 178, 414
relocation expenses, 252
re-mortgaging, 326, 344
renewable term insurance, 344
rental income, 166, 195–6, 265–7, 349,
    354
renting a room, 265, 354
rent relief tax credit, 238, 354
repayment mortgage, 136–7, 344
residency, 282–5
Residential Property Tax, 369
Residential Reversions, 159
respite care grant, 54
rest periods, entitlement at work, 62
retirement *see* pensions
retirement pension (social welfare), 46,
    54
retirement relief, 288–9, 365–6, 368–9
Revenue Affidavit, 315
Revenue Commissioners, 226, 259
    address, 392
    audits, 260–1, 370
Rights Commissioner, 64
rights of employees, 60–5
rights of financial consumers, 66–71

rock memorabilia, investment in, 187
ROS (Revenue Online Service), 226, 259
    contact numbers, 392

Salary Multiplier, 342
saving, 171–8, 414–16
    borrowing at the same time, 97–8
    children's saving, 416
    decision tree, 378
    emergency fund, 173–7
    Investor Compensation Scheme,
        70, 339–40, 389–90,
        414–15
    tax and, 177–8
savings bond/certificates (An Post), 177
SAYE (save as you earn) scheme, 254
schedules (income tax), 227–8
SCSB (Standard Capital Superannuation
    Benefit), 296–7, 352
seafarer's tax allowance, 242
search fees, 165
season tickets, and tax relief, 252
secret debts and savings, 28
Section 23, 196, 267, 349
Section 35 Investments, 242
Section 50, 196
Section 60, 363
secured loans, 105–6, 344
security, 344
seed capital scheme, 220–1
self-assessment tax system, 256–7
self-certification of earnings, 147
self-direct trusts, 138–9, 212–13
self-employed, and tax, 256–64
    employing children, 281
    employing family, 350
    employing spouses, 280–1, 350
    expenses allowable, 263–4, 350–1
    see also tax returns
separation, 298–302
serious illness insurance, 116, 118, 333,
    344
service charges, tax relief, 241–2

share incentive schemes, 254
share subscription schemes, 254
shared house ownership scheme, 167–8
shares, 344 see also stocks and shares
shopping, savings tips, 416, 420–1
short selling (shorting), 344–5
Sixty Plus Finance, 159
SKYPE, 419
'sniper' approach to debt, 100–1
social insurance benefit, 232
social welfare, 42–59
    assistance/benefits, 44–6
    Budget changes, 403–4
    contributory/non-contributory
        payments, 43–4
    means testing, 44–6, 56
    summary of payments, 46–56
    tax and, 57–8
special age tax credit, 235
specialised funds, 186
specialist (sub-prime) mortgages, 144–51
specified illness cover, 116, 118, 333,
    344
sports facilities, and tax relief, 252
sports persons, retirement and tax, 348,
    356
spread betting, 182
Springboard Mortgages, 149
SSAPs (small self-administered pension
    schemes), 212–13
    property and, 138–9
staff entertainment, 249, 263
stamp duty, 164, 224, 345
    farms, 290–1, 369
    Laser cards, 344
    transactions between relatives, 369
    transactions between spouses, 280
Standard Capital Superannuation Benefit
    (SCSB), 296–7, 352
standard rate cut-off point, 243–4
standing orders, 78
Start Mortgages, 148–9
stockbrokers, 192–3

Stock Exchange, 193
stock options, 254
stock relief (farms), 289, 358
stocks and shares, 189–94, 344
    'baskets', 187
    CREST, 333
    dividends, 191–2, 335
    employers' schemes, 253–5
    share price, 191
    specialised sectors, 187
    tax and, 192, 253–5
store cards, 109–10
    interest rates, 94, 103
strategic planning, 37
students
    budget account, 384
    tax relief, 239, 250
sub-prime lending, 144–51
subsistence allowances, 249, 351
Succession Act, 308, 309
    divorce and separation, 300
Sunday working, 61
supplementary welfare allowance, 48
surrender value, 345
survey fees, 164

tax, 219–91, 347–70, 380–2
    advisers, 219
    avoidance and evasion, 223, 345
    bands, 400
    certificate, 233
    computation template, 382
    credits and allowances, 233–42,
        246, 348, 380, 400
    divorce and separation, 299–301,
        305
    exemptions, 229–31, 353–4, 356,
        417
    expenses allowable (PAYE),
        247–53, 351
    expenses allowable (self-
        employed), 263–4, 350–1
    gross/net tax payable, 244

    havens, 260
    income exemption limit, 222
    levy, 400
    living abroad, 282–5
    marginal relief, 230–1
    mortgage relief, 165
    PAYE, 243–55, 351
    PAYE tax credit, 57–8, 237
    rates of tax, 400–2
    returns *see* tax returns
    savings, 177–8
    schedules, 227–8
    self-employed, 256–64, 280–1,
        350
    shares, 192, 253–5
    social welfare benefits, 57–8
    standard rate cut-off point, 243–4
    taxable profits, 262
Tax Clearance Certificate (probate),
    314–15
tax returns, 225–6, 256–64, 347–8, 370
    expression of doubt, 370
    important dates, 396–8
    non-disclosure, 370
    obligation to complete, 225–6,
        256
    online, 259
    penalties for late returns, 258–9,
        347–8, 397
telecoms, savings, 419–20
Tenants in Common, 316
term insurance, 119–20, 345
    increasing, 338
    renewable, 344
term loans, 109
terminal bonus, 187
terminal loss relief, 358
Terms of Business letter, 68
thatching grant, 168
tied agent, 345
tools, tax expenses, 251
top slicing relief, 296
tracker bonds, 185

tracker mortgages, 140, 345
trade union subscriptions, tax relief, 239
transport expenses, 250, 252
travel, free, 56
travel insurance, 130
traveller's cheques, 85
travelling expenses, 247–8
treatment benefits, 51
trustees, 308–9, 345
trusts, 124, 345

unemployed, and tax relief, 238–9
unfair dismissal, 62–3
unit-linked funds, 186
unit trusts, 186, 346
university fees, and tax relief, 239
unsecured loans, 105–6, 346

valuation, 346
variable rate mortgage, 139, 346
VAT (value added tax), 225, 359–61
    bad debts, 360
    farms, 289, 360–1
    foreign traders, 360
    important dates, 397

property, 360
rates, 361, 404
registering for, 261
turnover thresholds, 359
VRT (Vehicle Registration Tax), 412

wage, minimum, 60–1
warranties, extended, 129–30
whole of life assurance, 120, 346
widowed parent's grant, 55
widowed parent's tax credit, 235
widows and widowers pension, 47, 403
wills, 23, 307–18
    intestacy, 308, 379
wine, investment in, 188
with-profit funds, 186–7, 346
woodland investment, 419
work and employment rights, 60–5
work tools, tax expenses, 251
working week, 61–2

XD (ex-dividend), 192

yield, 191–2, 321–2

Your Financial Notes